THE SCIENCE OF CONFLICT

The
Science of Conflict

JAMES A. SCHELLENBERG

New York   Oxford
OXFORD UNIVERSITY PRESS
1982

Library of Congress Cataloging in Publication Data

Schellenberg, James A., 1932–
The science of conflict.

Bibliography: p.
Includes index.
1. Social conflict. 2. Violence. 3. Peace.
I. Title.
HM136.S283   303.6   81-4796
ISBN 0-19-502973-9   AACR2
ISBN 0-19-502974-7 (pbk.)

Printing (last digit): 9 8 7 6 5 4 3 2 1

Printed in the United States of America

Preface

A student in the Programme of Peace and Conflict Research at the University of Lancaster, England, gathers all the material he can find on simple societies without war or violence. At Bethel College, in Kansas, a student takes an undergraduate major in "peace studies" and does an internship at the Martin Luther King Center in Georgia. Elsewhere in America, graduate students write dissertations on such subjects as counterinsurgency warfare, the economics of disarmament, and the perceptions of international crises by makers of foreign policy. And at Oslo, Norway, peace researchers from around the world gather for a seminar at the International Peace Research Institute, where the scholarly *Journal of Peace Research* is also published.

These examples are illustrations of a growing worldwide interest in conflict and peace studies. Each year more colleges and universities offer courses of study in this general area, although the particular titles and emphases of programs vary greatly. Advanced research goes on too, especially in Western Europe, the United States, and Japan. With such work by scholars of varied disciplines at different locations, it is difficult to capture a sense of this field as a whole—its leading ideas, key research findings, and central continuing questions. Nevertheless, that is exactly what this book attempts to do. I have tried to provide, in terms understandable to undergraduate social science students or the intelligent layman, a reasonably up-to-date summary of conflict and peace studies.

This book is deliberately eclectic and interdisciplinary. A

great variety of scholars study conflict, and I have included as wide a representation as possible. And with the best work interdisciplinary in character, I have not focused upon a particular discipline, such as political science or sociology. The result is a broad overview of conflict studies which includes contributions from all kinds of social scientists—anthropologists, social psychologists, historians, economists, political scientists, and sociologists, and those of a few other fields as well. The attempt to be cosmopolitan extends to two other aspects: a review of important developments in both theory and research, without too much formality or technical emphasis in either direction, and an appreciation both for the classics of social thought and for some of the latest findings. I therefore will treat the ideas of Machiavelli or Marx with as much serious concern as those of contemporary game theorists or the researchers of recent collective violence.

In keeping with this eclectic approach, I have also tried to avoid presenting a clear ideological position. The dogmas of fixed positions tend to dissolve as we approach the complexities of social conflict with a broadly empirical spirit. Nevertheless, I believe that it is impossible to bring together such a broad array of studies as we find here without giving something of my own general framework of thought. Let me then forewarn readers of what they may expect from my (often implicit) presuppositions. One central theme in my approach might be labeled "social realism." I think we generally fail to inform ourselves fully of the objective basis for conflicts; we too easily assume that they are based on the bad intentions of wrong-headed leaders, who alone prevent some ideal world of peace and justice from flowering. Part of the problem is inadequate attention to the very real conflicts of interest that occur in all aspects of social life. Another part of the problem is a tendency to confuse our subjective experience (which leads us to view things as matters of individual psychology) with the actual underlying causal order of social forces (which is more collective in character).

However, a realistic understanding of conflicts does not require any particular methodological approach. In fact, a broad range of methodologies is precisely what is needed for an adequate understanding of social conflict. If we try to limit ourselves to the most rigorous forms of research, we usually find that our most important questions are scarcely addressed. What we may call a "soft-nosed empiricism" therefore joins "social realism" as an underlying theme characterizing the present work.

Partly to identify possible biases in the way this book is put together, but more to acknowledge important contributions to my thinking, let me mention a number of personal influences upon my work in social conflict. A religious and family heritage of pacifism is one important influence. So is my training as a sociologist, beginning with the important influences of my undergraduate teachers (L. Roy Just at Tabor College and Paul C. Kochan at Baker University) and continuing with graduate work at the University of Kansas; especially important here was the tempering of my youthful idealism with a respect for empirical research. Several authors were especially important in sharpening my interest in the area of conflict; among the most significant writings were *Conflict and Defense* by Kenneth Boulding, *The Functions of Social Conflict* by Lewis Coser, *Fights, Games and Debates* by Anatol Rapoport, and *The Strategy of Conflict* by Thomas Schelling. My classes in social conflict at Western Michigan University and Indiana State University have also been important in shaping my decisions as to what is suitable for a book such as this. Among other acknowledgments of help in preparing the present work, special mention should be made of the library facilities of Indiana State University; the skill at deciphering a very rough manuscript on the part of my typist, Lois Alberti; and the patient advice of my editor at Oxford University Press, Spencer Carr.

Terre Haute   J.A.S.
January 1981

Contents

Part One

Introduction

1

A New Science?

Lewis Richardson, a Quaker, was personally opposed to taking up arms in World War I. However, as a loyal subject of the British crown, he also felt a call to national duty. This, with his humanitarian impulses, led him to service as an ambulance driver, bringing wounded soldiers in from the front lines in France. During the lulls between battles, he amused himself by playing with numbers. He began to formulate mathematical analyses of war. Could we not quantify the patterns of action and reaction in war? Richardson thought that we could. And could we not derive mathematical equations to summarize such patterns—helping us to predict future events? He began thinking systematically along these lines.

After the war, Richardson spent many years gathering statistics of, as he called them, "deadly quarrels" and formulating mathematical models of conflict processes. Although he was respected for his work in physics and elected a Fellow of the prestigious Royal Society, very few people took seriously his conflict studies. Richardson himself considered them more important than his work in physical science (he retired early from teaching to be able to devote his full time to conflict research), but this appeared to matter little. Except for a handful of scholars, this painstaking work was simply ignored. He was unable to find a publisher for either of the two long manuscripts he produced in this area, and it was not until seven years after his death that his two main works (under the titles of *Arms and Insecurity* and *Statistics of Deadly Quarrels*) were finally published.[1]

During the last thirty years Richardson's work has finally been widely recognized, and he is now considered among the pioneers of a new field of scientific study. But why in his own lifetime did so few take seriously this work? Is the scientific study of human conflict so preposterous? It does not seem so today—at least no more preposterous than dozens of other areas in the social sciences. But during Richardson's lifetime the social sciences were apparently not quite ready for what he had to offer. His work was more mathematical than the social sciences were generally prepared to deal with; this is part of our explanation for the limited acceptance of Richardson's work. But another point is that in his day there was no established field into which his work might be placed. This has significantly changed since his death in 1953.

There has been an active growth in systematic studies of conflict since the early 1950s. Scholars have energetically pursued comparative studies of conflict behavior, laboratory investigations of negotiations, and theoretical models of conflict processes. Although worldwide, this burgeoning interest in conflict studies has been especially notable in American and European universities. Side-by-side with specialized pursuits of scholars has been the development of educational programs in what is often called "peace studies." Thus today at a few American colleges it is possible to complete an undergraduate major in peace studies, and at several universities one can now earn a Ph.D. degree in this area.

There are various names to refer to this new field. For purposes of public relations "peace" seems to be preferred over "conflict," though analytically conflict processes are often seen as more fundamental than those of peace.* So the work in conflict and peace studies goes on as people variously talk about "conflict studies," "conflict theory," "peace studies," "peace science," or the "peace research movement."

In taking seriously the question mark in the title of this

---

*This is not meant to suggest that the divisive forces of human society are more fundamental than those of cohesion. We only suggest that an understanding of peace usually requires an analysis of the underlying forces of conflict, while the study of conflict does not always imply a corresponding attention to peace.[2]

chapter, we are led to ask whether the new area of conflict studies is really a new discipline. Has it firmly established its own identity among the social sciences, or does it remain simply a point of convergence for scholars of various disciplines? A good argument could be made for either side in answering this question. Let us consider briefly both sides, presenting first—after the pattern of a good debate—the affirmative case for a new discipline.

Kenneth Boulding has solid enough credentials as an economist that he would not need to identify himself with another discipline. Still, as a leading participant in the peace research movement, he believes that a new discipline has been established. He has succinctly summarized this case:

> There are perhaps three tests of a discipline: does it have a bibliography? can you give courses in it? and, can you give examinations in it? A fourth criterion should perhaps be added: does it have any specialized journals? On all these four counts, conflict and peace studies can certainly claim to be a discipline.[3]

But does a common focus of interest and study necessarily mean a discipline? True, there are journals and organizations to represent peace research. But does membership in the International Peace Research Association (a worldwide organization sponsored by UNESCO)—or the Consortium on Peace Research, Education and Development (in North America) or the Peace Science Society (International)—require identification with a new discipline? As one approach to an answer, we can examine how authors of the leading journals identify themselves. As I write this, I have at my desk the latest issues of the *Journal of Conflict Resolution* and the *Journal of Peace Science,* as well as the latest volume of published *Papers* of the Peace Science Society (International). A quick count indicates that 33 authors are represented in these three issues, all but 3 having a university affiliation. Of the 30 university-based contributors, 21 are identified with standard social science disciplines (9 political scientists, 7 economists, 3 sociologists, 1 anthropologist, and 1 psychologist). The other 9 represent a miscellaneous assortment (including mathematics, law, industrial engineering, and "social systems science"). Only the authors of two articles are identified in a manner which suggests any formal institutional claims of peace research; one economist is also identified with Stanford's Hoover Institution on War, Revolution, and Peace, and the joint authors of another article are affiliated with the University of Pennsylvania's Regional Science Department and Peace Science Unit.

From this brief examination, we may conclude that most participants in the peace research movement have a primary scholarly identity in one of the standard social science disciplines. But we also recognize that the combination is quite varied; certainly no single discipline can claim peace research as simply an adjunct to itself.

So, do we have a new discipline here or do we not? Perhaps we need not decide clearly either for or against the disciplinary claim. We can recognize that scholars with diverse backgrounds have developed a common interest in conflict and peace studies. We can further recognize that in doing so they need not give up their identities as economists, political scientists, sociologists, or whatever. There is a high degree of interdisciplinary work and cross-disciplinary interaction. But the new focus in conflict studies has not yet been thoroughly institutionalized. If it is an emerging discipline, it is still not widely recognized as such.

The title of this first chapter ends with a question mark for more than one reason. So far, we have been concerned with whether or not we have *a* new science. The second word in the title might also be seen as problematic: do we have a *new* science?

The focus of scholarly interest in conflict studies and peace research has certainly grown dramatically since World War II. The research productivity of the last twenty years overshadows that of all previous periods combined. But are the fundamental ideas involved really new? Here, again, we shall hedge. As will be apparent in the remaining chapters of this book, the contributions of the last few decades are especially important. The most systematic empirical work has, with only a few exceptions, been carried out since the mid-1950s. But most of the fundamental ideas have been around for much longer. As we will see in the next four chapters, the fundamental perspectives we use today were already widespread during the nineteenth century. And we can go even further back in time (which we will do on occasion in this book) to get important insights for our studies. The analysis of the Peloponnesian War by Thucydides and Aristotle's reflections on revolutions provide two examples of writings which, though over two thousand years old, still provide vital insights in this area.

Finally, let us also question the last word in the title of this chapter. Do we really have a new science? If by science we mean merely systematic empirical research, there can be no question about it; much of this has accumulated, especially in the last decade or so. But is this research organized by a clear set of general propositions about human behavior? And are these propositions set forth as *positive* rather than *normative* principles? Here our answers are not quite so clear.

In the early development of most sciences, we find a strong concern for practical problems. Principles are seen as guides for dealing intelligently with these problems as well as guides for the understanding of fundamental truth. The propositions that sum up key ideas therefore have a *normative* (indicating what should be done) as well as a *positive* (simply describing how things are) character. As a science matures, however, it tends to lose this normative basis. The science seeks basic truth; its applications (though admittedly with normative components) are another matter, not to be confused with pure science.

The science of conflict is not at present generally regarded as a pure science in this positive and nonnormative sense. It may someday become such, for most of its research is cast in this mold. However, the normative approach to posing fundamental questions is still very much with us. We ask not only how nations in conflict actually carry on their contest but also how the conflict may or should be resolved. We ask not only how a revolutionary movement arises but what should be its actions if it is to succeed, or how the government should act if the rebellion is to be suppressed. Such questions are almost inevitably normative; and to the extent that the peace scientists deal with them, their science is not formed directly according to the pattern of the natural sciences.

But the field of conflict studies is not unique in having this problem of a normative-positive mixture. In this regard, it is simply mirroring the general state which is characteristic of most of the social sciences. And, as is the case with other fields, we learn here that normative issues may be as intellectually challenging as are those of a purely positive framework. Normative questions do not necessarily demand that we be wishy-washy.

The predominant spirit with which we embark on our survey of the science of conflict will be that associated with positive science. We are pursuing knowledge primarily for its own sake—which means primarily for our own understanding rather than for any particular applications. But there are limits to how far we can go with this framework in the study of conflict before we are brought eventually to normative issues. Perhaps this is a sign that the science of conflict is not yet a "true" or pure science. Perhaps. But the author prefers to think of it as a sign that we are struggling with issues that really matter, critically and directly, for the world in which we live. Rather than a matter for apology, we may consider the presence of fundamentally normative questions as a cause for excitement. They pose a challenge which is both intellectual and humane, for in the study of social conflict we deal with a most elusive intertwining of empirical facts and human values.

2

Overview

In this brief chapter, we present an introduction and overview for the main parts of this book. Part Two gives a background for understanding the leading theoretical approaches to the study of social conflict. Part Three surveys some of the most important empirical research of recent decades. In Part Four our attention shifts to general questions of strategy. And Part Five leads us through questions concerning conflict resolution.

FOUNDATIONS OF CONFLICT THEORY

Science is built from facts, but the facts are organized by a structure of ideas. In Chapters 3 through 5 we will review some of the leading ideas which have given structure to the emerging science of conflict.

As science develops, the structure of ideas becomes more refined and systematic. General ideas are reshaped into formal theories. To attempt to catalog or summarize all the theories of social conflict formulated by social scientists is beyond the ambitions of the present book. But we do believe that it is important to give some sense of the general structures of thought from which these theories have emerged. In order to do so, we will examine in some detail three perspectives from which the study of social conflict may be approached.

The first perspective is primarily biological. It is based upon the nature of humans as a species within the animal kingdom. It is assumed that different species are involved in a competitive struggle to survive, and that to some extent this struggle carries over to competition and aggressive behavior within the species. This competition between life forms (both between and within species) is the starting point for this perspective. Social conflict, in this approach, is a product of biological evolution; it represents the particular adaptations that the human species has made to its place within the framework of living forms.

The second perspective is primarily social psychological. It is based firmly upon the individual and the interests which each individual develops. That the interests of individuals are not always harmonious is the starting point for this perspective. Social conflict, in this approach, is based on the underlying conflicts of interest between individuals.

The third perspective is primarily sociological. It is based upon the structure of society and the interests of different groups within that structure. The opposition of interests between groups is the starting point for this third fundamental approach to social conflict. Social conflict, in this approach, is a product of human groups struggling for position within the overall framework of society.

Each of the next three chapters is based on one of these perspectives. To assist the process of fully absorbing a perspective, we will select the ideas of one person as the main or initial focus for each chapter. For this we will draw on three of the intellectual giants of modern thought: Charles Darwin, Adam Smith, and Karl Marx. Charles Darwin's conceptualization of organic evolution serves as the natural basis for a biological theory of human aggression and conflict; although its social implications take us far beyond Darwin, his posing of the fundamental issues provides a key to the understanding of social conflict. Some readers may be surprised by our use of Adam Smith, but his little-known social psychological views nicely supplement his better-known economic ideas to give a comprehensive basis for a theory of individual interests and conflicts of interest. Our treatment of Karl Marx is also selective, emphasizing Marx the sociologist over Marx the socialist; and we will find in his sociological thinking the foundations for a systematic theory of conflict between segments of society.

The development of ideas follows a somewhat different pattern in each of these three chapters. What we are striving to achieve in each case is the clear elucidation of a key perspective for viewing social conflict, along with a critical appreciation of its potential for guiding work in the social sciences of today. To do this, we will combine the ideas of an "old master" with more contemporary contributions in a similar tradition.

Each of these three chapters is devoted to one fundamental insight for understanding social conflict. All three of these insights point to an underlying basis of social conflict (in our nature as a species, in different interests of different individuals, or in different objectives of different groups), and all three are important for a thorough understanding of human conflict. This does not necessarily mean, however, that they are all *equally* important for all purposes. At least if our focus is on conflict within society, the Marxian tradition is more directly relevant than is that associated with either Smith or Darwin. We therefore may have more occasion to refer to the ideas of Chapter 5 in subsequent chapters than to those of Chapters 3 or 4. But that need not overly concern us at present. For now it is more important that we recognize that each of these perspectives has made a profound impact upon the social sciences, and that each serves as a valid base for building a scientific understanding of human conflict.[1]*

Selected Studies of Violent Conflict

In Chapters 6 through 8 our focus will shift from theory to research. We will leave aside most of the methodological questions posed by the researchers, and the research examined will be limited to that dealing with the most violent forms of conflict. But despite these limitations (imposed by the need to keep this work down to a manageable size and scope), the breadth remaining for these three chapters is still considerable.

---

*Notes at the back of this book include brief citations and bibliographic comments (such as this note and those for Chapter 1). However, the serious reader should also be alerted that the notes for subsequent chapters are varied in their content, including some matters of a technical nature. Occasionally these notes will be much more than incidental comments. In all cases, however, they go beyond what is necessary for the introductory reader. For this reason they are placed at the back of the book, where they need not overly burden the process of an initial reading.

Important foundations for the scientific study of conflict were laid during the second quarter of the present century. Among these foundations must be considered Lewis F. Richardson's pioneering work with mathematical models, Quincy Wright's exhaustive compilation of research on war, and Crane Brinton's comparative analysis of revolutions. These contributions are briefly surveyed in Chapter 6, "Three Pioneers." Chapter 7, "Further Studies of Strife," follows with a survey of more recent research on collective violence within nations. Here we give special attention to the more quantitative and comparative research on civil strife, such as that represented by Ted Robert Gurr and Charles Tilly. In Chapter 8, "Recent Research on War," we turn our attention to research of a similar nature (that is, quantitative and comparative) which focuses on the study of war.

Before we embark on this survey of recent literature on wars and civil strife, several qualifications and limitations about our treatment should be understood. We will be able to deal with only a small part of the available literature; that small part included will be outlined in only summary fashion; and many important questions about social conflict will be omitted. Let us amplify briefly each of these points.

Only a small part of the literature will be included. Out of hundreds of fine studies, we will select only a few for special attention. We have tried to include those which are the best known, but of course, different scholars have different lists of their favorite studies. Also, we have tried to represent something of the range of types of studies—from historically oriented research (like that of Brinton or Tilly), to cross-national statistical comparisons (such as those of Gurr and the Fierabends), to a comparative analysis of cases within a nation (for example, Spilerman's survey of American racial disturbances), to an exhaustive treatment of the background of a single conflict (such as work by Holsti or Choucri and North on the background of World War I). More on any of these topics, we hope, can be found in a nearby library for the reader who wants to delve more deeply into any of these areas of study.

Only brief sketches are given of each of the researches discussed. We try to give enough of a description so that the general methodology involved is apparent, for we want these researches to be viewed primarily as examples of empirical science. Although our attention is especially on the empirical side of the work discussed, we are also concerned with theoretical implications. We will therefore give at least some attention to the general theoretical models which these studies represent or have implications for. In the process, we hope that the reader learns enough to appreciate the kind of scientific work which these studies represent.

Finally, many important questions about social conflict will not be included in these chapters. Our attention will be focused on the most violent forms of social conflict—wars, revolutions, and other forms of collective violence. These most dramatic forms of conflict have especially drawn our attention and therefore have been the subject of more research than the less violent forms. But we should recognize that not all conflict involves violence.[2] If by violence we mean the willful injury to individuals or destruction of their property, it is possible to have very bitter social conflicts without violence. Two bitterly hostile factions may oppose each other in an organization and never come to blows, just as two organizations or two ideologies may have deep-seated conflicts without ever fighting physically. Violence, however, gives at least an objective indication of a significant degree of conflict, and major instances of violence like wars and revolutions always represent significant social conflicts. Therefore, our focus upon conflicts in society marked by significant violence should not be seen as representing all possible forms of social conflict, but it does allow us to give attention to some of the most important studies of some of the most dramatic forms of human conflict.

STRATEGY IN CONFLICT

In Chapters 6 through 8, our framework is clearly that of pursuing an objective empirical science. We search for generalizations which may help organize a great variety of empirical studies of conflict. In Part Four (Chapters 9 through 11), this focus changes to a significant degree. There we will concern ourselves fundamentally with the problem of participants seeking to pursue conflict in a rational manner. The common theme in these three chapters is "strategy"—generally understood as a carefully planned course of action toward a clearly identified goal, and specifically understood to involve conflict with another party.

Niccolo Machiavelli helps to open our thinking (in Chapter 9, "The Machiavellian Tradition") to the subject of strategy in conflict. A review of his recommendations in *The Prince* serves to alert us to the values (and some possible pitfalls) of an attitude of political realism. We then relate this attitude to more recent thinking in military affairs and foreign policy.

In Chapter 10, "The Theory of Games," we approach the subject of strategy in a much more abstract manner. We draw in fact primarily from mathematics in laying out the main elements and results of analysis of the theory of games. Although avoiding formal mathematical analysis, we present examples of the main approaches toward solutions in this abstract way of viewing social conflict.

We consider game theory further in Chapter 11 ("A Science of Strategy?"), seeking especially to relate it to real-world decision making. We also note some new developments in game theory which may be making it of greater value for empirical studies. Finally, we consider how the more formal types of strategy analysis (such as game theory) can be combined with the insights of the conventional social sciences in improving the art of practical decision making.

THE RESOLUTION OF CONFLICT

Conflicts are not only to be faced and fought, using whatever strategy may seem advantageous. Conflicts are also to be resolved. The need for conflict resolution brings issues to the fore that have been only indirectly considered previously. Among the questions to be considered are the following: How do parties typically proceed when they negotiate an end to a conflict in the real world? What are some alternatives to negotiations in terminating a conflict? Is physical force ever an effective means of conflict resolution? What role may third parties play in helping to resolve a conflict? And what rational standards of justice may be applied in resolving a conflict to make sure that it ends fairly? These are a few of the questions which help organize the materials of the final four chapters of this book.

In Chapter 12, "The Dynamics of Bargaining," we first examine the typical pattern of interaction in American labor-management negotiations. We then compare laboratory studies of negotiations to real-world settings in order to consider just how widely applicable certain models of the bargaining process may be.

Alternatives to negotiations are considered in Chapter 13, "Varieties of Resolution." Among the various forms of conflict resolution illustrated in this chapter are physical force, popular resolution through elections, the combination or assimilation of parties, the separation or segregation of parties, and unexpected external events. The possibilities of physical force for resolving conflict is a topic given special attention in this chapter.

In Chapter 14, "Resolution through Reason," we consider first the role of third parties in helping to resolve a dispute. They provide the possibility that broader considerations may be brought to bear in bringing a conflict to a conclusion. We then examine how ideas about justice may apply to issues of social conflict. Two main traditions of thinking about justice (each with its roots in ancient Greek philosophy) are examined for the light they may give in clarifying the various claims for justice in the rational resolution of conflicts.

In Chapter 15, "The Search for Peace," we draw a few concluding generalizations from the broad perspective given by the preceding chapters. Although we will resist the temptation to sermonize about the horrors of war and the blessings of peace, the reader should be warned that these final comments will be of a rather general nature. A few final points are made which the author believes are implicit in most of the current work in the systematic study of conflict.

Part Two

Foundations
of
Conflict Theory

3

Charles Darwin and the Biology of Human Aggression

Is a propensity for social conflict somehow rooted in our nature as members of the human species?

This question cannot adequately be answered with a simple yes or no. In pursuing an answer, we will first examine the revolution in thinking about human origins and human nature which is associated with the work of Charles Darwin (1809–82). We will then discuss some of the social implications of Darwinism as seen by other theorists in the second half of the nineteenth century. Finally, we will consider some of the Darwinian currents of thought today, and then draw our conclusions (tentative though they may be) about the biological basis of human conflict and aggression.

THE ORIGIN OF DARWINISM

The theory of evolution was no sudden hypothesis·in Charles Darwin's mind. The idea had long existed in one form or another (Darwin's own grandfather had written a book on the subject), and Darwin early questioned the assumption of permanently fixed species. It was during the five years that the young Darwin served as a naturalist aboard the *Beagle* (1831–36) that his thoughts on evolution began to take shape. However, he still lacked an explanation for why or how evolutionary change occurred.

The main purpose of the expedition of the *Beagle* was to survey the coast of South America. Darwin contributed to this purpose with important geological observations. These observations clearly supported the notion that present landforms were produced by slow evolutionary changes from previous forms, as was indeed claimed in the recently published *Principles of Geology* (first edition 1830–33) by Charles Lyell. But Darwin's curiosity roamed widely to other matters for observation—the various types of plants found in different places, the strange variations in forms of animals, and the strange customs of primitive Indians and only marginally civilized gauchos. He collected a fascinating variety of biological specimens, and his written observations in the form of his *Journal* (1839) were soon published.

But even more important than Darwin's discoveries on this expedition were the unanswered questions which arose. Different geological strata encased different forms of life; does this not indicate an evolution of life forms as well as the earth forms in which they are found? And how are we to understand the important similarities between extinct varieties and present plants and animals in the same area? Or the present differences between similar forms in different locations? Some form of biological evolution seemed a necessary part of the answer for each of these questions.

But Darwin still had no explanation of what could account for the major changes necessary to transform a species. For months after his return to England, Darwin pondered the subject of how evolution might take place. Changes in domesticated breeds of plants and animals offered some clues, and they demonstrated the importance of a careful selection of preferred types. But how could selection be produced in nature? The answer came to Darwin quite suddenly, as he recounts in his *Autobiography:*

> In October 1838, that is, fifteen months after I had begun my systematic enquiry, I happened to read for amusement Malthus on *Population,* and being well prepared to appreciate the struggle for existence which everywhere goes on from long-continued observation of the habits of animals and plants, it at once struck me that under these circumstances favourable variations would tend to be preserved, and unfavourable ones to be destroyed. The result of this would be the formation of a new species.[1]

Natural environments, in other words, select a new species by the gradual effect of differential death rates of the previous population. Those more apt to survive are "naturally selected" to become the emerging form.

Darwin was extremely cautious about this new idea, for he realized its sharp departure from the generally accepted opinions of fellow scientists. Then too there were other kinds of opinions—such as those of his devout new wife, to whom he had resolved to say nothing about his radical new ideas. It was not until four years later that Darwin set forth in a brief manuscript his idea of natural selection, but he made no move to publish this. What he did publish instead were such books as *Coral Reefs* (1842) and *Geological Observations on South America* (1846). In 1858, twenty years after he had first conceived the idea of natural selection, he at last worked on a book to present this theory. Then, however, in the mail came a letter from the East Indies, where Alfred R. Wallace was engaged in research as a naturalist. With this letter was an essay which, Darwin was horrified to discover, was almost an exact summary of his own theory. This moved Darwin into action. He sought the advice of scientific friends, who arranged for Wallace's essay and an abstract of Darwin's ideas to be presented together to the scientific world. Darwin then hurried to bring out a fuller statement the next year, which took the form of his celebrated *Origin of Species* (1859).

The full title of his book, *The Origin of Species by Means of Natural Selection or the Preservation of Favored Races in the Struggle for Life,* makes clear the central importance of natural selection in Darwin's theory of evolution. In his introduction he summarizes this idea as follows:

> As many more individuals of each species are born than can possibly survive; and as, consequently, there is a frequently recurring struggle for existence, it follows that any being, if it vary however slightly in any manner profitable to itself, under the complex and sometimes varying conditions of life, will have a better chance of surviving, and thus be *naturally* selected.[2]

In the hundreds of fact-filled pages that follow, the theory of biological evolution is systematically developed. Although natural selection is not presented as a total explanation, it is seen as the most important factor in the origin and change of species. "Thus," he says in his final paragraph, "from the war of nature, from famine and death, the most exalted object which we are capable of conceiving, namely, the production of the higher animals, directly follows."

In the *Origin* Darwin says nothing about the evolution of man. He does suggest that "much light will be thrown" in the future by similar analyses concerning "the origin of man and his history." But that is the extent of Darwin's discussion of human origins in that book. Twelve years later, in *The Descent of Man,* he attempted to follow up on this direction of analysis. While still the central theme, natural selection is here joined by a number of other ideas which were only briefly presented or hinted at in the *Origin of Species.*

The Descent of Man includes attention to, as factors in evolution, the inheritance of acquired characteristics, special accidents of heredity, what Darwin calls "correlated variation" (features which are not themselves adaptive but happen to be developed along with those which are), and differential fertility. Especially emphasized is "sexual selection" or preferential mating, which directly results in differential fertility. In fact, the full title of the book is *The Descent of Man and Selection in Relation to Sex,* and a discussion of sexual selection actually constitutes most of the book. It is among higher animals that sexual selection becomes important in evolution; among lower animals "perceptive and intellectual faculties are not sufficiently advanced to allow of the feelings of love and jealousy, or of the exertion of choice."[3] Sexual selection takes place in two kinds of "sexual struggle" between rivals: one is typically between males who seek "to drive away or kill their rivals," while the other is a more subtle competition for the attentions and favors of the opposite sex (male or female). In both cases, we have the basis of a rivalry between individuals within a species in seeking to mate which is a more direct confrontation than is the impersonal competition of natural selection.

SOCIAL DARWINISM

Other than in his extended discussion of sexual selection, Darwin had little to say about social or group factors in human evolution. He did briefly refer to the importance of "social instincts" which higher animals have acquired gradually "for the good of the community." Man, however, has "few or no special instincts"; social motives in humans, said Darwin, are much more influenced by learning than is the case with other animals. Other than making such general points, Darwin himself contributed little to what has come to be called "social Darwinism."[4]

Other writers were far less reticent in tracing the implications of Darwinism for society. One whom Darwin cited with general approval ("our great philosopher," he called him at one point) was his fellow Englishman, Herbert Spencer. Spencer was an even more thoroughgoing evolutionist than Darwin, extending this idea to the far reaches of human society and, indeed, the entire universe. Spencer also talked about the importance of "survival of the fittest" (a phrase which Darwin borrowed from him) before the *Origin of Species* appeared.

In his *First Principles,* published in 1862, Spencer sets forth a universal law of evolution. It is this:

> Evolution is an integration of matter and concomitant dissipation of motion, during which the matter passes from an indefinite, incoherent homogeneity to a definite, coherent heterogeneity, and during which the retained motion undergoes a parallel transformation.[5]

Such evolution was viewed as a cosmic law of nature—applicable alike to what Spencer distinguished as the *inorganic* (physical), *organic* (biological), and *superorganic* (or sociocultural) realms.

On the superorganic level, societies may be seen as significant integrations which continually increase in coherence and heterogeneity. This view of human society is parallel to the conception of biological organisms as emergent wholes. Societies, like individual organisms, develop their integrities or unities through a struggle for survival, a struggle which in large part pits society against society. Competition for survival is therefore characteristic of both individual organisms and societies, and in this struggle are forged the characteristic forms taken by animal species and/or human societies.

Fear is endemic in the uncertainties of early forms of human society, which leads to religious and political forms of social control. Especially prominent is a military form of social organization. Militarism makes possible the combination of smaller groups into larger units, thus extending the scope of social organization. With the expanding scope of social organization, however, more emphasis can be given to peaceful pursuits. Gradually, then, as the scope of human society expands, the plasticity of society increases and individual spontaneity and initiative assume more importance. Coercion becomes less and less necessary as a basis of social integration as more effective institutions of human cooperation prove their survival value. Spencer's view of the general evolution of society may thus be described as a transition from "military" (or coercively controlled) to "industrial" (or functionally cooperative) forms of social organization.

As we move more and more toward an industrial society—that is, one of peaceful interdependence—obvious conflict becomes more muted. But, according to Spencer, competition is still going on indirectly, pitting individual against individual and institutional form against institutional form. This is nature's way of discriminating between the more fit and less fit forms. And the less we consciously interfere with the process the better, for the most adaptive (and therefore best) forms are those which emerge gradually out of this long-term competition for survival. This, of course, led Spencer directly to the political position of *laissez-faire,* arguing for a bare minimum of governmental regulation. This should allow, he believed, maximum room for the competitive process, which produces the gradual improvement of human society.

In the United States, William Graham Sumner was soon arguing somewhat similar views. Conflict over the means of subsistence is the underlying fact which shapes the nature of human society, according to Sumner. But Sumner emphasized group factors (including the binding power of folkways and mores, which are arbitrarily evolved by groups) more strongly than did Spencer, and Sumner had less optimism about the direction of evolutionary change.

Spencer and Sumner were among the founding fathers of

the discipline of sociology in England and the United States, respectively. Both were thoroughgoing evolutionists, and both saw a central role for the application of natural selection to institutions of human society. Meanwhile, on the European continent an even more extreme form of social Darwinism was being propounded in the name of sociology by Ludwig Gumplowicz. In 1883 Gumplowicz published his most famous work, *Der Rassenkampf (Race Conflict)*, followed two years later by his *Outlines of Sociology*. He too tried to base his sociology upon natural science foundations; and for Gumplowicz, as for Spencer and Sumner, conflict between societies is a basic theme in social evolution. But especially unlike Spencer, Gumplowicz did not perceive these conflicts as becoming reduced and more individualized with the development of civilization. War between groups, in his view, has always been the main proving ground for the evolution of human social forms—and so it remains today.

At the heart of social conflict for Gumplowicz is conflict between races and nationality groups. To begin with, he assumes (in contrast to Darwin, incidentally) a polygenetic origin (that is, for different races at different times) of mankind. He further assumes the existence of an inherent animosity between persons of different races. Once the means of warfare became developed, it was only natural that war would be a constant feature of humanity. With war comes the possibility of the conquest of one group by another and the development of a strong state to ensure a means for domination. With the consolidation of larger political units (through war and conquest), a greater differentiation develops within the society. From then on, the range of conflict increases within societies to add to that between societies as, in the words of Gumplowicz, "the life and death struggle between hordes anthropologically different becomes a contest between social groups, classes, estates and political parties." [6] Class conflict is an especially prominent feature in developed states. In origin the dominant class usually represents a conquering group, but over time new classes develop to complicate the power relationships. Primary elements in the formation of the class system are opposing economic interests as well as the formation of alignments necessary to allow effective domination by a ruling group. The desire for greater material welfare for one's group and a drive toward domination over other groups provide the constant stimuli for further conflicts of class against class and nation against nation.

Throughout the writings of Gumplowicz runs a strong naturalistic emphasis. "The alpha and omega of sociology," as he summarized it, "its highest perception and final word is: human history is a natural process."[7] In this natural process, however, it is human groups, not individuals, which constitute the fundamental units. Indeed, according to Gumplowicz,

> It is not man himself who thinks, but his social community; the source of his thoughts is in the social medium in which he lives, the social atmosphere which he breathes, and he cannot think aught else than what the influences of his social environment concentrating upon his brain necessitate. . . . Man is not self-made mentally any more than he is physically. His mind and thoughts are the product of his social medium, of the social element whence he arose, in which he lives.

Given this social determinism, Gumplowicz can give no basis for considering social reality as anything other than it is. Conflict is endemic in the nature of human society, and there is nothing which we can do about it. Sociology can contribute nothing to help man resolve these conflicts, for they will continue to be resolved primarily through physical force. What social science can best contribute is understanding—and resignation. By adding to our knowledge of the basic laws of human society, according to Gumplowicz, "sociology lays the foundation for the morals of reasonable resignation, morals higher than those resting on the imaginary freedom and self-determination of the individual."

Today no sociologists apply the Darwinian ideas of evolution and natural selection to human society quite so thoroughly as did their late-nineteenth-century counterparts. No one generalizes so freely and with such optimism as Spencer, or so broadly and with such pessimism as Gumplowicz. Human society can be said to evolve, but in such an infinitely more complex manner than do biological organisms that sociologists generally hold that natural selection as a biological idea has little relevance. But does it not still have *some* value for understanding the nature of society?

Most sociologists today would admit some room for the principle of natural selection in the evolution of cultural traits—as *cultural* evolution, though, quite distinct from biological evolution. We are able to fly, for example, not because we have a pair of appendages which have been gradually adapted for millions of years to serve as wings, but because of tools produced by the human brain and hand. These tools themselves undergo a kind of evolution, as new forms of airplanes prove themselves better adapted to our needs than previous forms. So, a kind of natural selection goes on in determining the products of human culture which are most likely to survive. But note: we are not now talking of the survival of human individuals or groups. We are talking about the survival of cultural forms, forms which are generally shared by humans and which fairly easily pass from group to group. We are not talking of anything which is the special property of biologically identifiable groups, such as families, clans, tribes, or races.

Some social scientists have argued that cultural evolution has completely displaced biological evolution as a factor of significant change for humans. Weston LaBarre, for example, makes this claim:

> The human hand is the adaptation to end all adaptations: *the emancipated hand has emancipated man from any other organic evolution whatsoever.* With man, genetic evolution and organic experiments have come to an end. Without involving the animal body and its slow, blind genetic mechanisms, man's hands make the tools and the machines which render his own further physical evolution unnecessary; they replace the slow, cumbrous, expensive, uncertain, and painful mechanism of organic evolution with the swift, conscious, biologically free, and painless making of machines.[8]

Not all social scientists would agree that humans are now free from further biological evolution. Most would argue that such organic change is overshadowed by cultural evolution, but that biological evolution is still going on. Whether or not such organic change may be an important factor in our cultural adaptability and social behavior (other than by giving us our brains and hands in the first place) is one of the most hotly disputed questions among today's social scientists. Even those who most confidently ridicule the excesses of nineteenth-century social Darwinism find some of the same arguments coming from their colleagues in biology in the final decades of the twentieth century. Darwinism is once again becoming a center of controversy among scholars. In the next section we will examine how new currents of science—especially those bearing the names of "ethology" and "sociobiology"—are addressing themselves to the subject of the biology of human aggression.

The New Biology of Conflict

How much has happened in the hundred years since Darwinism became a major force in social science! Yet, strangely, how similar are some of the controversies engaging social scientists today to those of a century ago. The place of biological evolution in the understanding of human society is an issue which is still not at rest. This issue serves as the focus of renewed scientific and ideological debate, centering especially on the role of genetics in structuring human behavior.

As social science developed in the final decades of the nineteenth century and the opening years of the twentieth century, an evolutionary perspective provided a dominant framework for analysis. Early American sociology, for example, such as that represented by Lester F. Ward or William Graham Sumner, was cast solidly in the perspective of evolution—both biological and cultural. Early social psychology also followed an evolutionary perspective. Then, beginning in the second decade of the twentieth century and increasing in the 1920s and 1930s, came a disenchantment with such an approach. Evolutionary theory was viewed as too broad and all-encompassing for a scientific analysis of behavior. What seemed needed was a more limited framework, and anthropology, psychology, and sociology alike turned to the more patient accumulation of facts. Evolutionary theory was considered too speculative to have much to say for scientific studies of human behavior.

Then came the rapid advancement of genetic research in the third quarter of the twentieth century and, at the same time, marked progress in systematic behavior studies of lower animals. A new science called "ethology" was developed to study comparative animal behavior patterns, with a special emphasis upon the instinctive roots of such behavior. Popularizations of this work by Robert Ardrey, Konrad Lorenz, and Desmond Morris soon brought home to the literate public the implications of ethology for understanding human social behavior. Finally, in 1975, a still newer science, "sociobiology," was announced by E. O. Wilson and projected to take over eventually a broad area of science ranging from ethology to sociology. Immediate controversy soared about the pretensions of this newest science and especially about its claims regarding the genetic bases of behavior.[9]

Since central issues for the interpretation of human conflict and aggression are at stake, it is relevant that we at least review briefly this recent literature. Let us give special attention to Lorenz's *On Aggression* (a leading example of ethology). Later we will briefly examine Wilson's *Sociobiology*.

Much of *On Aggression* consists of a mature scientist's review and reflection on data with which he has first-hand experience—such as fighting behavior among cichlid species of fish or, his personal favorite, the greylag goose. Combining these with the research of others, he builds generalizations about aggression as a spontaneous response which is instinctively elicited by certain triggering occasions, with the occasions differing from species to species. Within each species there is a patterned regularity of the way aggression against fellow members of the species is expressed as well as the occasions for this aggression. Aggression is frequently highly ritualized, typically allowing for attack and submission to be expressed with little actual danger to life. Displacement of aggression upon substitute objects also frequently occurs, especially in highly social species.

In Lorenz's view, the natural mechanisms of aggression and its control are closely related to different forms of animal social organization. He points to four different types of social organization observed among various animal species. The simplest form is the anonymous crowd, a simple aggregation of members who band together for convenience or protection. Aggression is not characteristic within such simple "flocks" of birds or "schools" of fish. A second system of organization is the territorial group—members of a species which share a similar area, such as a nesting colony, which they defend against intruders. A third system is a tribal group, such as an extended family of rats which will attack any rat with the wrong kind of smell. All three of these systems of social organization are based on some vague consciousness of kind, but without requiring individual personal identities. The fourth system of social organization, the bond, is formed on the basis of individual identities. Here both love and hate become important features, with elaborate forms of courtship and intergenerational concern within the family group, along with highly expressive aggression against outsiders.

The particular forms of aggressive behavior, Lorenz holds, have been developed in each species through natural selection. They therefore always have some general evolutionary purpose, or perhaps a combination of particular purposes. The most general and common evolutionary function of animal aggression is the spacing out of the species. Such territorial dispersion facilitates population control (those more dispersed having lower life chances) and provides a reasonably effective environment for those remaining (enough food and mates, for example). More particular forms of aggressive behavior may function to facilitate sexual selection (such as access for a male to a particular female), brood defense, and the establishment of stable social relations (for example, through hierarchical "pecking orders"). Each species has its distinctive place in nature, and thus its distinctive combination of evolutionary functions fulfilled by aggression. And man? Says Lorenz:

> . . . it is more than probable that the destructive intensity of the aggression drive, still a hereditary evil of mankind, is the consequence of a process of intra-specific selection which worked on our forefathers for roughly forty thousand years, that is, throughout the Early Stone Age. When man had reached the stage of having weapons, clothing, and social organization, so overcoming the dangers of starving, freezing, and being eaten by wild animals, and these dangers ceased to be the essential factors influencing selection, an evil intra-specific selection must have set in. The factor influencing se-

lection was now the wars waged between hostile neighboring tribes.

At any rate, man is seen as having his aggression as strongly rooted in his biological heritage as is true for other species.[10] Indeed, he seems unusually murderous, for his development of weapons came so fast that he has not yet evolved the biological mechanisms of restraint—so common in the ritualized aggression of other species.

Humanity today, in the view of Lorenz, is left with a considerable burden in the control of its aggression. How are we to do this? In his final chapter, Lorenz considers a number of approaches toward controlling aggression. He dismisses simple moralistic condemnation and the elimination of aggressive cues as ineffective approaches, and the possibility of eliminating the aggressive drive through eugenic planning is also seen as a false lead (mainly because we do not know which desirable human traits might at the same time be lost). With what then are we left? Redirection seems to be Lorenz's main formula. He sees competitive sports as an especially promising area. He also talks about developing collective enthusiasm for causes of human betterment which can inspire us to heights of achievement and glory, as did the wars of old. Other forms of cultural control of aggression also should be furthered, he suggests. Finally, we are given the prescription of insight—to see our own behavior within a proper perspective. Two forms of this insight, either of which should aid our collective survival, are a sense of humor and a sense of our place in the natural order. Either assists us in developing the perspective necessary to help restrain that murderous impulse which lurks within.

◄§

The most problematic issue raised by Lorenz's work for us is that of the inherited nature of an aggressive drive, especially when we consider human behavior. Despite all the recent achievements in genetics, we are still a long way from identifying the precise genetic code for human inheritance. Even when we are able to derive a statistic called a "heritability index" (to measure the extent to which a given characteristic varies in response to known differences in heredity), its interpretation remains fraught with difficulties. For one thing, attempts to measure the heritability of aggression have not given either very high or very consistent results. This suggests that, at least for humans, aggression has a far greater learned component than Lorenz appears to allow.

However, we should recognize that in the higher vertebrates, including humans, there are rather clearly patterned neurological correlates of aggressive behavior. Centers of the brain associated with different kinds of aggressive responses have been identified and their functions described. Experimentally, it has been possible to manipulate aggression by hormone treatments and brain stimulation. But we should not neglect consideration of the sequence of events by which these physiological mechanisms normally operate. The brain centers most involved in aggression typically respond to signals given after some external stimulus is interpreted, and endocrine levels are typically affected in response as well. Aggression is not simply created from within; the physiological ingredients are themselves normally the result of perceptions about external events. As a leading student of animal behavior, John Paul Scott, concludes a discussion of the physiology of aggression:

> The important fact is that the chain of causation in every case eventually traces back to the outside. There is no physiological evidence of any spontaneous stimulation for fighting arising within the body.[11]

The points that we have just considered appear to be at variance with Lorenz's conception of aggression as a spontaneous response which is instinctively elicited by certain triggering occasions. At least for the higher vertebrates, the spontaneity appears in highly qualified fashion. Certain triggering occasions (for example, there is a fair amount of research to implicate aversive and frustrating stimuli with aggression) may indeed be associated with aggression, but this association depends significantly on past learning—especially in the case of humans.[12]

ENTER SOCIOBIOLOGY

Where *On Aggression* gives a leading naturalist's interpretations of aggression in humans and other animals, *Sociobiology* presumes to lay out a completely new science for the analysis of social behavior of animals of all types. Although conflict and aggression are not the central themes in this work, they are featured with enough prominence to make a few comments about this book relevant here.

Edward O. Wilson is an expert on insect societies, but his interests also cover broad questions of population biology and social organization in all species. These interests he proposes to bring together in the new science of "sociobiology." His enormous book, *Sociobiology: The New Synthesis*, reviews exhaustively the literature on the social life of animals, especially as interpreted within the framework of population biology. Within this framework, social evolution is viewed essentially as biological evolution. Genetic change is assumed to be the basis for changes in both the physical structure and the behavioral functioning of a species. Broadly speaking, then, features of social behavior are seen as genetically selected for, even if precise genes may not be identified. Wilson, however, is somewhat more cautious than Lorenz in talking about aggression as an instinct. Aggression is seen as genetic in the sense that, according to Wilson, "its components have proved to have a high degree of heritability," but he sees no general instinct of aggression. Rather, there are particular patterns of aggressive behavior which different species have found to be adaptive for their particular survival purposes. For example, displays of territorial defense are apt to be developed when the food supply is relatively limited and the costs of such defense are not too large. However, should defense prove too costly, a less territorial pattern is apt to be evolved. In evolving their particular patterns, says Wilson:

> Species are entirely opportunistic. Their behavior patterns do not conform to any innate restrictions but are guided, like all other biological traits, solely by what happens to be advantageous over a period of time sufficient for evolution to occur.[13]

Wilson identifies eight different categories of aggressive behavior: (1) territorial aggression, (2) dominance aggression, (3) sexual aggression, (4) parental disciplinary aggression, (5) weaning aggression, (6) moralistic aggression, (7) predatory aggression, and (8) antipredatory aggression. He emphasizes that aggression "is a mixture of very different behavior patterns serving very different functions" in different species. Even within the same species a wide variation in aggressive response is possible. He cites the example of how differently the rattlesnake will respond when wrestling with another rattlesnake, when stalking small prey, when dealing with a large animal, or when countering a rattlesnake-eating king snake. Four very different ways of fighting are all here shown by the same species of snake, each adapted to its special circumstances.

Wilson has little to say about human aggression, other than to assume that a characteristic "so widespread and easily invoked" can hardly be neutral or negative in affecting species or group survival. True, there is great variability in the aggressive behavior of humans. "But," continues Wilson,

> in order to be adaptive it is enough that aggressive patterns be evoked only under certain conditions of stress such as those that might arise during food shortages and periodic high population densities. It also does not matter whether the aggression is wholly innate or is acquired part or wholly by learning. We are now sophisticated enough to know that the capacity to learn certain behaviors is itself a genetically controlled and therefore evolved trait.

Here Wilson seems to be trying to avoid a heredity-versus-learning issue by viewing both as broadly within the adaptive processes of evolutionary change. He also suggests that the adaptive value of a particular behavior pattern for a species will not always be easily apparent to an observer.

In his final chapter, Wilson gives some attention to the distinctive plasticity and cultural nature of the human species, but his analysis of human social evolution is still essentially in terms of genetic evolution. Human institutions appear to have been selected for by the genetic advantages they gave to early human groups. Little room is provided for viewing cultural evolution as itself a primary determining force. It is this omission which most dismays sociologists and anthropologists about sociobiology.[14]

An example of Wilson's tendency to emphasize biological evolution to the neglect of cultural influences may be seen in his treatment of warfare. He suggests that war has played a significant role in the genetic evolution of humans, helping to spur general mental and cultural advance as well as selecting for military traits. Although possibly not universal (". . . some isolated cultures will escape the process for generations at a time, in effect reverting temporarily to what ethnographers classify as a pacific state"), warfare is viewed by Wilson as a significant general factor in human evolution. Anthropologists, however, have not shown any consensus in support of such an interpretation. Ashley Montagu counters with the view that "up to some twelve thousand years ago war played an insignificant role" in evolution, and that in the last 12,000 years war has become either biologically irrelevant or dysgenic.[15]

In pointing out various functions of war for primitive man, some anthropologists point to important contrasts between war fought within the tribe (often highly ritualized and associated with a male-supremacist cultural complex) and war between tribes (less common in the simplest societies than war within the tribe). It has been shown that these forms of warfare tend to be pursued in quite different fashions by rather different societies. Only in the case of intertribal war is the conflict relatively unrestrained and true victory or defeat a generally realistic outcome.[16]

Marvin Harris gives us an example of a largely cultural interpretation of early warfare. He views warfare within the tribe primarily in terms of cultural ecology. His analysis of warfare among the Maring of New Guinea, for example, suggests that it functioned primarily to prevent too great a pressure on the carrying capacity of the environment. It did this indirectly, by (1) placing a premium upon producing young men for fighting, thus leading to (2) infanticide or neglect of young females, thus (3) providing effective population control, and thus (4) reducing the pressure on available natural resources. War also more directly assisted the conservation of natural resources by keeping certain battle-related or recently abandoned areas out of cultivation for important periods of time. While such factors may have had some secondary significance for genetic selection (selecting males for fighting qualities), their main importance lies in the cultural order. Harris concludes that "war has been part of an adaptive strategy associated with particular technological, demographic, and ecological conditions" but that this does not require us to "invoke imaginary killer instincts or inscrutable or capricious motives to understand why armed combat has been so common in human history."[17]

We do not mean to present Harris' views as the final word on the meaning of primitive warfare; we use them mainly to contrast to the implications put forward by the sociobiologists. The general significance of such a contrast will be considered further in the final section of this chapter.

BEYOND NATURE?

Humans have often prided themselves on being more apart from than a part of nature. Recognizing our distinctive mode of adaptation—with conceptual thought, language, and a proliferation of tools—we are tempted to put ourselves in a very special place in relation to other forms of life. This leads to a desire to see our past as sharply different from that of other forms of life, to see our present as not bound by the constraints of our specific biological nature, and to see our future in terms of an infinite extension of our ability to control the forces of nature.

The Darwinian revolution—including its contemporary expressions in ethology and sociobiology—has forced us to reconsider this view of man. We now have another view of human origins, and our awareness of the biological limitations of our species has also grown. Even our vision of the future is more and more shaped by the recognition that we can continue to exist on our planet only as a part of an intricate web of life.

No doubt this renewed humility concerning our species is fundamentally good for us. But it is possible that we may be so caught up in the spirit of the Darwinian revolution that we might lose our sense of the peculiar distinctiveness of humans as cultural beings. We are a culture-creating species, whose linguistic patterns and systems of technology are as much a part of our world as are its flora and fauna. This is no doubt a result of our own distinctive prehistory of natural selection and evolution. But it also imposes limitations on the way we should see natural selection and evolution as applied to ourselves.

One of the mistakes we may make in uncritically accepting Darwinism is to overgeneralize the idea of natural selection. Natural selection does not necessarily imply some underlying primacy of conflict over cooperation. If nature is sometimes, as a Victorian poet put it, "red in tooth and claw," so too is it also often a symphony of marvelous coordination.[18] Survival is in part competitive, and the particular natures of species are shaped by this competitive legacy. But they are also shaped by the legacy of ways they have come to cooperate within the species and with other forms of life. When we come to humans, the role of cooperation within the species is greatly enhanced. To create and pass on a culture requires an unusual degree of common identity and group coordination. It is unlikely that such a culture-bearing species would have a greater endowment of aggressive genes than would most other mammals.

Another possible error which may be encouraged by an uncritical Darwinism is the assumption that biological evolution is the key to the future progress of our species. With this assumption usually goes the corollary that since biological evolution is not subject to any fundamental purposive control, there is little we can do to plan for our own long-term progess. We are, in this view, products of a blind progression, a progression which will continue to unfold blindly in the future according to the chance happenings of genetics and natural selection. But this view ignores the extent to which we are products of our culture as well as our genes, and it neglects the extent to which we can control and modify our culture. Human cultures do not suddenly transform themselves in response to human wishes, but there is at least some room for consciously guided change. To ignore this is to ignore what is probably most distinctively human.

Charles Darwin himself offers a beautiful example of what we are cautioning against. In one of his few pronouncements directly relevant to public policy, he said:

> Man, like every other animal, has no doubt advanced to his present high condition through a struggle for existence consequent on his rapid multiplication; and if he is to advance still higher, it is to be feared that he must remain subject to a severe struggle. Otherwise he would sink into indolence, and the more gifted men would not be more successful in the battle of life than the less gifted. Hence our natural rate of increase, though leading to many and obvious evils, must not be greatly diminished by any means. There should be open competition for all men; and the most able should not be prevented by laws or customs from succeeding best and rearing the largest number of offspring.[19]

The full logic of this position is difficult for us to accept in these days of contraception and planned parenthood. Darwin is actually suggesting a contrasting policy of encouraging "the largest number of offspring" to join in the struggle for life itself. Such a clear expression of social Darwinism can make sense only if we systematically turn our backs on our capacity as humans to exert control over the conditions of our life. This control does not always come easily. Much of it occurs through the collective accumulation of culture, of which we are not often very self-conscious. But there is room for at least a partly planned cultural supplement to the blind process of evolution through natural selection. This cultural supplement does not always incline us toward peace, but at least it raises the possibility of a more conscious creation of broader avenues of human cooperation than the age-old "survival of the fittest."

In the following two chapters, we analyze how the social forces which humans themselves create may be significant factors in their patterns of conflict and conflict regulation.

4

Adam Smith and the
Social Psychology of Interest Conflicts

Adam Smith (1723–90) is well known as the father of economics and the leading early spokesman for the capitalist system. Not so well known is his formulation of the psychological basis of economic interests and other sources of human competition. We will be emphasizing this less well known side of Smith's work in the present chapter. But before we do so, let us review a few key points about the general legacy of his social and economic ideas.

Each individual is basically a creature of self-interest; this must be recognized at the outset, for we cannot reasonably deny the fundamental egoism of human nature. Egoism leads individuals naturally to accumulate material goods, yielding a constant expansion in the scope of the market and of productivity. The man of business, in his search to accumulate wealth, is the central figure in this system, which is called "capitalism." The proper role of government in economic affairs is to do nothing, for all governmental activity tends to interfere with the laws of supply and demand and thus works against the purposes of national prosperity. Far better is it to trust in individual businessmen and corporations to carry on their activities as they see fit, for the competition of the marketplace will provide regulation enough for a system of free enterprise.

Such, we are commonly told, is the Gospel of Capitalism as set forth boldly in 1776 by Adam Smith, its first and foremost prophet. Smith's book, *The Wealth of Nations,* is the primary text which lays out these principles in detail. But this common wisdom about Adam Smith and *The Wealth of Nations* is more than a little misleading. For example, every sentence in the previous paragraph fails in some significant way to express correctly the views of this father of modern capitalism. He would consider each of them wide of the mark, containing at best only a half-truth. To clear up at the outset some of these popular misconceptions, let us review point by point the contents of the above paragraph.

1. As to individuals being creatures of self-interest, yes, this is the basic assumption of *The Wealth of Nations* (or, to give it its full title, *An Inquiry into the Nature and Causes of the Wealth of Nations*). But this self-interest is not assumed to rest upon simple egoism. It is assumed to be socialized by sentiments individuals acquire from living together in society, and it is expected to be bound by moral and ethical limits. These assumptions are not spelled out in detail in *The Wealth of Nations* because they had already been thoroughly discussed in Smith's earlier book, *The Theory of Moral Sentiments* (1759).[1]

2. True, human desires for material goods lie behind expansions in production. But the key cause of an expanding economy is, in Smith's view, an expansion in the division of labor. This does have its basis ultimately in human nature—in, as he put it, a "propensity to truck, barter, and exchange one thing for another"—but it is more directly determined by the scope of trade present at a given period in time.

3. The central figure of Smith's attention was not so much the man of business as the common laborer or, even more, the consumer. It is labor which Smith sees as the foundation of the natural value of commodities, and he sees wages as a clear indication of the general prosperity of a nation. But ultimately, for Smith, it is the consumer who is king. He expresses this most clearly: "Consumption is the sole end and purpose of all production; and the interest of the producer ought to be attended to only so far as it may be necessary for promoting that of the consumer." As for the specific term "capitalism," that came much later than Adam Smith. He preferred to call his approach simply the "system of natural liberty."

4. True, Smith argues for a drastic reduction in governmental involvement in economic affairs; that was his most basic message for public policy makers of his own day. But he was not a doctrinaire advocate of nonintervention or *laissez-faire*.

He readily granted the sovereign not only responsibilities for defense and general public order but also "the duty of erecting and maintaining certain public works and certain public institutions which it can never be for the interest of any individual, or small number of individuals to erect and maintain." Among such public works and institutions he explicitly recognized projects like roads and harbors, a postal system, public education, at least partial support for religious institutions, and some regulation of commerce. He even recognized the case for temporary monopolies in foreign trade. Also, his general approach was not that of advocating radical change but rather as setting forth the basic direction in which public policy should move.

5. Yes, Smith did trust generally in the competition of the marketplace to regulate commerce effectively. This would occur naturally through the laws of supply and demand. But he did not particularly trust in businessmen or their companies. He personally deplored "the mean rapacity, the monopolizing spirit of merchants and manufacturers," and he considered that forerunner of the modern corporation, the joint-stock company, as only of very limited promise.

Having clarified a few of the misconceptions we are likely to have when approaching the work of Adam Smith, we are perhaps more ready to examine his ideas with a fresh spirit. Our reward will be a fuller clarification of the dynamics of self-interest than is usually associated with the father of capitalist economics.

THE FATHER OF ECONOMICS

In 1764 Smith resigned from his professorship at the University of Glasgow in order to accept a more generous salary as tutor and traveling companion to a young nobleman. Accompanying the Duke of Buccleugh to France, Smith soon found himself with more leisure than he had expected. "I have begun to write a book in order to pass away the time," he wrote to his friend, David Hume. This writing project grew for a dozen years before it took its final published shape in *The Wealth of Nations,* and during these years Smith sorted out the fundamentals of the science of economics.

Although there already was a recognized field known as

"political economy," it was Adam Smith who laid out new and more solid foundations for this field in *The Wealth of Nations*. Here to organize his commentary, rich in concrete detail about the world of practical affairs, was a new structure of thought. This structure included an analysis of the processes of production, distribution, and consumption; the role of land, labor, and capital as factors of production; how prices are regulated by the supply and demand of the marketplace; how markets expand through the correlated processes of increased division of labor, capital accumulation, and technological improvement; and the principles of effective public finance and governmental regulation of economic affairs.

We do not propose to enter the debate of how relevant Adam Smith's principles of economics are for the final decades of the twentieth century. Experts obviously differ as to how far Smith's models of pure competition are applicable to the markets of our own day. Also debatable is his fundamental assumption concerning the beneficence of economic growth. Although we recognize his contributions in developing the science of economics, our present interest is more in Adam Smith as a philosopher of human nature. We are especially concerned with his views of how conflicts of interest may come about and how they may be resolved. In pursuit of this, we turn now to his portrayal of the dynamics of self-interest.

THE DYNAMICS OF SELF-INTEREST

It is not from the benevolence of the butcher, the brewer, or the baker that we expect our dinner, but from their regard to their own interest. We address ourselves, not to their humanity but to their self-love, and never talk to them of our own necessities but of their advantages. Nobody but a beggar chooses to depend chiefly upon the benevolence of his fellow citizens.[2]

In this famous passage Smith states his fundamental assumption about the self-interest basis of economic institutions. The context, however, is not a discussion of the fundamental nature of man; it is rather the more limited question of how a complex division of labor develops. Smith's answer is that it develops through the mutual self-interests people naturally have in trading with one another and in the gradual accumulation of more to trade as a more specialized division of labor develops.

The Wealth of Nations does not go far in developing Smith's analysis of self-interest. It is simply assumed that individuals have material interests which are continuously in conflict with those of others. The conflict, however, is not total; it is mostly indirect and impersonal, and it can be bridged through trade. And as trade develops, the market emerges to give natural regulation to these self-interests, directing them to serve also the interests of other people.

The greatest benefits of any market are shared with those closest at hand, for this is where interests are most immediate. This leads individuals to think first of directing their efforts to local needs, and to domestic production rather than foreign trade. In this, says Smith, man "intends only his own gain, and he is in this, as in many other cases, led by an invisible hand to promote an end which was no part of his intention." Smith pointedly adds that "by pursuing his own interest he frequently promotes that of the society more effectively than when he really intends to promote it."

The "invisible hand" here is, of course, the price system in a competitive market. It is a finely articulated mechanism which allows the public good to be served without any conscious control by public officials. All that is necessary is to permit "the obvious and simple system of natural liberty" to establish itself "of its own accord." Thus:

> Everyman, as long as he does not violate the laws of justice, is left perfectly free to pursue his own interest in his own way, and to bring both his industry and capital into competition with those of any other man, or order of men.

Such is the vision of Adam Smith of how individual self-interest provides the motive power for an expanding market system. But Smith never assumed that such self-interest constituted a completely unfettered egoism. Indeed, in the above quotation we note a significantly limiting phrase: "as long as he does not violate the laws of justice." Smith assumed that his finely tuned system must be based on justice as well as liberty.

In *The Wealth of Nations* we have little elucidation of this point. We are there given a discussion of the administration of justice in the context of Smith's attention to public finance; but for Smith's fuller views on justice we must turn to his earlier writings, especially *The Theory of Moral Sentiments.*

Justice is an essential foundation for any society, for, as Smith put it, "society cannot subsist unless the laws of justice are tolerably observed," and "no social intercourse can take place among men who do not generally abstain from injuring one another."[3] And it is most proper that the legal apparatus of the state be enlisted to define and punish crimes which would disturb the general welfare of society.

Balancing justice, which Smith saw as mainly a negative virtue (the avoidance of injury to other people), is the positive virtue of beneficence (seeking after the welfare of others). Both are necessary bases of moral judgment and natural products of humans living together in society. But justice and beneficence must both also be balanced with a third virtue, equally natural to man as a social animal; this third virtue Smith called "prudence."

While concern for other people leads to the virtues of justice and beneficence, concern for our own happiness and well-being leads to the virtue of prudence. Virtue? Yes, most certainly, affirmed Smith. To maintain oneself in health and comfort, to have sufficient wealth and security of personal resources, to make reliable friendships with others, and to behave with careful responsibility toward them—these examples of prudence do constitute a virtue. Prudence, Smith admitted, is never considered one of the most endearing of virtues; at best it "commands a certain cold esteem." Nevertheless, this virtue has a central place, for "every man is, no doubt, by nature, first and principally recommended to his own care" and, Smith felt sure, "is fitter to take care of himself than of any other person."

But in the prudent search for individual happiness there must be, as in practically everything else, balance. Although it is natural that every individual is "much more deeply interested in whatever immediately concerns himself than in what concerns any other man," he must still check this self-centered perspective. We must "view ourselves not so much according to that light in which we may naturally appear to ourselves, as according to that in which we naturally appear to others."

Smith's ethical theory does not rest on the foundation of any single or primary virtue. There is, for him, no primary ethical imperative from which other principles may be deduced. He assumed that there is room for several fundamental criteria for ethical conduct and that these naturally followed from the actual conditions of living. "The general maxims of morality are formed," said Smith, "from experience and induction. We observe in a great variety of particular cases what pleases or displeases our moral faculties, what these approve or disapprove of, and, by induction from this experience, we establish those general rules." But there is no rational first principle with which we start this process; we must start with our own moral feelings.

Smith also saw that there was room for a distinction between ethical judgments and how we actually behave; simple self-interest may be more characteristic of the latter than the former. But still there is a continuity between the *is* and the *ought to be*. Though our first impulses may be narrowly selfish, we learn to check them in terms of a more enlightened and socially conscious self-interest. When one, said Smith, "views himself in the light in which he is conscious that others will view him, he sees that to them he is but one of the multitude in no respect better than any other in it," and he must therefore "humble the arrogance of his self-love, and bring it down to something which other men can go along with."

We are now at the threshold of Adam Smith's central contribution to our understanding of the dynamics of self-interest. Before proceeding further, let us remind ourselves of what, following Smith's reasoning, we have established so far:

1. Self-interest provides the primary motive power for the effective operation of market systems, but this is assumed to be the enlightened self-interest of persons socialized to live in society.
2. The socialization of self-interest includes both the ac-

ceptance of legal controls upon undesirable behavior and the development of positive ethical standards which operate from within the individual.

3. Ethical standards from within develop naturally from living with others in society. Although there is always a tension between ethical standards and immediate selfish interests (in response to which most behavior represents a compromise), this tension is not between ourselves and some externally derived principle; rather, it flows from our fundamental nature as social selves.

But what is our fundamental nature as social selves from which ethical ideas derive? Here Adam Smith rejects the two lines of thought we might most expect him to follow. And in so doing he opens the way to a third approach, which we suggest is at the heart of his theory of human nature.

One approach which we might expect from Adam Smith at this point is that which locates an inherent moral sense in man, implanted there directly by God or by "nature." Certainly the history of philosophy gave Smith ample precedent for this kind of theory, but he rejected its simplistic appeal. It did not explain how the moral sense comes to function in the way that it shows itself.

Another approach which Smith rejected was ably argued by his good friend and fellow Scottish philosopher, David Hume. Morals, according to Hume, are drived ultimately from utilitarian considerations. We seek utility in the pursuit of whatever is pleasurable and in the avoidance of pain, and as we share our life with others, we also come to desire pleasure and deplore pain for others in our society. Our moral principles, in this view, are generalizations built upon these more fundamental pleasure-pain motivations. Much as this view might seem consistent with the "economic man" assumptions of modern capitalism, it was not a view that satisfied Adam Smith. He admitted that utilitarian considerations may enter into processes of moral judgment; but at its root, he believed, moral judgment is based on something else. We perceive what is to be properly approved of as distinct from what may be useful. "Originally," he says, "we approve of another man's judgment, not as something useful, but as right, as accurate, as agreeable to truth and reality"; utility "is plainly an after-thought." If not utility, what then is, for Smith, the basis of moral judgment? It is through our fellow-feeling and empathy with other human beings that we, according to Smith, derive our primary basis for moral evaluation. For this primary moral emotion Smith preferred to use the term "sympathy," but for him this included all basically shared feeling, not just pity and compassion.

"Nothing pleases us more than to observe in other men a fellow-feeling with all the emotions of our own breast," Smith observed; "nor are we ever so much shocked as by the appearance of the contrary." This empathy is at the root of our peculiarly human sensitivity, and it derives from our close association with others in society. Out of this close association also grows our sense of selfhood and, along with this personal identity, a foundation for moral judgment. How these two grow side by side is most clearly suggested when he tries to imagine what we would be like without society. Let us quote Smith fully here:

> Were it possible that a human creature could grow up to manhood in some solitary place, without any communication with his own species, he could no more think of his own character, of the propriety or demerit of his own sentiments and conduct, of the beauty or deformity of his own mind, than of the beauty or deformity of his own face. All these are objects which he cannot easily see, which naturally he does not look at, and with regard to which he is provided with no mirror which can present them to his view. Bring him into society, and he is immediately provided with the mirror which he wanted before. It is placed in the countenance and behaviour of those he lives with, which always mark when they enter into, and when they disapprove of his sentiments; and it is here that he first views the propriety and impropriety of his own passions, the beauty and deformity of his own mind. To a man who from his birth was a stranger to society, the objects of his passions, the external bodies which either pleased or hurt him, would occupy his whole attention. The passions themselves, the desires or aversions, the joys or sorrows, which those objects excited, though of all things the most immediately present to him, could scarce ever be the objects of his thoughts.

The idea of them could never interest him so much as to call upon his attentive consideration. The consideration of his joy could in him excite no new joy, nor that of his sorrow any new sorrow, though the consideration of the causes of those passions might often excite both. Bring him into society, and all his own passions will immediately become the causes of new passions. He will observe that mankind approve of some of them, and are disgusted by others. He will be elevated in the one case, and cast down in the other; his desires and aversions, his joys and sorrows, will now often become the causes of new desires and new aversions, new joys and new sorrows: they will now, therefore, interest him deeply, and often call upon his most attentive consideration.

In the above passage we see that the "mirror" which society provides is the basis of the individual's consciousness of self. It is because of the reactions of other people that an individual comes to reflect on his own motives. And it is because of these reactions too that he develops a sense of moral judgment to apply to his own actions. Gradually an individual develops an inner voice—"the man within the breast," as Smith termed what we would usually call conscience—to summarize these responses of other people. And as he develops his reasoning power, he is able to form a generalized judgment of how people tend to view different forms of conduct. This generalized judgment Smith calls the "impartial spectator," and it is "only by consulting this judge within . . . that we can ever make any proper comparison between our own interests and those of other people."

The impartial spectator only gradually becomes impartial, for it grows out of the direct fellow-feeling we have with others. Out of this mutual sympathy we gradually come to develop an internal image to reflect general approval or disapproval, which ultimately generalizes into a kind of all-purpose agency of moral judgment. This is the basis for Smith's theory of "moral sentiments," which can themselves be evaluated with precision only "in the sympathetic feelings of the impartial and well-informed spectator."

Although this impartial spectator within each individual takes him beyond a simple self-centeredness, it still bears the stamp of its social location. Although Smith did not develop this point, it seems apparent that persons who grow up in greatly different societies will naturally come to reflect somewhat different "impartial spectators" or ethical principles. What Smith did clearly recognize was that every individual "is naturally more attached to his own particular order or society than to any other"; and this led him to be skeptical about philosophies of universal benevolence. Also, the impartial spectator never displaces or completely curbs the individual's own interests. These direct interests remain the driving forces for the individual's own behavior, only moderated in degree by the force of "the man within the breast" (that is, one's internalized moral sentiments).

So far as specifically economic interests are concerned, Smith sees no sharp conflict between the claims of self-interest and those of conscience. Of course, unjust and illegal business practices are to be avoided, but there is nothing wrong with seeking to make a profit. Also, the very forces which tend to cultivate attention to our economic self-interest—"that great purpose of human life which we call bettering our condition"— is itself derived from sources not too different from our sense of moral judgment. Our economic striving, wrote Smith, is not primarily to satisfy our physical needs. Instead it is caused by a desire to be looked upon with approval by others. It is out of a regard for the opinions of others that we seek wealth and avoid poverty. "The rich man glories in his riches because he feels that they naturally draw upon him the attention of the world"; the poor man, in contrast, feels placed either "out of the sight of mankind" or, if noticed, the object of little sympathy. This attitude, in turn, is due to the tendency that people "are disposed to sympathize more entirely with our joy than with our sorrow."

It is therefore the desire for social approval that leads us to form both our economic ambitions and our higher ethical sensibilities. How neatly does Smith thus tie together the forces of greed and the more selfless impulses of humanity! All is rooted in the natural socialization of the individual as a self-conscious and approval-seeking member of society.

Society enters into Smith's system in two ways, one personal and one impersonal. *The Theory of Moral Sentiments* emphasizes the more personal aspects of society, how the individual, through interaction and fellow-feeling, develops into the kind of moral self that he or she becomes. *The Wealth of Nations* emphasizes the more impersonal aspects of society which are the ultimate effects of individuals pursuing their economic self-interest. Society in both of these aspects is for Adam Smith a wonderful system. He viewed it with few negative or even mixed feelings; man, said he, finds agreeable "the orderly and flourishing state of society" and "he takes delight in contemplating it."

It is also clear that Smith's view of society was always based on individual human beings. It is these, seeking their own concrete interests, that make the larger system work. And we should view with profound suspicion any suggestions that society can be remade without careful attention to its individual units, the human beings whose self-interests provide the motive power for the whole enterprise. We must therefore be on our guard against what Smith called the "man of system" who

> seems to imagine that he can arrange the different members of a great society with as much ease as the hand arranges the different pieces upon a chess-board. He does not consider . . . that, in the great chess-board of human society, every single piece has a principle of motion of its own, altogether different from that which the legislature might chuse to impress upon it.

When governmental policies and individual self-interests happen to coincide, then "the game of human society will go on easily and harmoniously." But when they "are opposite or different, the game will go on miserably, and society must be at all times in the highest degree of disorder."

CLASSICAL ECONOMICS AS CONFLICT THEORY

Occasionally Adam Smith made a comment about public order and social unrest (as in the most recent quotation) or war and international relations. In *The Wealth of Nations* he discussed in some detail the defense needs of society (in which he calls the art of war "certainly the noblest of all arts"), the possibilities of free trade for helping to overcome a petty nationalistic spirit, and the disadvantages of colonialism. *The Theory of Moral Sentiments* includes a perceptive analysis of national patriotism and a brief passage on international law. In still other writings by Smith, originally given as lectures, we have further discussions of international law, jurisprudence, and matters of defense. However, in none of Smith's writings do we have the kind of explicit attention to social conflict which he gave to economic competition in *The Wealth of Nations*. If we distinguish sharply between conflict and competition, we may be tempted to conclude that Adam Smith had little to say about conflict. But at least two qualifications stand in the way of such a conclusion.[4]

First, let us recognize that the distinction between competition and conflict is somewhat arbitrary. We most often talk about conflict when the contention between parties is direct and personal, which means that they are fully conscious (and often hostile) about their opposition. We talk about competition when the contention is indirect and impersonal, leading at best to only limited awareness of the opposition. Two farmers bringing corn to market have little sense of their underlying opposition in interests as they compete with one another and all other farmers to receive a good price for their product. The daughters of the two farmers, however, have a very different view of each other if they have both set their hearts on the same young man. Here the competition has a greater likelihood of turning into direct conflict as the rivalry becomes more personal, direct, and conscious. For some theoretical purposes it is important to distinguish between these direct and indirect forms of conflict. But it is also appropriate to begin with a recognition that they are both based on interest conflicts. At the foundation of both are parties pursuing interests which are not fully harmonious. Adam Smith was among those who saw interest conflicts as perfectly normal. It is natural that each individual has his own interests and that these may often be in some degree of conflict with the interests of others.

Fundamentally, therefore, Smith saw a potential for conflict as ever-present between humans. In this sense he was a conflict theorist. But it did not follow from this that there must be direct and open conflict. He saw two factors always limiting the range of direct conflict: (1) moral sentiments (based upon a fundamental empathy between persons) which provide ethical boundaries for the expression of antagonisms, and (2) forces of market competition (based on a system of prices and free exchange) which provide for an impersonal and indirect pursuit of conflicting interests.

We come now to a second qualification to the conclusion that Adam Smith was not a conflict theorist. The point to be made here is that he was less a theorist of conflict than a theorist of conflict resolution. Everything he said about the market system can be viewed as a theory of conflict resolution. Conflicts can be resolved through the impersonal and indirect mechanisms of the marketplace. This can occur without the costs of personal antagonism, and with the added virtue of an efficient allocation of resources for society as a whole. What a beautiful way to imagine conflicting interests working themselves out!

Smith, then, was a theorist of competition and conflict resolution rather than an analyst of conflict per se. But in his analysis of market mechanisms he created a powerful tool which can be applied to human conflicts of interest generally.

If Smith himself had little to say about direct struggles between human individuals or groups, others of a similar cast of mind have gone further. Classical economics (as Smith's model came to be called) has been applied to issues of war and peace and to sources of domestic discord. War is less likely to occur, it is pointed out, when there is free trade between nations. The interdependence created through trade and an international division of labor will strengthen the interests in a maintenance of peace. And in a corresponding manner within a nation, the pursuit of free enterprise will allow natural interdependence to develop, thus promoting both internal peace and prosperity.

But certainly there will still be important conflicts of economic interest in any society. Yes, of course. But the thing to be kept in mind, classical economists maintain, is that significant economic conflict arises only as a result of monopolistic organization or immobility of resources. If there is a system of truly free competition, a large number of prospective partners with whom to carry on exchange, and a free movement of persons and economic materials—when these conditions obtain, the market system removes the basis of economic conflict.

But does the market system not simply continue the inequalities already present in society? Different levels of society have different degrees of inherited wealth; different occupations have different incomes; different areas or regions have different degrees of economic development; different industries have differentials in their ease of obtaining capital; and so forth. Do these not all naturally set the stage for economic conflict, and justifiably so?

Adam Smith was less concerned with equality than he was with freedom. But he was generally in favor of both, and in his day he saw freedom as the primary way to achieve greater equality. A more equal society would be the result if only the artificialities of governmental favoritism were removed, he felt. In our own day we are apt to see government involvement in another light. The intervention of a modern welfare state *can* reduce the economic inequalities in a society. It can do this both directly (with taxes and grants) and indirectly (through a variety of economic policies and regulations). But in pursuing a political route, we are frequently sharpening the conflicts involved. And are the effects worth the struggle? Those among us who follow in the tradition of Adam Smith caution about the unintended effects of economic planning, and about how attempts at economic regulation so often end up benefiting those they were designed to limit rather than the general public. They suggest another approach to reducing the economic inequalities in society. Are we bothered by different income levels? Let the free marketplace reward persons for the actual value contributed, and persons who most need income will have an incentive to develop better-paying skills. Are we concerned about different degrees of development in different areas or industries? Encourage the free movement of labor and capital, and these inequalities will work themselves out. And so forth.

We do not presume here to settle difficult issues of contemporary public policy with a few sentences. Obviously our problems cannot be solved so simply. What we are trying to show is that the legacy of Adam Smith lives on in the twentieth century both as a method of economic analysis and as a general model to apply to public policy. As a model of public policy, this legacy gives one overriding message for how economic conflicts are to be managed and resolved: use the free competition of the marketplace as much as you possibly can!

FURTHER RAMIFICATIONS

Classical economics, beginning with *The Wealth of Nations,* views the economy as the aggregate result of the interests and actions of individuals. These interests are balanced through the automatic forces of the market. Although some later members of his school were not so concerned with social psychological assumptions, at least the father of classical economics went to some pains to argue that self-interests were not matters of unbridled egoism. As Adam Smith made clear in his *Theory of Moral Sentiments,* self-interests are themselves developed through interaction with others in society. Self-interests, for him, always rested on a base of prior socialization and within the framework of a legal order. Smith's two books, when taken together, produce a systematic framework for seeing self-interests emerging from interaction with others, for seeing conflicts rooted especially in the economic self-interests of individuals, and for seeing these conflicts regulated through exchange in the marketplace.

Practically all of Smith's thinking was focused clearly on the individual human being. Is it possible to take his ideas out of an individual context and apply them to broader units of analysis?

Smith himself saw some room for the economic analysis of units which were not individuals. Partnerships and joint-stock corporations were a part of his world, and he did not hesitate to include them in his analysis. But is there not a strain in continuing to extend this analysis to deal with today's giant multinational corporations? For legal purposes governments may recognize the corporation as a "person," but it is certainly a different kind of person from what Adam Smith had in mind. Economists continue to argue the extent to which these differences in size require different models of economic analysis from those introduced by Smith. Economists also argue the extent to which uncontrolled markets can effectively maximize aggregate economic interests in today's world. A whole generation of followers of John Maynard Keynes argues that classical economics is no longer sufficient for understanding "macro" or large-scale economic effects.

Even more controversial is the extension of a self-interest framework of analysis to noneconomic units. For example, we freely talk about national interests as if the nation were a being analogous to the individual. Smith himself did so in at least one passage, though elsewhere he resists seeing national interests in terms other than economic production and consumption.[5] But we must recognize the possibility that other units of human social organization may be analyzed within a framework similar to that suggested by Adam Smith. Groups, formal organizations, and even crowds may sometimes be analyzed as having interests which they act to satisfy. In contemporary game theory, as we will see later in this book, this process of extension has been carried so far that we may not even know what type of concrete entity is represented by a "player"; we may mathematically represent interests without even being particularly concerned about what kind of beings have these interests. Would Adam Smith be rolling over in his grave at the thought of such abstractions? Perhaps; but then again, perhaps not. Smith did not shrink from ventures into imaginative abstraction. However, he always came back in the end to his central concern for the individual human being.

If Smith's views of individual interests have been extended by others to other contexts, so too may we note that his conceptualization of society has been carried forward to new frontiers by others. First and foremost, he saw human society in process terms. Human selves derive from a process of interaction, and they are expressed in further interaction and exchange. Society, for Smith, is the overall summary of these processes of interaction and exchange.

A process view of society has had a wide following among sociological theorists. Georg Simmel and Leopold von Wiese in Germany and Robert E. Park and Ernest W. Burgess in Amer-

ica have been among the more influential twentieth-century sociologists who analyzed society largely in social process terms
and studied competition and conflict as key processes. Although it would be too much to claim that Adam Smith had a
great direct influence on these theorists, it is possible to point
to a general similarity between their assumptions about the nature of society and those of Adam Smith. Sometimes this comes
out in explicit discussions of the role of conflict in society. For
example, Lewis Coser, one of the better-known contemporary
sociological theorists, argues that conflict often has positive effects for society. This is especially so, he maintains, when a social system is relatively open to the natural expression of conflicts. Says Coser:

> Rigid systems which suppress the incidence of conflict exert
> pressure towards the emergence of radical cleavages and vio-
> lent forms of conflict. More elastic systems, which allow the
> open and direct expression of conflict within them and which
> adjust to the shifting balance of power that these conflicts both
> indicate and bring about, are less likely to be menaced by basic
> and explosive alignments within their midst.[6]

The content here is slightly different from Adam Smith's
Wealth of Nations, but there is at least a strong similarity to
Smith's basic argument about economic competition. Provide a
flexible system with free competition, advised Smith, and let
society develop and grow naturally as a result of these conflicting interests. This makes unnecessary the more "radical cleav-
ages and violent forms of conflict."

Among social scientists who emphasize a process view of society, there are two groups for whom the work of Smith should
strike an especially familiar note. One of these consists of those
social psychologists who call themselves symbolic interactionists.
They emphasize the emergence of the self through social interaction, the importance of self-consciousness in ongoing behavior, and the importance of language for self-conscious behavior. With at least the first two of these three themes, Smith's
Theory of Moral Sentiments, as we have previously indicated, is in
close harmony. And on the matter of language, Smith at least

suggested that speech was a key point for separating distinctively human interchange from that of animals.[7] Adam Smith deserves to be considered as an early symbolic interactionist to a far greater degree than contemporary adherents of this school acknowledge.

Then there is contemporary "exchange theory." Following the lead of George Homans and others, certain sociologists and social psychologists now are attempting to recast their key generalizations in terms at least analogous to economic theory. Individual interests, defined in terms of rewards and costs—social rewards and costs, which are far more extensive than economic rewards and costs—are used as the starting point for the analysis of social behavior. Even complex group networks are reduced to show the basic forms of exchange between individuals which they combine. Here is another stream of social science thinking which shows a strong similarity to ideas of Adam Smith.

But let us not end our attention to Smith's legacy for contemporary social science in general, and for conflict theory in particular, without a recognition that in some ways Smith is clearly out of step with prevailing thoughtways of today. For one thing, his general optimism about man and society is something we have trouble recapturing in the second half of the twentieth century. Although he was less naively optimistic than some of his age, his thinking still bore the imprint of the eighteenth century's Age of Enlightenment.

Human nature, in Smith's view, was quite benign. He had freed himself from traditional Christian assumptions about original sin, and he lived before the age when we were made aware of the dark forces of the unconscious mind. Further, since he saw man's basic nature as socialized by empathy with others, he could be quite optimistic about what would happen if individuals were permitted to pursue "the obvious and simple system of natural liberty."[8]

Smith's view of society was also rather rosy, at least in retrospect. He apparently noticed little of the seamy side of the industrial revolution which was then in process. Instead, he viewed the rich as indirectly but naturally helping the poor, as those with means gave employment to others while moving to greater heights of opulence. In general, he considered "the immense fabric of human society" as something especially favored by the "darling care of Nature" (note the capital letter) and somewhat like "an immense machine whose regular and harmonious movements produce a thousand agreeable effects." This is hardly the attitude toward society found in the most fashionable intellectual circles of our own day.[9]

One of the reasons why Smith seems naively optimistic to us today is due to our partial disenchantment with the faith of material progress. Smith saw no reason to doubt either that a general growth of material prosperity was natural (with expansion in the division of labor and the scope of trade) or that it was good. Today we are much more aware of the limited natural resources of our planet, which in turn set limits on our material prosperity. And we are also less apt than was Smith to prize material prosperity as good in itself.

We also tend to reject Smith's assumption of a relatively close correspondence between the world as it is and the world as it ought to be. Of course, he saw some tension between ethical ideals and the real world, but less than most thinkers either before or after him. He partly bridged the gap by the inductive basis of his ethics; ethics for him emerged from moral judgment, which in turn emerged through the natural forces of society. Such a foundation for ethical theory has much to recommend it. But it is not the most natural approach for most intellectuals of today, who insist on clearly distinguishing between ethical prescriptions and descriptive statements.

Finally, there is Smith's individualism. This seems badly out of step with the thinking of today. Or is it? There has been some renewed interest lately in Western Europe and the United States in the direction of his kind of liberalism. In general, however, his clear focus on the individual seems to leave out much of what stands between the individual and society at large.

How might one move to give greater attention to the complexities of social structure, thus bridging the simple individual-society dichotomy? How, in so doing, might we also recognize a greater role for more direct forces of conflict, and with a spirit which is less naively optimistic about human nature and society? In the following chapter we will pursue some possible answers to these questions, starting with the ideas of Karl Marx.

5

Karl Marx and the Sociology of Conflict

Karl Marx (1818–83) is usually considered as the direct opposite of Adam Smith, and Marxism is regularly set in contrast to classical economics. This is largely appropriate, but we must also qualify this contrast. Although Marx set himself in conscious opposition to capitalism and to the classical economists which he saw as its apologists, much of his economic analysis was borrowed from the classical tradition.

Marx did not specifically challenge the analysis of market forces of classical economics; rather, he sought to show that in the long run these forces served to undermine the capitalist system. He accepted classical analyses of the price of labor and turned the "iron law of wages" (the notion that wage rates, because of competition between workers, tend toward a level of bare subsistence) into a protest against the whole system. Marx's most distinctive economic contribution was his theory of surplus value (that labor was not given the full value of its production, with a surplus arbitrarily but regularly taken away by owners as profit); but even here he based his thinking on a labor theory of value (that the value of a product could be analyzed in terms of the labor embodied in it) which was quite similar to views set forth by Adam Smith. In technical details the economics of Karl Marx is not greatly different from the economics of the classical tradition.

But Marxism *is* different. It is different in the whole purpose for which economic analysis is undertaken—which for Marx was to understand the forces of social change and to help guide them toward a new framework of society. It is different in the view of the relationship of market forces to the rest of society; their temporary dominance, in Marx's view, was not an inherent necessity. And Marxism is fundamentally different in the attention given to the individual in relation to his social structure. For Marx the individual is no longer the focus. "The human essence," he wrote "is no abstraction inherent in each single individual. In its reality it is the ensemble of the social relations."[1] As we approach the work of Karl Marx, therefore, we must be prepared for a fundamental change of perspective from that appropriate for understanding the ideas of Adam Smith.

Probably the most fundamental respect in which Marx departed from the classical tradition was in his rejection of the individual as the appropriate unit for understanding economic forces. Economic forces, he held, need to be seen as institutions of society, based fundamentally upon the technology of material production which obtains at a given time. To focus upon the individual as a unit neglects the extent to which his actions are determined by broader collective forces of society. Besides, as Marx saw it, capitalism had grown by the mid-nineteenth century to a point where its scope of organization belied the validity of interpreting its dynamics simply in terms of the individuals involved. It was too big for that. A whole new view was necessary, placing the focus on collective forces beyond the individual.

Another difference that we must be prepared for is the extent to which Marx saw conflict throughout human society. He saw conflict and change all about, and he used the analysis of conflict as his central tool for the analysis of society. No longer must we strain to see, as we did with Adam Smith, conflicts of interest lurking behind the smoothly functioning institutions of society. Now conflict, more direct and more pervasive, is seen throughout the workings of the social order. Marx was a conflict theorist without apologies or reservations. In fact, he was thrice a conflict theorist. His analysis of contemporary society was grounded in the study of conflicting economic forces. His philosophy of history was grounded in a peculiar mental set (the dialectic) which affirmed conflict as a basic law of life. And his political stance as a revolutionary led him not only to analyze social conflict but to agitate actively for it. Each of these points will be developed further in the following section.

THRICE A CONFLICT THEORIST

One fairly straightforward interpretation of Marxian theory is to see it as based on a technological and economic determinism. The basis of any society must be seen in its system of material production. The "mode of production," as Marx sometimes termed it, determines the kind of economic system (or "relations of production") which may develop. A key aspect of any economic system is the definition of property, for this determines who holds primary rights over whatever is produced and who must work for whom. Because the economic relations are the primary determinants of other institutions of society—including the "superstructure" of political ideas, religion, morals, and art—it is extremely important to notice how these relations are structured. And the basic structure of these relations can most clearly be seen by recognizing the fundamental classes of persons involved. Almost always there are those who live by virtue of the property they own and another much larger group who must live by providing their labor to others. Although these two groups do not exhaust the varieties of social classes, in Marx's view, they are more and more coming to represent the predominant segments of humanity. And their interests are fundamentally opposed, whether or not they themselves recognize this.

Although Marx and Engels opened their *Communist Manifesto* with the assertion that "the history of all hitherto existing society is the history of class struggles," by the end of that document it becomes clear that they saw the struggle sharpened for the present (that is, around 1847) age.[2] The very success of capitalism had served to concentrate the control of property more sharply, with the less successful capitalists losing out to those who were more effective. The concentration of capital was accompanied by the concentration of the work force in larger and larger factories—under conditions where their class consciousness and mutual organization would be facilitated.

These factors should sharpen the struggle between the capitalist and working classes (or "bourgeoisie" and "proletariat") in the near future. For a variety of reasons (including an anticipated worsening condition of labor, periodic crises of overproduction, and a gradual recognition of the irrelevance of individualistic definitions of property over large-scale enterprise), Marx saw the outcome as bringing eventually a victory for the proletariat and with this the general abolition of private property.

What we have outlined so far is Marx's economically based conflict theory. It is most succinctly summarized in his *Critique of Political Economy* in the following words:

> In the social production which men carry on they enter into definite relations that are indispensable and independent of their will; these relations of production correspond to a definite stage of development of their material powers of production. The sum total of these relations of production constitutes the economic structure of society—the real foundation, on which rise legal and political superstructures and to which correspond definite forms of social consciousness. The mode of production in material life determines the general character of the social, political and spiritual processes of life. It is not the consciousness of men that determines their existence, but, on the contrary, their social existence determines their consciousness. At a certain stage of their development, the material forces of production in society come in conflict with the existing relations of production, or what is but a legal expression for the same thing—with the property relations within which they had been at work before. From forms of development of the forces of production these relations turn into their fetters. Then comes the period of social revolution.[3]

This is the Marx who has become one of the giants of modern social science, outlining the economic foundations from which flow his analysis of the class struggle.

But this is only one side of Marx, and only one basis for his theory of class struggle. A second side of Marx is that of a Hegelian philosopher. Marx had studied at the University of Berlin where Hegelian doctrines reigned supreme, and the German intellectuals who constituted the main audience for most of his writings were heavily influenced by the style of thought of Georg W. F. Hegel.

Hegel had seen the history of the world as the history of *Geist* or intellectual spirit. This spirit is in constant process of becoming, with its unfolding fitting into a dialectical process. The dialectical process always begins with something that exists ("thesis"), which brings with it the suggestion of its opposite ("antithesis"); and the interplay between these opposed ideas necessarily produces something new (a "synthesis," which may itself function as a thesis for further movement). Such is the nature of the never-ending progression of ideas which shape human history.

Marx, of course, did not see human ideas as primarily shaping history; but he could not shake off (if he ever wanted to) the basic Hegelian pattern of reasoning. His analysis of social conflict was therefore more than an analysis of economically based forces; there was also a quality of philosophical determinism. The bourgeoisie and proletariat were in conflict not only because they had different economic interests; they were in conflict also because Marx saw one of them (the bourgeoisie) as the embodiment of Hegel's thesis and the other (the proletariat) as contemporary history's antithesis. This gives a philosophical necessity for conflict over and above the economic and social necessity. For all life in its becoming is a process of conflict; such is the nature of the dialectical process. What this adds to Marxian conflict theory is both a more ponderous style and a more universal view of the nature of class conflict. This may be well illustrated in Marx's earliest (1845) statement of his theory of communism, as found in *The Holy Family:*

> Proletariat and Wealth are opposites. As such they form a whole. They are both forms of the world of private property. What concerns us here is to define the exact position each assumes in opposition. It is not enough to state that they are two sides of a whole.
>
> Private property as private property, as wealth, is compelled to maintain its own *existence* and thereby the existence of its opposite, the proletariat. This is the *positive* side of the opposition, private property satisfied in itself.

The proletariat on the other hand is compelled as proletariat to abolish itself together with its determining opposite, that which makes it the proletariat—private property. This is the *negative* side of the opposition, its restlessness within itself, dissolved and self-dissolving private property.

The possessing class and the class of the proletariat present the same human self-alienation. But the former class finds in this self-alienation its own confirmation and its own good, *its own power,* and possesses in it the semblance of human existence. The latter class feels annihilated in its self-alienation, sees in it its impotence and the reality of an inhuman existence. In the words of Hegel, the class of the proletariat is in its abasement indignant of that abasement, an indignation to which it is necessarily driven by the contradiction between its human *nature* and its condition of life, which is the frank, decisive and comprehensive negation of that nature.

Within this opposition, therefore, the owner of private property is the *conservative,* the proletarian the *destructive* party. From the former arises the action of preservation of the opposition, from the latter the action of its annihilation.[4]

We have quoted at some length to show both Marx's fondness for a dialectical style of thought and his particular application of the dialectic to the class struggle.

There is a third side to Marx as a conflict theorist (in addition to Marx the economic analyst and Marx the dialectician). This third side is Marx the revolutionary activist.

Marx was a revolutionary in style and substance before he developed his critique of capitalism or advocacy of communism. And his plea, "Workingmen of all countries, unite!" was not just a statement of economic determinism or dialectical necessity.[5] He was determined to change the world, and he enjoyed feeling himself a part of the struggle to do so. This sense of active participation gives an added dimension to Marx's theory of social conflict. He had not only a theory about how the world was, but also a theory of how to change it. Revolution was therefore an art dear to his heart, and not just something to be analyzed. This engaged spirit is well illustrated in the following passage of general advice to revolutionists:

Firstly, never play with insurrection unless you are fully prepared to face the consequences of your play. Insurrection is a calculus with very indefinite magnitudes, the value of which may change every day; the forces opposed to you have all the advantage of organization, discipline, and habitual authority; unless you bring strong odds against them you are defeated and ruined. Secondly, the insurrectionary career once entered upon, act with the greatest determination, and on the offensive. The defensive is the death of every armed rising; it is lost before it measures itself with its enemies. Surprise your antagonists while their forces are scattering, prepare new successes, however small, but daily; keep up the moral ascendency which the first successful rising has given to you; rally those vacillating elements to your side which always follow the strongest impulse, and which always look out for the safer side; force your enemies to retreat before they can collect their strength against you; in the words of Danton, the greatest master of revolutionary policy yet known, *de l'audace, de l'audace, encore de l'audace!* [6]

Marx certainly does not give us the last word on revolutionary tactics, and as a revolutionist his own efforts proved quite unsuccessful. But as both a participant and an observer of the revolutionary process, Marx gave us a view of social conflict in some ways richer and more comprehensive (and in some ways grossly one-sided because of his involvement) than any conflict theorist before or after him.

Marx's multiple status as a conflict theorist helps to explain his prominence in the social thought of the twentieth century. He is a pioneer in several lines of thought, all of which are combined in the ideology known as Marxism. As an analyst of the strategy and tactics of revolution, he has a place of distinction in a line of ideological heroes that continues through V. I. Lenin, Mao Tse-Tung, and Che Guevara. As a philosopher of the necessity for large-scale social change, his line of descent includes many prominent intellectuals, ranging from the democratic left (such as Erich Fromm) to the more extreme left (Herbert Marcuse), to the more orthodox theorists of twentieth-century socialist states. As a hard-headed analyst of the forces at work in industrial society, Marx has still another line of strong influence, which includes many social scientists for whom neither communism nor the Hegelian dialectic has much appeal. So dominating an intellectual figure was Karl Marx and so powerful is the combined impact of all of these lines of influence that many scholars today think of conflict theory and Marxism as almost the same thing.* But such an identification would not be useful for our present purposes. In order to use Marx's more scientific contributions as a key perspective for the study of social conflict, we must at least partly disentangle them from his dialectical rhetoric and revolutionary advocacy. To some this may seem like removing the guts from Marx's thought, but to us this seems a necessary prelude to recognizing the full value of Marx's sociological insights. This we will attempt to do in the next section, drawing heavily on the work of Ralf Dahrendorf.

MARX REVISED

He grew up in a city in the western part of Germany, early took a keen interest in social philosophy, and received a doctorate from a German university in his early twenties. Although attracted to a scholarly career, he also had a strong interest in politics; and he participated actively in efforts to make German political structures more responsive to fundamental social change. After his career as a political activist was largely frustrated in his own country, he turned his attention more to Europe as a whole. He moved with his family to England, and some of the most productive scholarly work of his mature years was done in London.

So could we summarize some of the key features of the life of Karl Marx. Precisely the same biographical description could be given for Ralf Dahrendorf (1929–   ), the contemporary sociologist who is probably most identified with conflict theory. Beyond these superficial similarities, however, the lives of Marx and Dahrendorf depart sharply. Marx, completely shut out of an academic career, turned to journalism and revolutionary politics. Dahrendorf was apparently much more successful in both academia and politics. He has had a distinguished career

---

*Sociologists sometimes use the phrase "conflict theory" to refer to a conflict-based theory of society. This usage should be distinguished from a theory of conflict, in which other factors are brought in to explain conflict. Marx was of course both a conflict theorist and a theorist of conflict.[7]

as a German sociologist and is now director of the London School of Economics, and his liberal political career with Germany's Free Democratic Party has been at least more immediately successful than was Marx's revolutionary activity.

In his thinking as in his life, Dahrendorf shows both strong similarities and contrasts to Karl Marx. Dahrendorf is often characterized as a "neo-Marxist," but he clearly rejects Marx's dialectical materialism, his revolutionism, and his communism. Dahrendorf might in contrast be most accurately characterized as a liberal pragmatist. Nevertheless, Dahrendorf acknowledges a profound debt to Marx, whom he calls "the greatest theorist of social change." [8]

Although other writings may be better in giving the full flavor of Dahrendorf's thought, his most important contribution to the analysis of social conflict remains *Class and Class Conflict in Industrial Society*. Here is reviewed at great length Marx's theory of social classes and class conflict. After presenting the main outline of Marx's theory and trying to separate out the unnecessary philosophical ingredients, Dahrendorf gives point by point the key sociological contentions of Marx.

First of all, there is the contention that social change grows out of social structure. This Dahrendorf sees as a central assumption of Marx's sociology, and he believes that Marx was fundamentally correct here. Social structures are not given in some permanent fashion; they grow out of their historical context. But as they emerge, they shape the behavior of men and women within that context, and they also carry with them the seeds of new social structures. Social structures, as Dahrendorf expresses this point, "reach, so to speak, beyond themselves; at any given point of time they either are no longer or not yet what they appear to be. Process and change are their very nature." Clearly Dahrendorf agrees with Marx on the central importance of social change and the primacy of social structure for understanding change. [9]

Marx, furthermore, saw the seeds of change primarily in the conflict between groups. And in the social structure at any one point in time, there is a tendency for groups in conflict to become polarized. One section of the overall social structure will be pressing for change, and another section will be resisting change. In this broad sense, Dahrendorf asserts in support of Marx, "any theory of conflict has to operate with something like a two-class model" and "there are never more than two positions that struggle for domination." Dahrendorf believes Marx can be generally sustained in seeing social conflicts as fundamentally rooted in class conflict. But Marx went too far, Dahrendorf believes, in more specifically defining classes in terms of property positions and in identifying the conflicting interests between such classes as the basis of all social change.

On several other key points Dahrendorf is sharply critical of Marx. Marx held that fundamental social change must be revolutionary in character, while Dahrendorf argues that change may occur in a more gradual fashion. Marx held that classes always tend to show strongly antagonistic relations ("class struggle"), but Dahrendorf claims that this is not necessarily so. Marx held that property is the basis of social class, but Dahrendorf considers authority the more general basis (of which property is only one possible form). Marx held that industrial power inevitably becomes translated into political power, while Dahrendorf holds that there is no reason that this is necessarily the case.

When we get down to details, then, we find Dahrendorf sharply critical of Marx. Still, in their broad outlines there is agreement. Both argue that social change tends to occur through conflict and that most social conflict is structurally based. It is presumably because of this agreement that Dahrendorf calls Marx a great theorist and others call Dahrendorf a "neo-Marxist."

There is, however, a difference in the degree to which Marx and Dahrendorf limit themselves to structural analysis. In this respect, Marx was perhaps the more thoroughgoing sociologist. As he wrote in his preface to *Capital:*

> . . . here individuals are dealt with only in so far as they are the personifications of economic categories, embodiments of particular class-relations and class-interests. My standpoint, from which the evolution of the economic formation of society

is viewed as a process of natural history, can less than any
other make the individual responsible for relations whose
creature he socially remains, however much he may subjec-
tively raise himself above them.[10]

Marx here had, Dahrendorf believes, a sound perspective, but
one that needs to be supplemented. Although we do not need
a dogma of collective determinism, we do need a thoroughly
collective mode of analysis; but, Dahrendorf insists, we also
need to be able to supplement this with an analysis of the relationships between social positions and the persons who occupy
these positions. It is the individual that Marx had largely ignored in his analysis. Without this consideration of individuals
and their differences, our understanding of their behavior—
even their behavior as members of conflicting social classes—is
bound to be incomplete.

THE CONFLICT MODEL IN CONTEMPORARY SOCIOLOGY

Just as Dahrendorf is selective in what he accepts from Marx as
a basis for a sociological theory of conflict, so also does he stop
short of posing a theory of conflict as *the* model for understanding society. He believes strongly that most modern sociological theories tend to neglect conflict, and Marxist theories
provide a corrective here. But he does not instead propose a
conflict model as a replacement for other theories. Rather,
what Dahrendorf proposes is the recognition of two leading
models of society, each of which is by its nature incomplete;
however, he further suggests that there is at present no good
way of combining them. One of these may be called the "integration" or "consensus" model, which may be summarized by
the following propositions:
1. Every society is a relatively persisting configuration
   of elements.
2. Every society is a well-integrated configuration of elements.
3. Every element in a society contributes to its functioning.
4. Every society rests on the consensus of its members.

Although such a model may help us to understand how parts of a society are interrelated, it is not very good for explaining social change. For this we need a "coercion" or "conflict and change" model, which may be summarized by the following propositions:

1. Every society is subjected at every moment to change; social change is ubiquitous.
2. Every society experiences at every moment social conflict; social conflict is ubiquitous.
3. Every element in a society contributes to its change.
4. Every society rests on constraint of some of its members by others.

Society should be recognized as always presenting this double aspect represented by these two basic models.[11]

The conflict and change model is clearly where Dahrendorf chooses to focus his own sociological work. Furthermore, this work emphasizes the structural basis of conflict. He poses in fact three key questions in response to which he builds his theory of conflict:

1. How do conflicting groups arise from the structure of society?
2. What forms can the struggles among such groups assume?
3. How does the conflict among such groups effect a change in the social structure?[12]

In explaining how conflicting groups arise from the structure of society, Dahrendorf starts from the insight that social organizations typically include those who rule and those who are ruled. Within any "imperatively coordinated group" (to borrow a phrase from Max Weber) there is a structure of authority consisting of those who dominate and those who are primarily subject to the influence of others. These constitute two "quasi-groups" whose interests are inherently opposed. They may not recognize, though, that their interests are in conflict. When conditions call attention to this conflict, they become "interest groups" and take on some form of self-conscious organization. This process of change from quasi-group to interest group is influenced by such factors as channels of communication, methods of recruitment, legal protection for forms of coalition, access to material resources, ideological support, and leadership.

Opposing interest groups are naturally in a state of conflict. The form of conflict and its intensity may depend on a variety of conditions. Social mobility of individuals, for example, may reduce the level of expressed conflict; and there are always social mechanisms available for regulating conflict, which function with greater or lesser effectiveness. When these regulating mechanisms fail to work, violence is a possible accompaniment of conflict—though Dahrendorf takes pains to distinguish between the variables of conflict intensity and violence.

As to the forms conflict may take, they are many and varied. The form depends, of course, on the social units which are in conflict. At one point, Dahrendorf gives a classification of five types of social units which may be involved in superordinate-subordinate conflict: roles, groups, sectors of society, societies, and suprasocietal relations.[13] The middle three of these can all be identified as producing forms of what Dahrendorf broadly calls class conflict, and it is in the analysis of such class conflicts that Dahrendorf has made his primary contribution. His book *Class and Class Conflict in Industrial Society* presents his fullest discussion of class conflict, including a summary set of propositions which specify his main definitions, assumptions, and predictions.

Some conflicts are resolved, but Dahrendorf (in contrast to Marx) holds that class conflicts never are. They are only regulated, not resolved; and they are most effectively regulated when both sides recognize the nature of the conflict, are systematically organized, and are willing to follow certain rules of the game for carrying out the conflict.

Class conflict is of such central importance for Dahrendorf because of its role in facilitating social change. Two of his key propositions hold that more intense class conflicts produce more radical structural changes, and that more violent class conflicts produce more sudden structural changes. This perception of the close relationship between social conflict (especially class conflict) and social change represents the key point of continuity between Marx and Dahrendorf. It also represents the key contribution of both to modern sociological theory.

Contemporary sociological theorists do not see all of social change as a product of class conflict. Nor do they see conflict in general (including conflicts not based on class differences) completely accounting for patterns of change. But most share the assumption that the most central factor in social change is structurally based conflict. The detailed way this assumption will be represented varies considerably from theorist to theorist. Not all will acknowledge Marx as a source for this assumption, nor will Dahrendorf necessarily be cited. But this assumption represents the solid core of Marx's sociological thinking, which has at last entered the mainstream of contemporary sociological thought. And Dahrendorf has played a key role in identifying this central sociological insight by separating it from the less useful elements of Marxian ideology.

From Economic Man to Political Man

In any society there is a political order which is expressed in the state. This may take various forms—such as monarchy, aristocracy, or democracy—but in every case there is a "ruling element." This ruling element is always the strongest and most powerful segment of society, and it is the interests of this segment that predominate in the formulation of the rules of the state.

So argued Thrasymachus of Chalcedon in one of the dialogues of Socrates recorded in Plato's *Republic.* "By making these laws," he went on,

> they define as "right" for their subjects whatever is for their own interest, and they call anyone who breaks them a "wrongdoer" and punish him accordingly. That is what I mean: in all states alike "right" has the same meaning, namely what is for the interest of the party established in power, and that is the strongest. So the sound conclusion is that what is "right" is the same everywhere: the interest of the stronger party.[14]

Plato does not allow Thrasymachus to win this argument. Instead he describes Socrates as making a clever refutation to require "justice" and "right" to be identified with the needs of society as a whole. But is the position of Thrasymachus so easily put down? Twenty-four centuries later, most of us are still made uneasy by the argument of Thrasymachus.

Marx was not uneasy with this argument. It fit precisely his analysis of capitalist society. All he needed to specify was that "interest of the stronger party" really means "economic interests of the propertied class." It is economic interests which provide the basis for any political structure, according to his view. Only as a new class (itself a product of economic changes) shows itself as more powerful (by revolutionary action) can we have a new political and social system.

Dahrendorf also finds this argument hospitable, as he makes clear in his essay, "In Praise of Thrasymachus." Of course, as we noted earlier, Dahrendorf would not agree with Marx's insistence upon the primacy of economic factors. "Whatever changes are introduced or prevented," Dahrendorf has written, "governmental elites are their immediate object or agent"; though it is "admittedly not sufficient to identify a ruling class solely in terms of a governmental elite," it is still "necessary to think of this elite in the first place, and never to lose sight of its paramount position in the authority structure of the state."[15] Dahrendorf seems here to be asserting, in contrast to Marx, the primacy of political factors. This puts him in a position to agree even more directly with Thrasymachus than with Marx. "So long as the ruling groups are effectively superior to the ruled," Dahrendorf states in summary, "we can analyze the course a society takes in terms of the interests, goals, and social personalities of those in power." When, however, the position of those in power becomes more precarious, their opponents prepare to "take over and translate their interests into norms." Social structure broadly determines the lines of cleavage in this struggle, according to Dahrendorf. "Those in power pursue certain interests by virtue of their position; and by these interests certain groups in society are tied to them. Similarly, opposition is based on interests, and social groups with these interests adhere to the opposition cause."[16]

Although he mentions that persons in power translate their interests into norms, Dahrendorf does not give a great deal of attention to this process. He could, and sometimes did, cite the important work of Max Weber in this regard. Weber, the great

German sociologist of the early twentieth century, discussed at great length the importance of legitimating authority. Every system of authority, he said, "attempts to establish and to cultivate the belief in its 'legitimacy.' "[17] It does so by appeals to tradition, to reason, and to emotion. Coercion, Weber maintained, inadequately explains social order, for power based solely on coercion is unpredictable and ineffective. To be effective, power must be socially harnessed in a manner that encourages people to give their voluntary assent to those in command.

Dahrendorf pictures contemporary sociology as split between two viable models of society. The consensus-and-equilibrium model is followed by many sociologists most of the time, but Dahrendorf prefers (as did Marx) a conflict-and-change model. He leaves the impression that there is no good way to bridge these two models. However, it can well be argued that the bridge had already been built by his fellow German sociologist, Max Weber. Weber's work provides a thorough analysis of diverse forms of social organization and how in them social norms come to be stabilized so that raw social conflict is rarely observed. But Weber's theory also is based upon assumptions about the fundamental role of power and conflict in society.

James Duke is among those who recently have pointed out the bridge which Weber provides between conflict and consensus theories of society. In his able review of sociological theories of conflict, he shows a special appreciation for Weber both as a sociologist of conflict and as a sociologist of social order. The propositions Duke uses to paraphrase and summarize Weber's conflict theory can be used as well as a summary of the neo-Marxian position we have seen developed by Dahrendorf:

1. Conflicts of interest are endemic in social life.
2. Power is differentially distributed among groups and individuals in any society.
3. Social order is achieved in any society through rules and commands issued by more powerful persons to less powerful persons and enforced through sanctions.
4. Both the social structure and the normative systems

of a society are more extensively influenced by powerful persons than by weaker persons (true by definition), and come to represent the interests of these more powerful persons.

5. Social changes are often more disruptive to powerful persons than to less powerful persons. Powerful persons therefore generally favor the status quo and oppose changes that would reduce their power.

6. However, changes in a society occur as the result of actions by persons who stand to benefit from these changes and who accumulate power to bring them to pass.

Part Three

Selected Studies
of
Violent Conflict

6

Three Pioneers

In Chapter 1 we mentioned the work of Lewis F. Richardson, the World War I ambulance driver who developed an enthusiasm for the mathematical analysis of human conflict. He is certainly one of the pioneers of contemporary conflict studies, and his work deserves to be presented in greater detail than the brief mention given earlier. Two other pioneers whose work will be given special attention in this chapter are Quincy Wright and Crane Brinton.

STATISTICIAN OF DEADLY QUARRELS

One of Richardson's typical efforts was the determination of just how many people are killed by their fellow human beings. He went about this very systematically, attempting to get all the data possible for the years 1820 through 1945. First, he gathered information on all wars fought during this period, with estimates of the war dead in each instance. Then he examined statistics on murder rates for a number of countries and from them derived an estimation of world murder rates. Between murders and wars, however, there was a gap. There were no good records of deaths from most episodes of large-scale banditry, local riots, and other disorders short of civil war. But Richardson noticed a strikingly regular pattern between the level of magnitude of a fatal quarrel (summarized as the base ten logarithm of the number of people killed) and the frequency of quarrels at this level. For example, he found the following frequencies in relation to magnitude:

Magnitude	Frequency
7 ± .5	2
6 ± .5	5
5 ± .5	24
4 ± .5	63

Only two wars (World Wars I and II) were of the highest magnitude, with fatalities in the 3 to 32 million range. Slightly more common were wars of magnitude 6 (in the 316,000 to 3 million fatality range), such as, for example, the American Civil War. Still, more common were wars of lesser magnitude, such as those of 31,000 to 316,000 (magnitude 5) or 3,000 to 31,000 (magnitude 4) fatalities. At the other end of the scale, Richardson estimated there to have been about 6 million quarrels of magnitude 0, that is, involving 3 or less fatalities. Extending the data to fill in the middle ranges, where the data are less readily available, we get the following estimates:

Magnitude	Frequency
3 ± .5	354
2 ± .5	5,630
1 ± .5	397,000
0 ± .5	6,000,000

Altogether, we get a total number of fatalities of slightly over 59 million during this 126-year period—with over half of these the result of World Wars I and II.[1]

This exercise gave a more precise measure of man's inhumanity to man (in terms of persons killed by fellow human beings) than had been previously available. More exciting to Richardson, however, were the mathematical properties of the results. They indicated a certain lawfulness about episodes of unruly violence. If we can describe the relation between magnitude and frequency of violent conflicts with a precise mathematical formula (which Richardson did), might not there be many more features of human conflict susceptible to summary by mathematical models? And as we identify these, should not our ability to predict—and ultimately control—these conflicts be greatly increased?

Lewis Richardson's compilation of statistics on past wars indicated a number of other interesting patterns. He showed, for example, that nations with a high number of neighboring countries generally tend to have a greater number of wars—though there are several notable exceptions. On the general question of whether warfare is increasing in modern history, Richardson's figures are ambiguous. Though some of the more recent wars tended to be larger (especially World War II), there was no pattern within the time studied for an overall increase in frequency. There were, however, indications that wars of major destruction tended to occur in cycles, with about one generation representing the interval between periodic highs.[2]

Probably Richardson's most famous work was his attempt to develop mathematical models of arms races. He started by representing key factors in an arms race in mathematical terms. For example, let x represent the arms production rate of an imaginary nation and t represent time. A change in armament production could therefore be represented as dx/dt, or a difference in arms production for a given difference in time.

In searching for what might affect such armament changes, Richardson narrowed his attention to three primary variables. One would be the arms level of a potential enemy nation, which could be represented as y. Another would be the cost to one's own nation of producing a given level of armaments (such armament rates, we remember, are represented by x). Finally, there is a factor to represent the accumulated grievances against a potential enemy (call this g). With such assumptions, it is a simple matter to put them together into a mathematical equation, such as:

$$dx/dt = ay - mx + g$$

To translate this into words: the change in armament levels (dx) of a given country over time (dt) is seen as a result of:
1. the armament levels of a rival (y) times a constant (a) representing the tendency to be influenced by the rival,
2. less the amount of one's own production (x) times a constant (m) which describes the costliness of different production levels,

3. plus the amount of the accumulated grievances (*g*,
   which would be subtracted instead of added in the
   event that there is a net surplus of good will).

In developing this formula, we have already partly taken
into account the armaments of another nation (our *y* term). To
fully represent an arms race, we need to include both rivals.
We can therefore use corresponding terms to represent this
second nation or bloc. This leads to the following pair of equations to represent the arms increases of *x*-land and *y*-land, respectively:

$$dx/dt = ay - mx + g$$
$$dy/dt = bx - ny + h$$

Notice that we use new coefficients *b* and *n* for *y*-land in the
second equation (instead of *a* and *m*), because we do not wish
to assume that both sides are equally responsive to arms of the
other (*a* or *b*) or that they find armament increases equally
costly (*m* or *n*). We would expect some similarity in these responses, but not necessarily identity. We even assume that the
grievance levels may be different for each side (*g* or *h*), recognizing that different nations may have different past experiences affecting how they see grievances.

Apparently, all we need now is a set of measures to plug
into our formulas, allowing us to predict the future course of
an arms race. Such predictions can then be tested against reality and refinements can be devised to make the formulas ever-
closer approximations of the real world. Such, it would appear,
is the main value of mathematical models such as Richardson's
representation of arms races.

However, appearances here would be deceiving. True,
Richardson himself went to great lengths to find measures of
his arms race terms, and he obtained a fairly precise prediction
for the arms race just before World War I which fit observed
facts quite well. But the problem of obtaining measures for the
terms of such equations is so enormous as to make them of
limited value so far as practical prediction in the real world is
concerned. But this is not the greatest value of this particular
contribution of Richardson. Rather, the chief value of such
models is to help us see in principle the main types of outcomes

that occur in arms races. This contribution is more directly theoretical than empirical. By using formulas such as Richardson's and grinding out their consequences with a variety of different inputs, it soon becomes apparent that the main outcomes fit a very limited number of basic patterns. We can identify the main patterns of arms races, recognizing what outcomes are most likely to be characteristic of each. We can then compare real situations generally with these types, without necessarily presuming to measure accurately all the detailed terms of the equations.

Omitting some mathematical work that we need not review in detail here, the arms races described by Richardson's formulas tend to fall into one of four types:

Type 1. In this type $mn > ab$, $g > 0$, and $h > 0$. Here, cost considerations of armament production are more important than considerations of arms superiority. Also, there is assumed to be an accumulation of mutual grievances.

Type 2. Here $mn > ab$, $g < 0$, and $h < 0$. Again, cost considerations predominate over those of arms superiority; but now there is a net accumulation of good will rather than a legacy of grievances.

Type 3. In this type $mn < ab$, $g > 0$, and $h > 0$. Here, arms competition is more important than considerations of armament costs. Also, there is assumed to be an accumulation of grievances.

Type 4. Here $mn < ab$, $g < 0$, and $h < 0$. Arms competition is again of central importance, but there is a net legacy of good will rather than grievances.

For each of the first three types above, there is a clear arms production pattern over time—contrasting neatly with the other types. Type 1 moves quickly to a stable equilibrium, with both nations or blocs stabilizing arms production at fairly constant levels. In contrast, Types 2 and 3 have no such equilibrium. Both of these may be seen as runaway arms races—though running in different directions. In Type 2 the movement is benign, toward total disarmament. In Type 3 we obtain the classic runaway race toward increasing armaments—with mutually accelerating arms production curves continuing until both sides are exhausted (or at war).

Type 4 presents an especially interesting pattern. Here the situation is ambiguous—but in a clearly determined way. It all depends upon the starting point. If the initial level of armament production is above a certain point for both sides, they will fall into a runaway arms race. But if it is below that critical level, then the reverse occurs, and there is mutual disarmament.

There is a deterministic quality about the outcome for each of the above cases. In each there is a relentless logic. which forces the consequences from the assumed conditions. There is an aura of inevitability, as each case presents its own pattern of momentum. Perhaps this helps us perceive something of the quality of the momentum which large-scale international events may have, leaving the individual decision maker in a position where he feels he cannot go against the pattern already in motion. Lewis Richardson, however, would make a qualification here. True, there is a mechanical and deterministic quality about processes such as those represented by his arms race models. But this should not be confused with real-world inevitability. According to Richardson, the models show only what would happen if we do not stop to think. They show a pattern of events which must be taken into account in the formulation of effective policy—but not one with such total inevitability that there is no room for conscious human choice.

A MONUMENTAL STUDY

In the peaceful 1920s, while Lewis Richardson was still unrecognized for his mathematical models, a group in the United States began pursuing an even more ambitious study of war. It was in the spring of 1926 that faculty members and graduate students of the University of Chicago initiated a plan for a series of studies on the causes of war. Although first led by Charles E. Merriam, a political science professor, the project soon passed to the leadership of Quincy Wright, an expert in international law. About 75 studies were planned, most of which were eventually completed in the form of graduate theses (45 different theses of the University of Chicago were from this project) or scholarly articles and books. Pulling all these studies together was the gigantic task of Professor Wright. A preliminary attempt took the form of a series of lectures published as *The Causes of War and the Conditions of Peace* (1935), but the final compilation did not appear until 1942, when the two-volume *A Study of War* was published by the University of Chicago Press. Here was a truly monumental compilation of theory and research in approximately 1,500 carefully written pages, including 77 tables and 44 appendices which summarized enormous amounts of statistical information. No single work of this scope on the subject of war has been published either before or since.[3]

We will not here attempt to summarize this many-sided work, but we will pull out a few of the contents that may be of special interest.

First, we may note some patterns in the incidence of war. Warfare is not randomly distributed in space and time. Certain nations—especially those larger and stronger nations known as great powers—are involved in more wars than other nations. For example, in the first three decades of the twentieth century, nations classed as great powers averaged 46 military campaigns with a mean duration of 14 months. Secondary powers averaged 19 campaigns each with a mean duration of 8 months; and lesser powers averaged 10 campaigns with 6 months as the average duration. Clearly, the larger powers fight more often and longer than do other nations.

Fighting between nations also shows important temporal variations. Before the twentieth century most battles were contained within a single day, and night battles were rare. In the twentieth century, however, battles have become longer, most lasting beyond a single day. The campaign period has also increased, with winter campaigns less rare than had previously obtained (spring or summer being historically the most preferred seasons for fighting). There seems to be little overall patterning in terms of the length of wars, though there does appear to be some periodicity in the intensity of wars. Wright points to data which suggest a peak in battle casualties about every 50 years—not with enough regularity for prediction of future wars but with enough of a pattern to warrant speculation about its possible causes (such as the time necessary for

economic recovery and for political preparation of the population to endure a major war).

As we survey the modern period (Wright's detailed compilation of wars begins in 1480), are there any quantitative trends
describing changes in warfare? Yes, there are several. Armies
have tended to become larger. There tends to be a slightly increasing period of peace between wars, thus fewer wars. But
battles during war are more intense and longer. There also is
an increasing tendency for fighting to spread, including more
nations in a given war. The economic and human costs of war
also appear to have increased during the period of modern history. All of these documented trends appear to be intertwined.
In a summary statement Wright characterizes war as becoming
"more intense, more extended, and more costly" at the same
time that it has become "less functional, less intentional, less
directable, and less legal." What is behind this pattern? According to Wright:

> The accelerating speed of technological and social change in
> the modern world, the more rapid geographical diffusion of
> ideas and methods, the increasing economic and political in-
> terdependence of separated areas, the growth of population
> and standards of living, the rise of public opinion and popular
> initiative in politics, have together tended to concentrate mili-
> tary activity in time and to extend it in space; to make it less
> easy to begin, to localize, and to end; to make it materially
> more destructive and morally less controllable; to make it ap-
> pear psychologically more catastrophic and less rational; to
> make it more difficult for any state to isolate itself from mili-
> tarization in time of peace and from hostilities in time of war,
> once the controls of international law and organization have
> been successfully defied.[4]

Such, at any rate, was the summary pattern which appeared to
represent the past few centuries.

A Study of War, however, was not limited to an examination
of wars of modern history. There are also chapters on animal
fighting and warfare among primitive peoples, as well as consideration of the wars of ancient civilizations. Deadly violence
among animals is shown to be rare within the same species.
There is sometimes a heightened aggressiveness (especially of

males in certain species of birds and mammals) in defense of mates and/or home territories. This serves to space out the species involved and thus assists its survival; but rarely does it involve killing or group fighting. Certain insect societies provide perhaps the closest parallel to human warfare, but here the mode of organization is very different—based as it is upon genetically given social categories in insect societies. Human evolution appears to lead in a different direction.

Patterns of primitive warfare vary greatly from group to group, indicating varied social foundations of human fighting. Wright gives primary emphasis to maintenance of social solidarity as the basic foundation of primitive warfare. Particular techniques vary according to the traditions of the tribes involved, though tending to become more specialized and more deadly with advances toward civilization. Indeed, it is only with the rise of civilization—and with the associated specialized development of permanent military organizations—that warfare on a really large scale becomes possible. And thus comes the beginning of a general trend continuing into the modern age— toward warfare of a wider scope, with greater destructiveness, a more explicit separation between periods of war and peace, and a greater recognition of the need to control and limit the enhanced destructive potential of war.

Throughout *A Study of War* is a recognition that peace as well as war is under discussion, and that both grow out of a complex interrelationship of human institutions. To prevent and limit the destructiveness of war has been as much a part of institutional development of modern nations as has the preparation for war. And Wright sees the process extended more and more to include the international organization of peace. International law, as we indicated earlier, was Quincy Wright's academic specialty. His first book, *The Enforcement of International Law through Municipal Law in the United States* (1916), pointed out a wide variety of ways that supranational law impinges upon American domestic law. Subsequent works on *Control of American Foreign Relations* (1922) and *Mandates under the League of Nations* (1930) continued his careful scholarship on international law. Much of the theoretical work in *A Study of War* also grows out of this international law framework, and it is quite clear that Wright supported strongly the need for a further expansion of such law. He saw that national sovereignty must be increasingly limited by this wider body of supranational law, which would have to be made more binding if the forces of war were to be contained.

Quincy Wright was not a utopian. He saw war as arising not so much from basic human nature as from features of the complex interrelationship of human social institutions. The more effectively these human insitutions function—the better they approach a working equilibrium—the less likely that war will erupt. But these institutions (combining technologies, legal systems, and popular attitudes and sentiments) are extremely complex. It is difficult to shape them into the forms we might wish. It therefore behooves us to study them carefully, with sensitivity to the many causal forces at work. This is the spirit with which *A Study of War* examines the causes of war and the conditions for peace.

For Wright the main thrust of our efforts toward building peace is quite clear: we must develop more effective forms of international organization and world law. Peace, more than war, must be artificially created, but it is not to be gained so much as an end in itself. Rather, it must come as a "by-product of a satisfactory organization of the world."[5]

A Comparative "Anatomy"

Lewis Richardson pioneered in the quantitative study of conflict. Quincy Wright included quantitative research in his studies of war, but his work also broadly reflected other methodological approaches as well. The third pioneer we wish to recognize in this chapter, the historian Crane Brinton, represents a much more qualitative kind of study. He is, in fact, better known as a general historian of modern Western history than as a conflict "scientist." However, we will ignore most of the distinguished career of this Harvard historian (who died in 1968 at the age of seventy). We will not mention nearly a score of other books he wrote in order to discuss just one, *The Anatomy of Revolution*. First published in 1938, this study of revolutions was a landmark in the comparative historical study of social conflict.

Brinton deliberately took a scientific stance for his comparative analysis of revolution. Although conceding that laboratory experimentation is not feasible in the study of revolution, he held that a *clinical* science based upon the observation of carefully selected cases is another matter. Such a clinical approach is closely akin to natural history investigations in the biological sciences and the case studies of medical science. It includes a hard-headed respect for the accumulation of facts, the organization of these facts in terms of leading concepts which sensitize us to dominant patterns, and a spirit of relative detachment in organizing and interpreting the facts.

Brinton selected four modern revolutions for analysis—the British Civil War of the 1640s, the American Revolution, the French Revolution, and the more recent Russian Revolution. A number of reasons support this selection. In the first place, these all were important revolutions in the history of the modern world. As significant revolutions, each has been the subject of an extensive accumulation of factual data which may be used for secondary analysis. When Brinton first published his work in 1938, the Russian Revolution was still recent enough that many of the facts were still widely disputed; nevertheless, even for the Russian case, there was no shortage of data for analysis. Finally, Brinton was no doubt guided to cases which fit with the most common connotations of the term "revolution" in the contemporary context. All four cases were popular revolts, generally supported by a majority, carried out in the name of liberty, and at the expense of an entrenched minority. They were all therefore "democratic" revolutions, in at least the main connotations of that term. They were all also successful, in that a transfer of power to the rebels was accomplished in each case.

Not all revolutions are of such a nature. Brinton recognizes that many kinds of revolution are excluded—such as revolutions of the right carried out in the name of a conservative ideal, territorially based nationalistic revolutions (though the American Revolution was a partial example of this), or revolutionary attempts which proved unsuccessful in their efforts to overturn the power system. Also left out are still other forms of political events or social turmoil to which the term "revolution" is sometimes attached.

Nevertheless, there remains considerable diversity among

the four significant modern revolutions which Brinton includes. They represent different countries, different centuries,
and a wide diversity of particular events. If they all share basic
characteristics in their overall patterns, we may at least tentatively put these forth as features of what might be called "the
revolutionary process."

Brinton proceeds to examine the course of the revolutionary process, summarizing at each stage the data of each of the
four cases. He starts with an analysis of the old regimes and
follows with the first stages of revolt. After initial success, the
revolutionary movements involved typically show a trend toward radicalization; this culminates usually in a crisis period
followed by a return to normalcy.

In his final chapter, Brinton seeks to summarize apparent
uniformities in the four cases. He does this quite tentatively,
for he recognizes no grand laws of revolutionary dynamics.
Nevertheless, he believes that a number of features do stand
out which characterize the onset and course of at least these
four revolutions.

Among the symptoms of societies on the verge of revolution, Brinton calls attention to five specific points. All of these
revolutions involved societies which were generally progressing
economically, but in which important elements (certainly not
the most poor, but important segments still not satisfied in their
aspirations for wealth and recognition) felt their opportunities
unduly restricted. All of these societies had rather bitter class
antagonisms. All showed a general disenchantment of intellectuals with the old regime. All involved regimes with a great
deal of governmental inefficiency. And all involved ruling
classes in which important segments had come to doubt their
way of life and right to govern. The general picture thus given
of the prerevolutionary society is not one of overwhelming
oppression so much as it is of uneven progress and a widespread loss of faith in old institutions and those who run them.

As for the course of these revolutions, Brinton also found
common elements in their early stages. A financial crisis for the
government is typically part of the opening series of revolutionary events. The organization of discontented elements develops to the point where revolutionary demands are openly

set forth. These are typically met with by force from the government, but this governmental repression proves ineffective. In a short time, the reins of government then pass to the rebels.

At first, it is the moderates among the revolutionaries who hold power, but the momentum of the revolution moves it gradually to the left. After a time, there is a crisis period in which extreme measures are deemed necessary to promote the new revolutionary goals (in all cases but that of the American Revolution, this crisis period introduced a reign of terror in which revolutionary extremists seemed temporarily unchecked in their exercise of power). Following this period, however, the society grows weary of revolutionary activity, and there is a return to normalcy. The network of normal social relationships reasserts itself, the more extreme revolutionaries lose favor or are forcibly put down, and the revolution passes into history. It leaves, however, a new government in which the worst abuses and inefficiencies of the old regime are no longer present. It also leaves men and women in a different ideological climate and with new symbols of political legitimacy (all four revolutions at least temporarily displaced monarchies); but in the everyday life of the average person there is no dramatic change. As Brinton puts it, "Our revolutions seem in many ways to have changed men's minds more completely than they changed men's habits."[6]

Such conclusions are not put forward in the sense of rigorous scientific laws. Rather, they seem to be rough generalizations which are supported by the four revolutions studied. They are not theoretically precise, so we are given little guidance for how widely they may be expected to apply to other revolutions. Brinton does not even give us a clear definition of the term "revolution." His spirit is much more that of empirical exploration than theoretical refinement, and his exploration gives us only tentative leads toward generalization. The question remains open as to how widely these patterns may apply to other revolutions—especially to revolutions different in type from those four (all leftward moving, widely supported, and mainly successful) which he studied.

7

Further Studies of Strife

People willingly cooperate to form and preserve those institutions, political or otherwise, which they see as supporting their happiness and well-being. If large numbers feel their happiness is not being served, they will endure for a time; ultimately, however, they will come to regard their institutions as oppressive and raise their voices in protest. When such protests are heard, reforms may be the result, as leaders of society accept changes (often slowly and with grudging hesitation). But sometimes the protests—even when voiced by the great majority of citizens—are not attended to, or perhaps the response is so slow that the proponents of change lose patience. Then they will take to the streets to express their discontent and defiance; turmoil and strife will be the natural consequence. When discontent is especially severe the result will be rebellion, often including a political revolution.

So runs what is probably the most popular interpretation of the basic sources of civil strife. This interpretation can be applied alike to general turmoil, to collective movements aimed at changing established institutions, and to revolts aimed at displacing a governmental regime. The underlying proposition in all cases seems to be: the greater the discontent, the greater the pressure for change. Furthermore, the more the pressure for change is resisted, the greater will be the violence of the resulting explosion.

Such a theory of riot, rebellion, and revolution is especially commonly stated in societies with a democratic tradition. It usually helps to rationalize the establishment of their political system in the first place (as in, for example, the American Declaration of Independence), and it supports the idea of keeping the system open to continual change. The theory emphasizes that those in power must (to continue in power) be constantly receptive to the desires of their people—certainly a central democratic idea.

But how true is this theory? Is it supported by the best data we are able to muster in studying the conditions of collective violence? Or does some other set of ideas fare better? These are the fundamental questions posed in the present chapter, and we use them as a vehicle for examining several impressive empirical studies of the backgrounds of rebellion.

HARVESTS OF DISCONTENT

We start with the basic hypothesis that the amount of discontent present in a society is the best predictor of civil strife or rebellion. The greater the discontent, the greater the likelihood of a major rebellion. But we must be careful in our identification of discontent. As Crane Brinton reminded us in the last chapter, major revolutions do not necessarily occur when or where economic hardship is most pressing. Alexis de Tocqueville, in his classic analysis of the French Revolution, makes a similar point about political oppression:

> . . . it was precisely in those parts of France where there had been most improvement that popular discontent ran highest. This may seem illogical—but history is full of such paradoxes. For it is not always when things are going from bad to worse that revolutions break out. On the contrary, it oftener happens that when a people which has put up with an oppressive rule over a long period without protest suddenly finds the government relaxing its pressure, it takes up arms against it. Thus the social order overthrown by a revolution is almost always better then the one immediately preceding it, and experience teaches us that, generally speaking, the most perilous moment for a bad government is one when it seeks to mend its ways.[1]

Is it possible that discontent may be generated by something besides objective conditions? If so, how can we give this insight a theoretical formulation?

James C. Davies has attempted to explain de Tocqueville's paradox by suggesting that the subjective discontent of a people is frequently greatest only after they have seen some improvement in conditions. When the improvement stops, however, or slows considerably, then the expectations of progress are especially frustrated. Revolutions, therefore, "are most likely to occur when a prolonged period of objective economic and social development is followed by a short period of sharp reversal." He calls this a J-curve pattern because a graph of progress in objective conditions looks like an inverted J. He has discussed a series of case studies which show support for this idea.[2]

A similar idea was put forward by Ivo and Rosalind Feierabend in comparing conditions of political stability or instability in different nations. Although they did not make any comparisons over time which might test the particular predictions of a J curve, they did hold that subjective factors of relative satisfaction would be effective predictors of order or disorder. Furthermore, they used some rather ambitious quantitative techniques. Their central measure was an index of political stability for each of 84 nations for the seven-year period 1955–61. They used this index to search for related background conditions. They combined a number of measures into an index of "systemic frustration," which was interpreted as a ratio of want formation to want satisfaction (for example, literacy and urbanization were used as indicators of want formation, while income level was one of the variables used for indicating satisfaction). The resulting nation-by-nation measures of systemic frustration correlated quite well with measures of political stability, as Table 7.1 shows. Only 62 nations had enough information to be rated on both variables shown in Table 7.1, but this is enough for the predominant pattern to be clear; those nations with high levels of systemic frustration tended to show subsequently more political instability. Conversely, those nations with less systemic frustration (mostly the more developed or modern nations) tended to show greater subsequent stability. There were, of course, exceptions to this pattern. Tunisia and the Philippines were politically stable despite high systemic frustration, and several other nations (such as Argentina, France, and South Africa) were unstable despite low frustration levels—at

Table 7.1 Number of nations in different subcategories of systemic frustration (1948–55) and political stability (1955–61)

Level of systemic frustration	Index of political stability	
	Unstable	Stable
Low	6	20
High	34	2

Source: Adapted from Feierabend and Feierabend (1966).

least as measured by this study. This pattern is seen as confirmation of a general frustration-aggression model (suggesting frustration as a basic psychological condition for aggression) for interpreting basic causes of political unrest and violence.[3]

Starting with a somewhat similar orientation to that of the Feierabends, Ted Robert Gurr has even more thoroughly studied the conditions of rebellion. For Gurr the main theme—at least for understanding the psychological basis of civil strife—is "relative deprivation." When people feel deprived relative to what they expect, the potential for civil unrest and violence grows. Of course, it is not possible to use such a general statement for predicting degrees of unrest or violence, and Gurr goes to great pains to define a set of variables and the conditions under which they will predict civil strife. This is most systematically presented in his book *Why Men Rebel*. A brief summary of this framework is given by Figure 7.1. As shown in this figure, relative deprivation sets the stage for collective violence.

Figure 7.1 Gurr's basic model of why men rebel. (Adapted from Gurr, 1970)

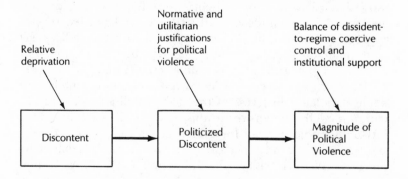

The intensity and scope of relative deprivation determine the potential for collective violence. Whether or not this discontent turns to political violence depends on a number of conditioning factors related especially to justifications for political violence. If political violence is widely approved and also appears likely to be successful, discontent can easily be channeled into political violence. But how much political violence will actually occur? This depends not only on the extent of politicized discontent but also on certain societal variables. Especially relevant here is the relative balance of coercive power held by the regime in power, and also the scope of the regime's institutional support. If the regime really has an effective monopoly of coercive power (army, weapons, police, etc., with dissidents completely unarmed), relatively little political violence will appear. Likewise, it is true that little violence will be expected when institutional support (business, labor, the church, academic and professional groups, etc.) is solidly behind a regime—or solidly against it, for that matter. Political violence is at its maximum when a regime and dissidents approach equality in either or both of these two areas (coercive control and institutional support).

Such, at any rate, is the general causal model sketched by Gurr to explain why men rebel. Each of the links in this model has been further developed by Gurr into subhypotheses, with a variety of evidence pointed to for support.[4]

Gurr's own work in exploring these relationships has been primarily devoted to a quantitative and comparative analysis of political violence in different countries. Measurement of key variables has posed very difficult problems, but Gurr has worked hard to overcome them. How, for example, do you measure the magnitude of civil strife? Gurr has tried several approaches for this, but he finally ended with two indices: (1) an estimate of man-days of strife per 100,000 population, and (2) deaths from strife per 100 million population.[5]

How well can we explain the differences between nations in political violence in terms of the main conditions specified in Gurr's model? The answer to this question depends on which of Gurr's studies is used for evidence. For our present discussion, we will depend especially on a cross-national analysis he did of 21 Western nations for the period 1961–65. As a point of comparison, the United States during this period was in the high middle range of nations in terms of magnitude of civil strife. By the criterion of man-days of participation per 100,000 population, the United States ranked tenth out of the 21 nations; and by the criterion of deaths per 100 million, it ranked sixth. By neither criterion was the United States as violent politically as Belgium, France, or Rhodesia—nor as peaceful as New Zealand or the Scandinavian countries (which had essentially no political violence during this period). By combining the two criteria in equal weights into an overall magnitude-of-strife score, we get the following rank order for the 21 nations analyzed by Gurr:

1. Rhodesia
2. Belgium
3. France
4. Italy
5. Greece
6. South Africa
7. Israel
8. West Germany
9. Austria
10. United States
11. Canada
12. Australia
13. United Kingdom
14. Ireland
15. Finland
16. Switzerland
17. Denmark, Netherlands, New Zealand, Norway, Sweden

Five nations tied for last place; all showed no sign of civil strife for the years indicated. Incidentally, this total set of nations is generally more peaceful internally than most nations of the world, with political violence in Europe and North America less, on the average, than in Asia, Africa, and Latin America.

Gurr developed a number of quantitative indices to represent conditions predicted to produce strife. We will not detail exactly how this was done, but one example may suffice to show that this was not a simple task to accomplish. "Short-term economic deprivation," to select one summary measure, was represented by an index which combined scores on the following five indicators:

1. Trends in trade value of 1957–60 compared with 1950–57;
2. Trends in trade value of 1960–63 compared with 1950–60;
3. Inflation in 1960–63 compared with 1958–61;

4. Gross national product growth rate in 1960–63 compared with the 1950s; and

5. Rating of degree of adverse economic conditions reported in the world news for 1960–63.

In similar fashion, indices were developed for other key variables suggested by Gurr's overall model. Table 7.2 gives some partial results, showing the simple correlation coefficients between these variables and the summary magnitude-of-strife scores. As can be seen in this table, the strongest direct predic-

Table 7.2 Correlations of various conditions with total magnitude of civil strife for 21 Western nations, 1961–65

	Correlation with civil strife
Relative deprivation variables	
Persisting deprivation	.39
Short-term political deprivation	.50
Short-term economic deprivation	.06
Variables of justification	
Governmental legitimacy	.67
Extent of past strife	.62
Historical success of strife	.53
Variables of power and support	
Coercive capacity of the regime	−.23
Coercive capacity of dissidents	.67
Institutional support for the regime	−.57
Institutional support for dissidents	.72

Source: Adapted from Gurr (1972).

tors were the variables of justification and the variables reflecting dissident strength. Collective violence was especially likely to occur when (to mention all variables with correlations of .60 or more): the legitimacy of the regime was in question, there was a considerable history of strife, dissidents held a large measure of force at their command, and/or institutional support was especially strong for dissidents. It may be noted that, compared to these variables, the relative deprivation measures do not come through very strongly. Especially notable is the absence of a strong association between short-term economic deprivation and strife. Gurr's relative deprivation theory would lead us to expect a stronger link than the negligible relationship (a correlation of .06) actually found.

Data which Gurr presents elsewhere, including most nations of the world, show a somewhat stronger relationship between deprivation measures and level of civil strife. Some of these data are summarized in Table 7.3. This table shows that there is a general pattern for nations with the highest levels of deprivation showing the highest levels of civil strife. This pattern holds for nations at all levels of economic development and for both short-term deprivation (this measure combines political and economic factors) and long-term deprivation. This

Table 7.3 Correlations of selected variables with magnitude of civil strife, 114 nations, 1961–65, by level of economic development

	Level of economic development			All nations (114)
Variable	High (37)	Medium (39)	Low (38)	
Short-term deprivation	.57	.58	.23	.47
Persisting deprivation	.34	.29	.31	.35
Legitimacy of political system	−.20	−.52	−.23	−.38
Extent of past strife	.65	.01	.37	.29

Source: Adapted from Gurr (1969).

Gurr sees as support for his general emphasis upon relative deprivation. Table 7.3 also shows that the legitimacy of the political system is negatively correlated with the magnitude of civil strife and that the extent of past strife is a good predictor for at least some nations—especially those with the most highly developed economies.[6]

So far, we have discussed only a general overall measure of civil strife. Gurr also broke down this variable into subcategories of turmoil (including, in turn, nonviolent protest and violent turmoil) and rebellion (including conspiracy, if by a small group, and internal war, if large numbers of participants are included). Gurr also examined the effects of background variables upon each of these subcategories of strife. In so doing, important differences between these subcategories were found. Without going into detail, we may indicate what some of the main patterns were in comparing these subcategories of strife:

1. Rebellion is more strongly associated with deprivation measures than is turmoil or (especially) nonviolent protest.
2. Turmoil generally (and nonviolent protest in particular) is more strongly associated with justification measures than is rebellion.
3. Rebellion is more strongly associated with measures of coercive balance than is turmoil.
4. All forms of strife are about equally associated (strongly negative in all cases) with measures of institutional support for the political regime.

The implications which Gurr draws from such findings (especially as reflected in his study of 21 Western nations) are that:

> The less intense forms of strife in Western nations—demonstrations and most riots—are more the result of how people think about governments and the desirability of protest than of intense grievances. . . . But the most serious forms of strife—terrorism, anti-government conspiracy, and the more violent riots—are in Western nations a direct response to intense and persisting frustrations, not much affected by political loyalties or traditions.[7]

DISORGANIZATION AND COLLECTIVE BEHAVIOR

We pause to remind ourselves of the model underlying the work cited in the previous section. The central theme was that discontent produces strife, with the underlying psychological assumption that of the frustration-aggression hypothesis. Strife is viewed as an aggregate result of the frustrations (or relative deprivations) of individuals. When many individuals share a sense of deprivation or frustration, the result is likely to be some form of civil strife. True, we did include some additional factors—especially when we considered the work of Gurr—but the central theme has always been the accumulated dissatisfactions of individual men and women.

Is there an alternative way of conceiving of our problem?

Yes, there is an alternative, and one which has a very rich history in the discipline of sociology. We refer to what is usually called "collective behavior." Actually, this term is more than a little misleading, for only certain behaviors of people acting collectively (and usually the less clearly articulated collective actions at that) are included. Basically, the defining distinction made is between institutionalized behavior and collective behavior. For every society a great deal of behavior is highly regulated by established norms; we can refer to this as "institutionalized behavior." For some occasions, however, the norms are not very clear; when these occasions affect a large number of people together, the emerging result is collective behavior. Crowd behavior is the most classic type of such collective behavior, as a group gradually forms and its distinctive behavior emerges from the situation.

What produces civil strife or violent rebellion, according to the collective behavior model? Frustration may well be involved—but is not some degree of frustration almost always present? More important, in the collective behavior model, is the absence of clearly articulated norms. In this view, it is when people are relatively uncontrolled by norms that we are most likely to find violent group outbursts. Such expressions of conflict reflect essentially an absence of viable social organization.

Not all collective behavior expresses violence or rebellion. Sometimes it may be simply expressive, as in the frenzy of a religious revival. But to the extent that there is shared anger (which itself may be due more to acts of official repression than to initial hostility), a crowd may begin to focus itself violently. Sometimes a large section of society may be involved in such crowdlike behavior. If so, the result may be the beginning of a political revolution.

An especially influential analysis by Neil Smelser includes a definition of collective behavior as "mobilization on the basis of a belief which redefines social action." Smelser further qualifies this definition by specifying that such beliefs must include the "existence of extraordinary forces" which are at work and the possibilities of "extraordinary consequences which will follow if the collective attempt to reconstitute social action is successful." The beliefs which are the focus of collective behavior are unusual in their power to invoke faith and provoke action. Furthermore, the behavior organized by these "generalized beliefs" is "not institutionalized." To the degree to which the behavior is institutionalized (that is, regulated by norms and expectations established by past practices), it loses its character as collective behavior.[8]

In his analysis of determinants of collective behavior, Smelser gives particular attention to six factors. They are: (1) structural conduciveness, (2) structural strain, (3) growth and spread of a generalized belief, (4) precipitating factors, (5) mobilization of participants for action, and (6) the operation of social control. "Structural conduciveness" refers to the background conditions of a society which may prepare the way for one or another form of collective behavior. "Structural strain" refers to ambiguities, deprivations, conflicts and discrepancies which arise within the social order. The "generalized belief" which becomes widely shared (and serves as the central concept in Smelser's theory) is one which identifies both causes of the strain and possible responses to remove it. "Precipitating factors" refer to events which bring into concrete focus the generalized belief and provide an opportunity for giving some kind of response. "Mobilization" for action involves people coming together and, guided by whatever leadership becomes recognized, preparing to take action. The "operation of social control" refers to those forces of regular law and order which may limit or suppress emerging collective behavior.

The above six factors operate in a cumulative process, according to Smelser. A full-fledged collective behavior movement which successfully changes the social order (for example, a popular uprising which culminates in a political revolution) must include them all, and essentially in the order indicated. That is, the generalized belief depends on the nature of the strain; what successfully "precipitates" a response depends on the belief; mobilization depends on the particular precipitating factors; and so forth. If any one of these is notably missing, the collective behavior process will be aborted. For example, there may be a generalized belief about the injustice of a regime which, however, never becomes dramatized in any particular incident; or a movement may go on to be fully mobilized but then be suppressed by the official agencies of social control, such as the police and army.

The initial background in Smelser's model of collective behavior is social disorganization or strain. The focus of attention becomes a belief about that strain and what may be done to relieve it. The ensuing action is a movement for social change, however successful it may prove to be in the end.

Let us follow such a collective behavior model in seeking to derive general predictions about rebellious behavior. Given the combination of contingencies for fully developed collective behavior, we would not expect a very precise predictability regarding when and how violent group outbursts might occur. However, we would expect to find evidence for some broad patterns. Some kinds of individuals should be more likely than others to be involved. Essentially, we would expect persons less fully integrated into the prevailing social structure to be most represented in violent crowd behavior or movements of social rebellion. In addition, as Eric Hoffer has suggested, they are likely to be persons with a fundamentally soured self-image; or as Erich Fromm has pointed out, they may be persons who are especially insecure about their place in the social structure.[9] Therefore, some segments of society—essentially those most out of the mainstream, such ar racial or ethnic minorities—are expected to be more likely to be involved than others. We would also expect areas with significant signs of social disorganization (regions of chronic poverty, or those undergoing very rapid social changes, for example) to be natural areas for riots and other violent outbursts. Finally, certain kinds of societies should show these patterns more clearly than others (especially should we find them in rapidly modernizing societies, in which traditional institutions have been eroded and modern industrial institutions are not yet fully established).

A collective behavior approach has appeared most successful when applied in retrospect to particular instances of violent group outbursts. Case studies of riots offer particularly good opportunities to use this model. They seem to show the same characteristics of human behavior which are emphasized by collective behavior theorists. But do the predictions of this approach stand up to the test of quantitative data? For instance, are they supported by the most systematic of the numerous studies of recent American racial disturbances?

Before we examine in greater detail the evidence in response to this question, let us recognize several problems about scientific research in the area of riots. First of all, a riot is not an ideal setting in which to conduct objective scientific research. Considerations of personal security probably outweigh those of careful observation for any social scientists on the scene, and of course very seldom are social scientists on the scene anyway. So, data come indirectly—primarily from accounts put together by journalists, from police records, and from interviews conducted later with people involved. These secondary reconstructions are always selective about what facts are included in the record. Journalists highlight whatever is dramatic and unusual. Police records reflect the particular forms of police involvement. And all participants tend to recall whatever will most make their own behavior consistent and justifiable. These are not reasons to avoid systematic study of riots or other forms of collective behavior; but they do caution us that there are real difficulties to be overcome in getting a clear hold on objective facts.

Among the simplest kinds of facts to obtain are those of the incidence of violent group outbursts. Significant riots will be reported in the press, and with enough detail to make at least a reasonable rating of the extent of violence. For example, Sheldon Levy combed old newspapers for reports of violence during sample time periods in American history and obtained indices for different forms of collective violence. Figure 7.2 gives a summary of some of his results, showing the second half of the nineteenth century to be generally the most violent.[10]

Another example of research based largely on newspaper accounts can be seen in Seymour Spilerman's analysis of the incidence of American ghetto riots in the late 1960s. He identified the number of disorders experienced by each of 673 American cities (which ranged up to a high of 11 disturbances, though 504 cities had none). Then he investigated the characteristics of these cities which might be associated with their "disorder-proneness."[11]

A variety of specific measures were derived to represent

Figure 7.2 Relative frequency of deaths through civil strife in the United States for different periods of history. (Levy, 1969, p. 88)

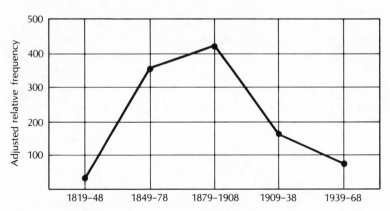

conditions in each city. These were then grouped by Spilerman into clusters, each cluster reflecting one of the more popular interpretations for the incidence of ghetto riots to be found in the social science literature. For example, the following three variables were all considered in a "social disorganization" cluster (which would be especially appropriate for a collective behavior interpretation):

Percent change in total population;
Percent change in nonwhite population;
Percent of persons living in dilapidated housing units.

In comparison, a "relative deprivation" cluster was composed of the following variables:

Relative proportion of nonwhites to whites employed in traditionally Negro occupations;
Relative size of nonwhite to white median family income;
Relative size of nonwhite to white unemployment rates;
Relative educational levels of nonwhites to whites.

Should one of these two clusters seem to be especially good for predicting the incidence of disorders, this would tend to confirm one of the popular theories of riot causation (for example, that the more disorganized urban conditions are likely to produce riots, or that black-white inequality is the root causal factor).

Spilerman's findings, however, did not show a strong predictive power for the variables of either of the two clusters mentioned above. The incidence of disturbances in a city also fails to show a strong relationship with either of two other clusters of variables—one consisting of measures of "absolute deprivation" and another reflecting the particular "political structures" characteristic of the city. Instead, two miscellaneous variables not usually much emphasized in discussions of causes of racial disturbances showed much higher predictive power than any variables in the above four clusters. Far and away the best single predictor of the incidence of racial disturbances was the absolute size of the nonwhite population. In other words, there was more riot activity where there were more blacks. This variable alone accounted for 46.8 percent of the city-to-city variation in incidence of racial disturbances. Another variable which was only very roughly measured also proved surprisingly strong. This was whether the city was in the North or the South, with northern cities much more prone to disturbances than southern cities.

Table 7.4 summarizes some of the results included in Spilerman's analysis. The first cloumn of figures shows how much of the city-to-city variation in the dependent variable (incidence of racial disturbances) can be accounted for by combining all the variables of that cluster. At first glance, it appears that at least modest success is to be found in the "relative deprivation" and "political structures" areas. Still, however, these are both much weaker than either of the two miscellaneous variables previously mentioned. If we first measure these two variables— absolute size of the nonwhite population and region (South or North)—and then add the variables of a cluster, how much additional variation in the dependent variable may be accounted for? Answers to this question may be seen in the final column of Table 7.4. These figures show that very little variation in the incidence of racial disturbances can be accounted for by any of these variables if they are considered *after* taking account of nonwhite population size and region. In other words, most

Table 7.4 Relative ability of different clusters of variables to account
for variations in disorder proneness of American cities

Cluster of variables	Percentage of total variation between cities accounted for	
	By cluster alone	By cluster when entered after two miscellaneous variables
Social disorganization	6.0%	2.3%
Absolute deprivation	6.3	.1
Relative deprivation	20.4	1.3
Political structures	28.5	.9

Source: Adapted from Spilerman (1970).

of the predictive power originally seen attached to variables of these clusters is probably better seen as reflecting one or the other of the two miscellaneous variables: nonwhite population size and/or region.

The general conclusion most properly drawn from Spilerman's analysis is that "the racial disturbances of the 1960s were not responses to conditions in the local community"; instead, disorder proneness seems to be better pursued as an attribute either of individuals or of American society as a whole.[12]

Let us for the moment put off consideration of how riot proneness may be seen as a characteristic of American society as a whole. Instead let us pursue the possibility of an explanation in terms of individuals.

The kind of research which is most relevant for this line of inquiry is that on riot participation. The question here to be translated into research is: What distinguishes riot participants from other persons of the same neighborhood? Are there systematic differences which would reflect some of the general explanations previously mentioned (for example, that persons most deprived or frustrated would be the most likely participants, as relative deprivation theory might argue, or, as the collective behavior approach might suggest, that persons least integrated into the social structure would be most apt to participate in a riot)?

There have been quite a number of research studies on riot participation. Probably the best overview of this research is provided by Clark McPhail. His review of the literature shows that predictions derived from a frustration or deprivation model are weakly supported by most of the data. Although most studies show a positive association between frustration or deprivation measures and riot participation, almost no research confirms this as a strong pattern. In other words, riot participants are not very likely to show more personal deprivation or frustration than others who do not riot.[13]

What about the hypothesis that those who are more socially isolated are more apt to be riot participants? Among more than two dozen studies which attempted to gather evidence on this question, McPhail found only one with a moderately strong association in its results. In this one study, an index of social isolation (based on whether individuals were single, lived alone, were without organizational memberships, and had lived in the city less than ten years) was positively correlated with arrests in Detroit for rioting (as compared to characteristics of a control group). However, here each of the ingredients of the index was only weakly associated with riot participation—and some other studies actually found the opposite pattern in regard to length of residence in the city.

McPhail suggests that most of the research on riot participation has been geared to the wrong question—namely, what are the psychological characteristics or the personal frustrations and deprivations of rioters? Instead, he suggests, a more fruitful question would be: What settings at what points in time yield large numbers of available persons in general proximity to one another? And rather than focus upon the inner natures of persons who participate, we might better focus on the sequence of events that transform an assemblage into a riot.

McPhail's review does not indicate that no personal characteristics are strongly associated with riot participation. Indeed, in black ghetto riots, there are two characteristics very strongly associated: age and sex. Young males are much more strongly represented among rioters than nonrioters. But this, in McPhail's view, largely reflects the simple fact that young males are more likely than others to be on the streets when an occasion for a riot presents itself.

McPhail's review of riot participation studies ends with the suggestion that perhaps an even more radical collective behavior approach may be in order. He suggests focusing on "the assembling process" through which large numbers of people happen to come together at the same place, and how people come to interact with each other at such places. He suggests that giving primary attention to attitudes or predispositions which people carry around with them may be misplaced. Such attitudes or presumed predispositions (especially when measured after the fact) may be more products of behavior than causes of it. At any rate, their ability to predict something like riot participation is quite low.

Another possible conclusion is that the research reviewed by McPhail simply did not use sensitive enough measures of attitudes and predispositions. Perhaps. We do not have the basis of judging this possibility. We can, however, point to other studies which relate the personal characteristics of individuals to ideologies of radical political action and protest behavior. In the most systematic of these studies, there is little evidence for a general pattern of relative deprivation or social isolation associated with approval of radical or violent action. Instead, persons who support such positions tend to be those whose friends and associates also do.[14] This suggests the possibility of viewing violent outbursts in society as extensions of more ordinary processes of social organization and socialization. We will pursue this possibility in the next section.

DISORGANIZATION OR REORGANIZATION?

So far in the present chapter, we have been operating with a model such as that of Figure 7.3 in the back of our minds. Strife has been viewed as a product of discontent, whether discontent is seen in terms of relative deprivation (as suggested by Davies or Gurr) or of social dislocations (as the collective behavior approach seems to suggest). To be sure, we have recognized that it isn't quite this simple. For example, with Gurr's model, we considered relative deprivation as the underlying cause of rebellion, but we also recognized other contributing conditions, such as political legitimacy, range of institutional support, and coercive capacity. And in Smelser's collective behavior model, though we saw structural strain as a key background feature, we also identified a number of steps which were seen as necessary before the strain becomes transformed into an active movement which challenges the social order. But we have in both cases still operated with deprivation or strain as a general background cause. It may be viewed as an underlying condition or root cause.

The empirical evidence we have examined, however, has been considerably less than totally supportive. Most of the hypotheses generated by our previous models have been in the right direction, but seldom has the support been very strong. This leads us to wonder whether we might have left out of consideration some major factor.

Figure 7.3 A simple model of collective violence.

We now prepare to shift our attention in a rather major way. A new theme will be brought to center stage. This is the theme of social organization. Instead of focusing on disloyalties created by individual discontents within the social order, we focus upon loyalties to new forms within the social order. Instead of considering responses to breakdown and strain, we consider how new forces of social organization may help engender breakdown and strain in older forms. Social organization itself is our key, not the aggregation of individual responses; and the emphasis is upon forces of reorganization rather than disorganization.

In Figure 7.4 we sketch an outline of such an alternative social organization model of collective violence. In the background is structural change, which leads to changes in the nature of group organization. New groups, or groups which have increased in following due to changes in society, actively press their interests. They mobilize themselves and available re-

Figure 7.4 Chief factors leading to collective violence. (Adapted from Tilly et al., 1975)

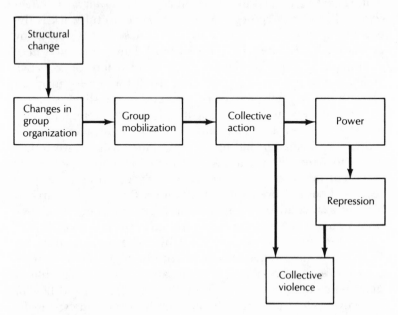

sources in support of their interests, and they engage in various forms of collective action. The ultimate objective is usually power—either the power to resist certain dominant groups or a greater share in the power available through the central political system. At some point, this search for power brings a repressive reaction from the already established centers of power. Out of the interplay between collective action by new segments of society and repression by older established segments comes the product of collective violence. Collective violence tends to be high when both emerging forms and established forms of social organization tend to be strong; here social conflict is most intense, and such conflict is often accompanied by violence.

Among the theoretical perspectives previously mentioned, those of Marx and Dahrendorf would both broadly fit with this new model. However, for somewhat more detailed research in this direction, we turn to the work of Charles Tilly and his associates. Tilly is a sociologist and historian who has specialized in the study of modern Europe. His most important theoretical writings are contained in a book titled *From Mobilization to Revolution*. For our purposes, however, a more useful work is the more empirically focused study, *The Rebellious Century*, by Charles Tilly, Louise Tilly, and Richard Tilly. The Tillys here attempted a comprehensive coverage of all actions of collective violence during the 100 years after 1829 for three European nations: France, Italy, and Germany. They exhaustively combed old newspapers and other documents in attempting to enumerate every disturbance above a minimum level (50 or more participants, including at least some civilians, were necessary for most enumerations, and some force upon persons or objects of property must have been involved). After identifying several thousand events in this manner, the authors searched for both qualitative and quantitative indicators of the conditions under which such events were most likely to occur.[15]

Of the three countries studied by the Tillys, the data for France are most systematically quantified. This allows careful time series analyses of the French data to see what conditions may rise or fall in close correspondence to the ebb and flow of collective violence. A most notable result of such analysis is the absence of correlation with variables of economic deprivation—either with or without allowances for a time lag preceding collective violence measures. Much more closely related to violence were measures reflecting political conditions. The big peaks in collective violence, for example, were clearly associated with periods of major political contention.[16] Although the quantitative data on this are more clear for France than for Germany and Italy, all three nations generally show similar patterns in the correlation of collective violence with significant periods of political transition.

The Tillys suggest that we should be careful about too sharp a division between collective violence and nonviolent collective action. They point out that "the great bulk of collective violence in France, Italy, and Germany since 1830 has occurred within the context of well-established forms of collective action which are not intrinsically violent." In fact, there was little if anything to set off the initial stages of the events ending in violence from those which remained peaceful. Violence was the exception; for example, less than 2 percent of French strikes involved violence, and many that remained peaceful started out much the same as the few which developed violence. What seems to be the historical pattern is that there is a general rise in collective action during periods of political transition. Various groups in society become more highly politicized as they press their claims and counterclaims. Where there is a high volume of such collective action, there is also a higher likelihood that some of the events will turn into violent encounters.

The Rebellious Century shows no consistent overall trend in the level of violence. There is some suggestion that the average number of participants may have increased along with a growth in urbanization. Deaths, however, have probably declined, even while the number injured has increased. This is due not only to advances in the care of injuries but also to the increased use of police forces in repressing collective violence ("troops fired; police clubbed," as the Tillys summarize this difference). Incidentally, much more frequently have deaths and serious injuries come from the actions of "peace-keeping" forces than from actions of rebellious groups of rioters. But all these are secondary points; in general, there is little evidence of either an overall rise or fall in violence during the period examined. Instead, there seems to be a fluctuation closely paralleling important political realignments for each country concerned.

Although the general level of collective violence did not seem to change during the century under examination, the Tillys show important changes in the forms of collective action involved. Early in the period "reactive" forms of collective action seemed to predominate. That is, the issue was largely resistance against the advance of central political or economic power; resistance to conscription and taxes were examples. By the early 1900s a "proactive" form of collective action seemed to be associated with more of the violent episodes. That is, the issue was to meet he demands of groups wanting to be more fully included in the central political and economic system; most strikes and political demonstrations are of this type. The

Tillys associate this change in emphasis with the general emergence during this period of the predominance of the state in the institutional structure of society. Early in the nineteenth century this was often resisted; but by the twentieth century it was generally an accomplished fact, and the more important issue was who would be fully included in the system. This transition occurred earliest in France, closely followed by Germany, and last for Italy; and the patterns of change of reactive versus proactive forms of violence showed a roughly similar order for the three countries.

The work of Charles Tilly and associates makes a good case for the reasonableness of a social organization model of civil strife when applied to broad historical patterns. The model we presented in Figure 7.4 fits quite well with the broad sweep of collective violence in France, Germany, and Italy during the late nineteenth and early twentieth centuries. But perhaps the very breadth of the Tillys' empirical scope—their wide historical and geographic sweep—helps make such a model credible. Would it have held up so well if attention were focused on a single case of collective violence?

In the following section, we use a particular case to examine in greater detail how well our reorganization model fits the events described. The case we select is that of the Irish Land War of 1879–82. Fortunately, this has recently been the subject of a rather thorough sociological and historical analysis by Samuel Clark, and we shall draw heavily upon his work.[17]

A PARTICULAR CASE

The most direct challenge to established power in Ireland during the second half of the nineteenth century occurred in events generally known as the Irish Land War. Throughout the nineteenth century, Irish agriculture was mainly organized in a landlord system, but for a few years this system was subject to violent attack. We will first summarize the events of this attack upon established power; then we will attempt to assess the causes of this attack.

Ireland experienced severe crop failures during 1877–79, when prices of farm produce were already depressed. Landlords, tenant farmers, and farm laborers were all faced with economic crisis, and all sought means to reduce their hardships. Some landlords sought to remove their less efficient renters, but this was strongly resisted. Ordinary farmers (who lacked ownership of the lands they worked) demanded that rents be reduced and that their rights to more permanent tenure be recognized.

Quickly the rift deepened between landlords and tenants, and the struggle was on. Where a few years before there had been only about a score of active farmers' clubs in Ireland, by 1880 hundreds of local chapters of the newly formed Land League were militantly opposing landlord interests. Their actions included massive public demonstrations, boycotts (the term in fact originated at this time in well-publicized actions against an Irish landlord named Boycott), and sporadic violence. Although the leaders of the Land League disclaimed any responsibility for the violence, they sought to justify the moral outrage expressed in occasional murders and instances of mob violence. They set up local "courts" to judge cases in which their model rules for land tenure and rent reductions were not followed, and they organized boycotts to punish tenants and landlords who opposed their mandates.

Landlords, meanwhile, were not simply passive in the face of this challenge. Most accepted at least some reduction in rents, but they opposed any general change in their rights and privileges; and, by and large, they had the established powers of law and order on their side. Sometimes, however, it was difficult to enforce the letter of the law—such as when police at Carraroe in County Galway were routed by a mob of about 3,000 persons armed with whatever they could find to use as weapons.

The end of the Land War came gradually in 1881 and 1882. Harvests were improved during these years, leaving less of a sense of economic crisis. Official coercion continued, including finally the outlawing of the Land League and imprisonment of many of its leaders. Parliament, however, concerned itself with reform as well as repression. In addition to acts which gave further powers to law enforcement agencies, Parliament enacted the Land Act of 1881. This was a rather far-reaching attempt to establish more rights for tenant farmers in their relations with landlords (including fixed rents and arbitration for cases of dispute) as well as provisions for public loans to tenants to help them buy the lands they farmed. There was no sudden shift away from the landlord system, but the reforms enacted in 1881 were at least significant changes in that system.

⋙

How do we explain the onset of these events? Why did so many farmers of Ireland rise in revolt at this time? That they were distressed seems evident, but what was the basis of this distress? Economic hardship seems to be the obvious answer. There was a sharp reduction in yields of most crops in 1877 and again in 1879, and for that mainstay of Irish diets, potatoes, the 1879 crop was the lowest in many years. Meanwhile, there was a further decline in livestock prices, and there was also less demand for Irish seasonal labor in Great Britain. All of this had an effect upon the farmers of Ireland.

There are, however, several qualifications which need to be made for this interpretation in terms of the economic hardship and distress of tenant farmers. First, all segments of Irish agriculture were hit—landlords and farm laborers as well as tenant farmers—but it was mainly the tenants who revolted. Second, economic hardship was not necessarily worse in 1877–79 than in previous bad years; it was of course far less serious than during the Great Famine of the late 1840s, and even the post-famine years 1859–64 saw a greater decline in farm production—but the landlord system was not directly challenged in these earlier periods. Third, there is no sign that there had been a political or social decline in the position of tenant farmers in the 1870s. Although the landlords still had far greater power and status, their predominance was showing at least small signs of erosion. Finally, not all economically distressed farmers joined to fight the Land War. Tenant farmers varied greatly in their attitudes toward Land League agitation, and in some parts of the country (especially in Ulster) the agitation had very little support.

A collective behavior approach offers another way to explain the Irish Land War. In this approach, the economic downturn is seen less as a direct cause than as a symptom of more general social strain. The social order of Ireland was undergoing change. The old certitude of a social system based on the two power bases of the Catholic Church and the Protestant Ascendency, while still in place, was beginning to lose its sense of inevitability. The agricultural crisis simply highlighted the strains already present. Gradually a generalized belief took hold which blamed the landlords for the difficulties of Irish farmers. The answer then began to spread as people came together: check the power of the landlords! Make them reduce their rents, and keep them from evicting tenants who fail to give all rents demanded. And let mass action take its course upon any who stand up against these demands. The contagion of this program of action spread gradually from initial uprisings in the West of Ireland (especially in County Mayo) until most of Ireland was involved. After a time, however, the excitement of the new movement declined; also, the forces of repression (combined with some reform measures) made themselves felt. Then the countryside of Ireland returned to a more normal pattern of life for the rest of the century.

But there are also problems with a collective behavior approach. For one thing, there is little evidence that Irish society was more disorganized at the beginning of the Land War than at any other time. Also, the local patterns of association of those engaged in this controversy followed generally the same patterns as other social activities—friends banded together with other friends, mostly at the level of the local parish. As to the idea of a generalized belief emerging out of their interaction, this too seems an exaggeration. The cause of the farmers was really nothing new; the demands for fixity of tenure and what they considered to be fair rents were their traditional goals. The only change was that they were now pursued with more concerted energy and determination than before. And what of the violence? When placed in perspective, the Land War was not even especially violent. There had been more rural violence in earlier periods of the century which were never given the title of "war."

No.

Finally, let us consider a social organization interpretation of the Irish Land War. This happens to be the approach primarily taken by Samuel Clark, who goes into considerable detail to trace changes in the social structure of Ireland. Important changes after the Great Famine reduced the number and variety of tenant farmers and brought them more fully into the market economy. There was therefore a stronger basis than before for collective action on the part of farmers. Their greater involvement in the market economy made them more vulnerable to an agricultural depression, and the welfare of townsmen (who now depended largely on purchases of farmers) was also affected. The result was a coalition of farmers and townsmen in opposition to landlord interests. Clark documents how the Land League reflected this coalition during the Land War (along with rather hesitant support from the Catholic clergy and Irish politicians—and with very little involvement of farm laborers). This coalition continued in the political agitation of subsequent decades for the cause of Irish nationalism and in opposition to British power and Irish landlord interests.

Clark's analysis does well what he set out to do, namely, to show in a particular historical instance how groups of people came together with their shared discontents. The primary theme in his analysis is how changing patterns of social organization made possible more effective antilandlord agitation. But this social organization or "mobilization" approach also has its weaknesses. It helps to explain the general overall pattern of the Land War, but it cannot explain the particular expressions of outrage. Why did violence occur on some occasions but not on others? How was the particular technique of the boycott developed, and what conditions especially facilitated its use? And why do we have the Land War especially active in the West of Ireland, when other areas had in the past shown greater political activity? All of these questions suggest the usefulness of a collective behavior model to supplement Clark's social organization approach.

Even within a social organization approach, there are factors which are not easily susceptible to precise explanation. There remains the question: Under what conditions will economic hardships be endured, and when will they result in public protest? The organization of collective action in the Irish Land War was spotty and not highly consistent from area to area. What we are suggesting is that there was considerable room for local leadership and improvisation. There was therefore not a highly predictable order for these events. This very lack of predictability added to the sense of disorder, which brought public attention to the plight of Irish tenant farmers. It also gave an opportunity to politicians such as Charles Stewart Parnell to place their personal imprint upon events in a way which otherwise might not have been possible.

In conclusion, we find the main lines of Clark's analysis quite persuasive for putting the Irish Land War into the context of the evolution of Irish social organization in the nineteenth century. His social organization analysis probably explains more than rival models. But this explanation does not completely displace other approaches.

Let us recapitulate very briefly how we have proceeded in the present chapter. We have used the primary research or reviews of studies by the Feierabends, Gurr, Smelser, Spilerman, McPhail, the Tillys, and Clark as a means of broadly testing the implications of three leading models of how collective disturbances develop in a society. These have been the deprivation-frustration, collective behavior, and social organization approaches (promoted especially by Gurr, Smelser, and Tilly, respectively). The deprivation-frustration model is very close to the discontent-causes-civil-strife assumptions which constitute the most popular explanation among laymen. However, it has generally fared less well in systematic research than have the other two approaches. As a broad framework for predicting patterns of strife, the social organization approach appears especially useful.

But the literature we have reviewed in this chapter does not signal any final victory for any of these three approaches. For one thing, these approaches are not mutually exclusive; there is a great deal of overlap between them. Also, from none of these do we obtain very precise predictions of behavior. Explanations for collective disturbances, using any of our models, seem better when applied after the fact and in general than when applied to the precise details of such events. Apparently the phenomena of civil unrest are more complex and varied than have been our attempts to get a theoretical handle on them.

Does this same low predictability for domestic upheavals also extend to war and international conflict? Or will the fact that here the major parties are established governments (not rather amorphous segments of society) give us a greater basis of precise explanation? We shall see in the next chapter.

8

Recent Research on War

When Lewis F. Richardson died in 1953, little more than Wright's *A Study of War* existed as a major published contribution to the scientific study of war. Wright himself made another key contribution by helping to edit Richardson's work for posthumous publication in 1960. Ten years later the situation was very much different. The late 1950s saw the emergence of a peace research movement, which rapidly expanded in the 1960s. When Quincy Wright died in 1970, his work was far from unknown. Indeed, a special issue devoted primarily to him and his work was immediately turned out by the *Journal of Conflict Revolution*.[1] More importantly, the scientific approach to the study of war which Wright had pioneered was bearing fruit in numerous new studies. Several of these studies in progress at the time of Wright's death may be briefly described to characterize this continuing movement toward a scientific study of war.

THE CORRELATES-OF-WAR PROJECT

The recent study most obviously in the Richardson-Wright data-gathering tradition is the correlates-of-war project carried out by J. David Singer and associates at the University of Michigan. At this writing, the most notable product of this study is a descriptive statistical analysis by Singer and Melvin Small of the most significant wars of the period 1816–1965 (titled *The Wages of War 1816–1965: A Statistical Handbook*). Building upon the earlier work of Richardson, Wright, and others, Singer and

Small have added their own refinements for classifying and measuring the 93 international wars of this 150-year period.

Using a rather careful set of limitations (to be included, a war must have at least one party officially recognized as a part of the international system of states, and battle-connected deaths must exceed 1,000), Singer and Small identify 93 wars for this period. They subdivide these into 50 "interstate" wars (in which both parties were part of the international system) and 43 "extrasystemic" wars (colonial wars or wars with small states, with in either case only one of the sides recognized as a regular part of the international system). Excluded from analysis are civil wars, no matter how extensive, and revolutionary upheavals, no matter how bloody. For example, neither the American Civil War of 1861–65 nor the Russian Revolution of 1917 is included in the Singer and Small list of wars.

For each of these wars, Singer and Small derived some basic descriptive statistics. These included, to begin with, indicators of the duration and intensity of each war. Duration was measured in nation-months, thus considering both the time period and the number of nations involved. Intensity was measured by the number of battle deaths. Table 8.1 lists the most severe wars according to several possible variations of these two criteria. World War II was the most severe war according to the two most direct applications of these criteria, involving as it did approximately 15 million battle deaths and 876 nation-months. World War I, with approximately 9 million battle deaths and 608 nation-months, was second on both counts. By other criteria, however, some little remembered wars may surpass either of the two world wars in severity. For example, the most intense war, according to the criterion of battle deaths per duration in time, was a single-day conflict in which about 3,180 persons were killed—mostly Turks who were resisting a combined British, French, and Russian blockade at Navarino Bay in southern Greece. And the most bloody conflict in terms of the population base of the nations involved was the Chaco War of 1932–35, in which Bolivia and Paraguay (nations with rather small population bases at the time) killed about 130,000 of each other's military personnel in a territorial dispute.

One of the most frequent questions asked about the inci-

Table 8.1 Most severe wars, 1816–1965, according to different statistical criteria

Total battle deaths
  1. World War II (1939–45)
  2. World War I (1914–18)
  3. Korean War (1950–53)
  4. Sino-Japanese War (1937–41)
  5. Russo-Turkish War (1828–29)

Total nation-months in duration
  1. World War II (1939–45)
  2. World War I (1914–18)
  3. Korean War (1950–53)
  4. South American Pacific War (1879–83)
  5. LaPlata War (1864–70)

Total battle deaths per nation-month
  1. Navarino Bay (1827)
  2. Russo-Hungarian War (1956)
  3. World War II (1939–45)
  4. Russo-Turkish War (1828–29)
  5. Second Balkin War (1913)

Total battle deaths per capita for involved nations
  1. Chaco War (1932–35)
  2. World War I (1914–18)
  3. World War II (1939–45)
  4. LaPlata War (1864–70)
  5. Ten Years' Cuban War (1868–78)

Source: Adapted from Singer and Small (1972).

dence of war is whether or not there is a general increase in warfare. Within the 150 years examined, Singer and Small can find no evidence of this. They conclude, on this point:

> Whether we look at the number of wars, their severity or their magnitude, there is no significant trend upward or down over the past 150 years. Even if we examine their intensities, we find that late wars are by and large no different from those of earlier periods.[2]

It is true that gross measures of battle deaths and war frequency show increases in the twentieth century over previous periods, but these need to be interpreted in terms of the growing size (in number of nations and populations involved) of the international system.

Although they find no general trend toward an increase or decrease in war, Singer and Small do find some evidence for destructiveness coming in cycles. The clearest evidence comes from annual measures of the amount of war underway, which suggests a cycle of approximately 20 years for peaks in warfare. Such a cycle, however, is not clearly indicated by other measures of incidence or by statistics for individual nations. It remains, therefore, a suggestive pattern to be explored more fully in further analysis.

A number of other interesting patterns are indicated by the data reported by Singer and Small. Among them are the following:

1. Although there is no clear seasonal pattern for terminating war, wars are especially likely to begin in spring or autumn (with April and October the most favored months).

2. The most frequent participants in war have tended to be the most powerful nations of their period. European powers such as Britain and France are especially frequent participants. Also, as Table 8.2 shows, most of the frequent participants have a high rate of victory—which may help to explain their high participation.[3]

3. There is a wide variation in the amount of war destruction experienced by different nations. Three na-

Table 8.2 Most frequent participants in international wars, 1816–1965

Nation	Total number of war-months	Total number of wars	Number of wars on victorious side
France	494	19	14
Britain	410	19	16
Turkey	339	17	5
Spain	262	9	5
Russia	249	15	12
China	205	8	3
Japan	196	7	5
United States	166	6	5
Italy	156	12	9
Germany	140	6	4
Greece	104	7	4
Austria-Hungary	78	8	5

Source: Adapted from Singer and Small (1972).

Table 8.3 Most consistent enemies among pairs of nations

Pair	Number of months at war with each other, 1816–1965
China–Japan	122
Britain–Germany	119
Russia–Turkey	91
Germany–Russia	87
France–Germany	75

Source: Adapted from Singer and Small (1972).

tions (Russia, Germany, and China—in that order of severity of punishment) have suffered over 60 percent of all battle deaths. In contrast, about half of the nations listed had no war experience included in the tabulations.[4]

4. Although there are a few cases in which traditional enemies may be identified (see Table 8.3), the general ability to predict future enemies from the past does not stand up well in the data. Opposing nations in war are as likely to have been allies in a past war as to have been enemies. "Most nations," say Singer and Small, "show a remarkable flexibility in 'selecting' their partners and adversaries."[5]

5. Although there is some tendency for vanquished nations to have more battle deaths than victors, this pattern is by no means universal. Furthermore, the vanquished-victor ratio seems to be rather unpredictable and shows little systematic variation with the type of war.

6. When an initiator of hostilities can be clearly identified, there seems to be some advantage associated with such initiation. These nations suffer on the average about half the fatalities of their victims. On the other hand, the initiator loses in over one-fourth of the wars studied. Singer and Small conclude that "the initiation of military hostilities has not been a particularly safe activity in the past."[6]

The above generalizations grow out of laborious statistical analyses of 93 wars, but these analyses are primarily descriptive. The initial "statistical handbook" does not go very far into the main task of the correlates-of-war project: the identification of conditions most likely to lead to the onset of war. What, in other words, are the other variables which influence the frequency, magnitude, and intensity of war? At this writing there is still no final general report on this larger analysis, though an early interim report does give a few preliminary findings.[7] These findings only underline the complexity and difficulty of making statistical generalizations about the conditions of war. We are told, for example, that "the amount of inter-governmental organization has no visible effect on the incidence of war," but there is little opportunity to include a consideration of the quality of such organization. Generally, though, such preliminary results as are available would lead us to discount some of the assumptions about war found in the conventional wisdom. Wars are not primarily between nations of incompatible social systems; instead we find that "most inter-state wars are between nations which are not only close geographically, but quite similar on most other attribute dimensions." And despite the common assumption of a link between population pressure and war, Singer reports that "there appears to be no significant association between a nation's growth rate in population or density and its war-proneness."

Trying to Explain One Major War

Singer and Small have initiated a statistical analysis into background factors for approximately 100 wars. Another notable project in the quantitative analysis of war focuses on the backgrounds for a single war, that of World War I. We may refer here especially to the work of Nazli Choucri and Robert C. North as contained in *Nations in Conflict*.

Most of the first half of this book is a detailed examination of historical events of 1870–1914, which might be seen as the causative period for this war. International events of six nations (Britain, France, Germany, Austria-Hungary, Italy, and Russia) are carefully set forth which seem especially relevant to the authors' primary assumption:

In general there seem to be at least three major processes that generate conflict and warfare among nations: domestic growth and the external expansion of interests; competition for resources, markets, superiority in arms, and strategic advantage; and the dynamics of crisis.[8]

Choucri and North, however, go beyond a general review of the presumed causes of World War I to develop and test an explicit model of the effects of key variables. This work occupies most of the second half of the book, though the key variables are introduced in their first chapter.

The key variables may be briefly identified (using terms which slightly modify those of Choucri and North) as the following:

1. Colonial expansion—the amount of expansion of the authority of a state beyond its home country;
2. Colonial conflict—the amount of conflict with other major powers over specifically colonial issues;
3. Military capability—the amount of effort to maintain military power;
4. Alliances—the amount of strength which may be present in alliances with other nations;
5. International violence—the amount of violence involved in actions toward all other nations.

A quantitative index of each of the above was derived and applied to each of the six nations studied for each year of the 1870–1914 period. For example, colonial expansion was measured simply by the total square miles of colonial territory held at a given time. Military capability was estimated by U.S. dollar equivalents of military expenditures for a given year. The measure of alliances was simply the number of formal alliances active at the time. And so on.

The above five variables were assumed to be the central variables for study, and the most likely causal variables for each were identified. For example, colonial expansion was assumed to reflect some influence from at least the following: population density, national income per capita, trade per capita, and military capability. International violence, to take another example, was assumed to reflect colonial conflict, military capability, alli-

Figure 8.1 Choucri and North's basic model of international conflict. (Choucri and North, 1975, p. 168)

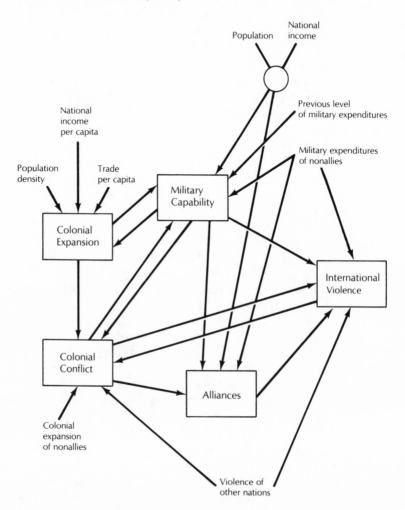

ances, the military expenditures of nonallied nations, and the violence of other nations. These primary influences can be summed up in a single model, as presented in Figure 8.1. This figure presents a summary of Choucri and North's assumptions about international conflict behavior. It should be understood that an arrow represents a positive direction of influence between variables. In some cases, arrows may go in both directions; this indicates that these variables are seen as significantly causing each other. Where no arrow is drawn, no direct influence is assumed.

Choucri and North next developed a system of simultaneous equations for predicting each of the five key variables. They developed most of these equations from data on Britain and then sought to see how well they would predict the behavior of other nations. Although we need not go into detail concerning the statistical methodology involved, we may in passing point out a few things of which the general reader should be aware:

1. The equation used to predict each key (or "dependent") variable includes the addition of a series of distinct terms. There is one term for each predictor (or "independent") variable, including a coefficient to represent the relative strength of that variable in the prediction equation. There is also a term to represent error (or "residual") variation.

2. There is not just one dependent variable, but rather a whole system of variables being predicted by each other ("endogenous" variables within the system of equations) as well as by some additional ("exogenous" or outside) variables.

3. Solving such a set of simultaneous equations for time-series data involves some extremely difficult mathematical problems. Certain simplifying assumptions always have to be made to solve the equations, and there are important differences of opinion about which of these simplifying assumptions are the most reasonable to make.

4. Despite the technical problems involved, such causal models (combining interrelated predictions for a set of variables) have become increasingly common in the social sciences in recent years. They represent an attempt to grasp the interrelationships of a *system* of variables, as opposed to the simpler analysis of relationships one at a time (represented by more tradi-

tional forms of variable analysis, such as the simple correlations cited in our last chapter).

The five main predictive equations (each predicting one of the key variables of Figure 8.1) were applied equally to each of the following six nations: Britain, France, Germany, Italy, Russia, and Austria-Hungary. This assumed a constant set of dynamics for each of these nations continuing throughout the 35-year period before World War I. Although this assumption is probably unrealistic, it does provide a single set of equations against which we may measure the actual facts. In other words, we have a mathematical model—albeit with simplifying assumptions included—to give predictions about basic changes in the system; how well this model actually predicts outcomes should indicate the correctness of the assumptions which went into the model.

How well *did* the model actually predict the prewar trends for the six nations to which it was applied? Here we can give no simple answer, for the analysis is quite complex. We can, however, say for a start that for each of the five key variables the predictive equation proved statistically significant for most countries considered. But even here there were exceptions: Germany did not significantly fit the predictive equations for colonial expansion or alliances, and Italy did not fit the equation for colonial conflict. Furthermore, statistical significance is a rather weak criterion for success; it means only that factors must be strong enough to show an influence clearly beyond what might be normally expected by chance.

A stronger criterion for the success of a model would require that each element in each predictive equation be statistically significant in results for each nation. By this criterion the Choucri-North model rather clearly failed. Practically no term in any equation proved universally significant.[9] Nevertheless, there were a number of factors which generally showed strong predictive power. Among them the following should be mentioned:

1. Colonial expansion was generally best predicted by population density.
2. A nation's colonial conflict was most successfully predicted by the violence of other nations.

3. Military capability is largely determined by past capability. Beyond that, the combined influence of population and national income also generally proved to be an effective predictor of military capability.
4. The extent of alliances is generally most successfully predicted by military expenditures of nonallies and by colonial conflict.
5. The amount of international violence a given nation shows is most successfully predicted by the violence of other nations.

Since international violence is probably the most central variable in the system (at least in terms of our interest in predicting the conditions of war), it is of interest to note that the variables which were its best predictors seemed to vary greatly from nation to nation. Even for the same nation there is significant variation from one time period to another. This suggests to the authors that "international violence can be reached from different initial conditions and along different paths."[10] It also suggests that the idea of a single overall model for predicting international violence was not very successfully achieved. Let us, however, let Choucri and North give their own summary:

> Violence-behavior [or, in our terminology, international violence] generally is a reactive process. The level of violence is not as strongly linked to [other variables] . . . as we had hypothesized. Nevertheless, increases in these dimensions often provoke some response by a rival power, which in turn stimulates violence-behavior—clearly an action-reaction process. Thus, our hypothesized links throughout the model still appear to be extremely important, but in an indirect and always complex form.

If we were looking to Choucri and North to give us some magic formula by which we could predict the onset of war, we must admit disappointment. Their own assessment of the most important finding of their work was that "domestic growth (as measured by population density and national income per capita) is generally a strong determinant of national expansion." This finding, however, may be particularly relevant to the late nineteenth century, which constituted most of their study. But Choucri and North fail to link it in any very convincing way to the onset of World War I. In fact, although all that they describe and analyze may well be an important part of the background for that war, there is little in their numerous tabulations of data to suggest any success in predicting the onset of that war. On the contrary, they specifically point out that their data *"do not show any exceptional increases in violence between nations of the Triple Alliance and those of the Entente or between key rivals."* Accordingly, World War I, far from being predetermined by background factors, appears as something which occurred through a sudden and largely unpredictable escalation of hostilities.

MORE ON WORLD WAR I

In contrast to the approach of Choucri and North is the work of Ole Holsti on the origins of World War I. Holsti, formerly a graduate student and close associate of North at Stanford University, developed this contrasting approach as an explicit part of North's "conflict project"—a series of studies on the backgrounds and patterns of onset of major international conflicts. Holsti's work focuses on the process of escalation which marked the onset of World War I. His book, *Crisis Escalation War,* gives primary attention to the way in which an unexpected event on June 28, 1914, set in motion a process which within five weeks developed into a major world war. Holsti studied the foreign policy decision-making processes during this five-week period, examining in particular the role of stress in affecting the quality of these decisions.

Holsti first examined anecdotal and experimental evidence on the effects of stress upon decision making. This led him to infer that crisis situations tend to be characterized by an overload of communication and a restriction on the ability to perceive accurately what communications are intended to convey. Furthermore, a crisis (defined as "a situation of unanticipated threat to important values and restricted decision time") is apt to lead to a decline in certain abilities important for effective decision making, such as the identification of possible courses of action and assessment of the gains and costs of alternative policies.[11] Such influences lead to the increased likelihood of action which prematurely closes out important policy options.

Next, Holsti examined the details of European decision making in the summer of 1914 to show the relevance of the above ideas to those events. Included in his analysis is a systematic content analysis of diplomatic communications during this period which shows both a dramatic increase in the volume of messages and a sharply heightened sense of time pressure for action. He suggests that the consequences for decision making were such as to lead the nations of Central Europe rapidly into World War I. The particular chain of key variables is pictured in Figure 8.2. In concluding his chapter on "Crisis, Time Pressure, and Policy Making," Holsti holds that:

> The evidence indicated that time pressures—especially those arising out of immediate rather than long-range considera-

Figure 8.2 Holsti's model of decision making under stress. (Holsti, 1972, p. 122)

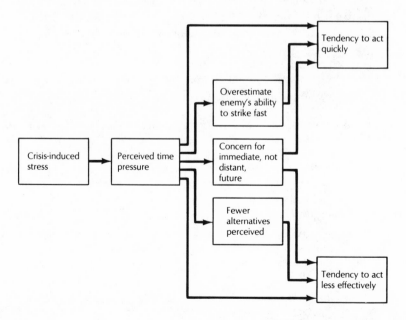

tions—increased sharply during the most intense stages of the crisis. Furthermore, time pressure appears to have been a central factor in the decisions which led to a general European war in 1914.

Holsti does not hold that all international crises have the same effects upon the quality of decision making. In fact, he examines the Cuban missile crisis of October 1962 as an example which contrasts in many ways to the World War I case. He finds in the Cuban conflict evidence that escalation to war is not an inevitable result of crisis decision making—if crisis management techniques are intelligently applied. In a final chapter, he spells out what such crisis management techniques may be and how they can be made part of a nation's ongoing international policies.

We have not gone into detail on the methodological aspects of Holsti's work. As an illustration of the kind of detailed quantitative work included in his analysis, let us consider the following hypothesis: "As stress increases in a crisis, the volume of communication tends to increase." To test this hypothesis for the 1914 crisis, Holsti examined all documents available in Austro-Hungarian, British, French, German, and Russian collections for this period. This involved a total of 5,620 documents. He found that these tended to be processed at the daily rates indicated by Table 8.4. It is at once apparent from Table 8.4 that the volume of communication increased in the summer of 1914 as the crisis deepened. But these are rather gross com-

Table 8.4 Average number of Foreign Office documents processed daily, major European powers, 1914

	27 June to 28 July	29 July to 4 August
Officials abroad to foreign office	48.2	217.6
Foreign office to officials abroad	30.3	139.0
Messages within foreign office	13.0	37.3
Direct messages from foreign leaders	2.0	20.5
Direct messages to foreign leaders	2.4	18.0

Source: Holsti (1972).

parisons. Holsti also made daily measures of the content of communications, deriving from these a rating of stress. Table 8.5 shows measures of association with such daily measures of stress and volume. All the measures indicated by Table 8.5 are significantly positive. There is, in other words, a close relationship between the daily flow of messages and the stress rating of the typical message content. This tends to support further the general hypothesis that communication volume increases with stress.

Table 8.5 Median strength of association between daily measures of message volume and stress, five major European powers, Summer 1914

	Message volume measured by:	
	Number of documents	Number of words
Officials abroad to foreign office	.50	.42
Foreign office to officials abroad	.57	.47
Messages within foreign office	.64	.54
Direct messages from foreign leaders	.55	.49
Direct messages to foreign leaders	.67	.58

Source: Holsti (1972).

If the volume of communications increases in a crisis, and if communication overload heightens the sense of being in a crisis, we see that a foreign policy crisis may in part feed upon itself. The greater the communication volume, the greater the sense of pressure, and the more likely will decision makers consequently reduce their sights to coping with the immediate situation. The outcome in 1914, Holsti strongly suggests, was a result of such processes—a world war that none of the nations involved really desired.

REVIEW

In the present chapter, we have briefly reviewed three books which apply quantitative techniques to the study of war. In the previous two chapters we reviewed other work of a quantitative nature, mostly bearing on the conditions of collective violence. In this concluding section, we will try to sum up some of the findings and implications of these rather varied empirical studies.

Much of what we have surveyed in these three chapters has been descriptive in character. Before we can go very far in explaining the causes of war or internal collective violence, we need to have clear measures of such violence. Although different measures have been used by different investigators, great strides have been made toward the kind of measurement which will allow us to make effective comparisons. This is the foundation for a scientific analysis of conflict, for without such primary data, explanations cannot be effectively tested.

As we have reviewed measures of violence, most of us have been impressed by some of the statistics. Had we realized that there had been so many episodes of major violence (Richardson, for example, counted 94 "deadly quarrels" in the period 1820–1945 in each of which at least 3,000 were killed), or that some wars had been so bloody (such as 15 million deaths in World War II, not counting civilian casualties)? And had we realized how universal has been the presence of civil strife? The Feierabends, for example, found only one nation in 1955–61 (New Zealand) completely stable politically—and even there they probably would have found some political strife had they looked hard enough. And Gurr has asserted that no country in the modern world has been essentially free of civil strife for as long as a generation at a time. Such statistics may well lead us to think of collective violence as a normal part of our world and age, not something abnormal or bizarre.

Recognizing the full incidence of violence in recent history—as the statistics of these chapters have recounted—we may still seek some comfort by assuming a favorable overall historical trend. If we believe firmly enough in progress, we may see signs of a coming age of peace—reflecting on some of the grosser barbarities of ancient wars which are no longer practiced. Or, more disenchanted with modernity, we may assume the recent period to be an unusually violent one, leaving the possibility of a more peaceful world once we dismantle the present system. But alas for either view, our survey of the evidence gives us no reason to assume any long-term trend in the incidence of war or domestic violence on this planet. Singer and Small, as well as Wright, specifically refute any long-term trend of increase or abatement in the incidence of wars. And the work on domestic violence which covers the broadest historical scope, that of the Tillys, gives us no reason to see any long-term historical trend in the overall amount of collective violence.

Are we then to look upon organized or collective violence as an inevitable feature of the human condition? To so conclude would probably be going too far. Violence is widely present and persistent in human experience, but it is also highly variable in amount and form. Nothing with this degree of variation can be considered as inevitable, and an examination of the conditions of variation should help us understand how at least some of our more destructive forms of strife might be eliminated.

Except for seasonal variations in the outbreak of wars and some slight suggestion of a generational cycle in war intensity, wars seem to be almost randomly distributed over time. But major wars are not randomly distributed over the face of the globe. The most extensive wars have been fought where major world powers have existed in close proximity—especially in Europe and East Asia. Wars involving lesser powers—especially those relatively isolated by geographic barriers—have been less frequent and have generally been less destructive when fought. A few nations, in fact, have avoided war for well over a century.

When we examine patterns of civil strife within nations, we are much more struck by great differences. Within a given nation, there are great variations from one period of time to another. The United States, for example, had its heyday for violence during the latter part of the nineteenth century, though little of it involved any challenge to the prevailing political system. American collective violence in the late 1960s seemed severe partly because it followed two decades of almost unprecedented domestic tranquility.

There are also striking differences between nations. Some

nations have gone for generations without major domestic violence, while others seem to be in almost constant turmoil. Generally, there is some correlation here between economic development and political stability, as the Feierabends have shown, though other factors have also been suggested. Indeed, in some nations there may even be traditions of strife continuing from generation to generation—such as for the revolutionary and conservative traditions in France or between republicanism and unionism in Ireland. In these cases, there is a ready-made political context for strife which may be relatively absent elsewhere (such as in Denmark, Switzerland, or New Zealand).

Collective violence shows significant variation not only in amount but also in form. Wars, as Quincy Wright has shown, follow broad historical trends toward becoming more concentrated in destructive power and broader in the range of their involvements. In a host of detailed ways, many of which reflect modern weapons technology, there is a great difference between recent wars and those of centuries ago. Domestic strife, even more than international wars, comes in a variety of sizes and shapes. Gurr, for example, uses the categories of nonviolent protest, violent turmoil, conspiracy, and internal war, and he points to significant differences in the conditions for different forms. The Tillys, in even more concrete detail, point to different forms of collective violence and the conditions under which each tends to occur. Some (such as food riots) have become almost extinct in Western nations, while others (for example, political demonstrations which spill over into violence) have become more common.

Once we can identify and measure variations in wars and other forms of group violence, our next problem becomes the explanation of this variation. How do we explain the degree to which group violence manifests itself at one time and place rather than at another?

In Chapter 7 we considered three main approaches to explaining the incidence of collective violence. These may be referred to broadly as (1) deprivation or frustration, (2) breakdown or disorganization, and (3) mobilization and power models. These approaches toward explanation can also be applied to international conflict.

Let us consider first the deprivation or frustration model, clearly the most popular of the three in commonsense thinking. Violence, it is held, is a product of deprivation and frustration, and collective violence is a product of a widely shared sense of misery. We have created in the modern world greatly expanded means for the satisfaction of human wants. But many wants still remain unsatisfied. That knowledge is available about the means which would bring satisfaction makes the frustration of those so "relatively deprived" all the more difficult to bear. Is there really any surprise that such frustration from time to time expresses itself in collective violence?

This perspective on collective violence is more apt to be argued by liberals than by conservatives. Implicit is an assumption that social change is a normal part of the world and that people are suffering from inadequate rather than too much change. An outdated structure of established power controls how the benefits of the modern world are distributed, and too many are left with too little. Thus their frustration and collective resentment are part and parcel of their being left out after promises of progress.

How well does this perspective fit with the facts? In the case of international war, it immediately faces a problem. Contrary to the common stereotype, international wars have been more often initiated by the "have" nations than the "have-nots." There is simply no good statistical evidence to support the generalization that more miserable populations create nations which are particularly war-prone. On the average, the really poor countries have appeared more peaceful than the wealthy ones.

But what about internal order? It is true that the Feierabends show a relation between "systemic frustration" and political disorder. However, most of this relationship reflects the difference between Western democracies (with less frustration and disorder) and less developed nations (with apparently more of each). When Gurr made comparisons among 21 Western democracies, his relative-deprivation approach yielded much more limited success. In this analysis, the variables of legitimacy, institutional support, and coercive balance appeared more strongly able to predict civil strife than any measures reflecting the relative deprivation of the population. Also, Spilerman and McPhail found very little success using deprivation or frustration hypotheses to identify the incidence of or participation in American racial disturbances. And the Tillys found practically no correlation between measures of economic hardship and European outbreaks of collective violence.

All in all, the evidence to support a deprivation or frustration explanation for collective violence is not very good. Perhaps the popular preoccupation with psychological conditions has misled us here. Because we are individually angered when deprived or frustrated, and because then we recognize our own impulses toward violence, we imagine that collective violence may be just an aggregation of such impulses. We are not arguing that such an aggregation of individual sentiments is never an important factor in war or collective violence. We are, however, suggesting that the accumulated facts do not well support this type of *general explanation* for either war or internal strife.

Perhaps what we need to explain social violence is a more directly social model. For example, violence may be viewed as a symptom of social disorganization, as a general breakdown of the normative order.

Let us recognize, for this approach, what a sensitive web of relationships modern society is. We have, over a period of many generations, constructed a social order, which includes a framework of established institutions and roles and rules for living according to these institutions. When institutions operate in harmony with each other, and when persons within them know and follow the appropriate roles and rules, then there is relative peace. When, however, there is a breakdown in the system—when institutions work at cross purposes to each other or when persons are given their roles and rules with inadequate persuasiveness or authority—then the human propensity for violence asserts itself. Some of the violence is simply individual, but some of it also takes collective forms as people together attempt to force their interests against the loose and deteriorated fabric of the normative order.

What we have just sketched is a breakdown-of-normative-order theory of collective violence. It is a perspective especially dear to conservative hearts, for it usually is convenient for conservatives to assume that the established institutions are workable if only persons would give them more faithful allegiance. It is the thirst for change and innovation, they hold, the seductive glamour of a new idea or an untried new procedure, that so frequently leads men and women astray—dissolving workable systems of social order before new ones can be created. The key culprit therefore is social change. This being so, we should know where to look for empirical generalizations. Where there is unusually rapid social change, there should we find a high incidence of collective violence. Wars, revolutions, and collective unrest might all be reflections of the same general conditions of uncontrolled social change.

How well do the facts of war and peace support this perspective? Some of Quincy Wright's interpretations in *A Study of War* are along similar lines—such as peace requiring a complex interrelationship of institutions and war resulting from a severe disruption—but his statistics on war frequency do not give us any clear test of the idea. Indeed, the most frequent and severe international wars (for example, World Wars I and II) have involved, at the outset at least, relatively well established institutional systems. Perhaps there was a breakdown in the *international* system, such as it was (Holsti's evidence suggests that this was at least true for European diplomacy in the summer of 1914), but this would be hard to predict by the kind of evidence gathered by Richardson, Wright, Singer and Small, or Choucri and North. Also, war seems to be no more likely to occur in segments of the world with less developed international institutions than in those with more developed diplomatic traditions. As preliminary findings of the correlates-of-war project show, the amount of intergovernmental organization seems unrelated to the incidence of war, and rapid change in population also seems unrelated to war involvement. Our data for international wars therefore do not notably confirm predictions implied by our societal-breakdown perspective.

The facts on domestic violence may harmonize a little better than those on international war with these assumptions. Political instability, as the Feierabends have shown, is a more common feature of developing than economically developed nations. The work of the Tillys suggests that European collective violence has tended to be associated especially with political change and with a broader background of societal change. But "social disorganization" variables appeared relatively powerless to indicate the incidence of American racial disturbances in Spilerman's data, and the Tillys find a social organization approach (generally seeing violence as expressing the influence of *organized* social forces) more useful to explain their data on the incidence of European disturbances than a social-order-breakdown perspective. In sum, our social-breakdown perspective receives only modest support as we review the materials of these last three chapters.

Another approach to explaining social violence is in terms of the claims to power of new social groups. As the social order changes, new groups attain access to greater resources—physical, social, and symbolic. They seek to mobilize these resources to attain greater power and influence. In doing so, they tend to be opposed by those who are already entrenched in power. The result is therefore a struggle for relative power, which from time to time takes the form of collective violence.

In Chapter 7 we, following the Tillys, found this approach relatively successful for interpreting the ups and downs of collective violence in modern Europe. We also found it a useful model to apply to the Irish Land War. We did not specifically examine studies of American collective violence from this perspective, but data on the racial disturbances of the late 1960s seem at least as harmonious with this model as with either the deprivation-frustration or the disorganization-breakdown approach. Other American evidence supporting this approach has been obtained in research by William Gamson, who has shown an interesting correlation between the success of social protest groups and their propensity for violence.[12]

But how well does the mobilization-and-power model fit the facts of international violence? Probably even better than on the domestic level. It is in conflicts between the claims to power of rival nation-states, and in their mobilization of resources to assert their power, that most wars originate. This is so commonly true that we seldom think of such a generalization as an explanation. But interpretations don't have to be convoluted to be worthy of our respect, and good explanations don't have to be elusive. It is in the rival organizations of power of nation-states that the modern world has its greatest source of violence. It is in their ability to so readily mobilize human and physical resources in support of their claims that they have such a capacity for massive violence. This is quite clearly supported in Quincy Wright's analysis of the evolution of modern warfare. Singer and Small's strong correlation between great-power status and war participation also is consistent, as is the statistical and historical evidence for the onset of World War I given by Holsti and Choucri and North.

We do not want to conclude, however, that any single model well summarizes the data on group violence given by the studies we have reviewed in these chapters. Although we believe that a power-mobilization approach is more directly fruitful than either a deprivation-frustration or a breakdown-disorganization approach, we still fail to attain the precise specification of predictions which we seek in a well-developed science.

Perhaps what is needed is a more complex model, or set of models, for explaining variations in social violence. We have noted several attempts in this direction. The work of Choucri and North and that of Gurr give us examples of models that use a set of variables—rather than a single factor—to explain variations in violence. Although this multi-factor approach holds greater promise for scientific explanation than more simplistic generalizations, we must recognize some problems in these more complex models too. Assumptions must always be built into the model. There are assumptions, to begin with, about what are the most important relevant variables to examine. There are also assumptions about lines of influence between variables, since not all possible formulations for even a few variables can be tested.[13] A lot of possibilities must therefore be left out of the model; the best that can be hoped for is that the most important variables are included. But here we come to another problem: The most important variables for one occasion may not be generalizable to another. Choucri and North, for example, found highly variable degrees of success of their key variables (singly or as a combined system) for predicting the behavior of different European nations in the period preceding World War I. And even for the same nation, their equations worked very differently from one time period to another.

We do not want to end this discussion with an impression of an inherent unpredictability of social violence. It is true that violence is by nature less constrained by routine norms than most human behavior; therefore, we should not expect violent behavior to be quite as predictable as, say, food consumption or recreational endeavors. But there *are* patterns of statistical relationships pointed to in this chapter. Social violence does not have a purely random character. Where we fail to have a high predictability may reflect the limited identification of the conditions of conflict. The work discussed in this chapter has mostly dealt with rather gross measures of variables, without the fine tuning required for more exact prediction of events. Even so, we have come up with a healthy number of generalizations which at least hold up in a broad probabilistic sense. We know, for example, that wars are more likely between major powers in close geographical proximity than for lesser and more dispersed nations. We know that periods of collective violence tend to be more likely during periods of change in central political organization. We know that rebellion is more likely to occur in nations where regimes lack legitimacy and institutional support. And so on. This does not mean that dispersed and lesser powers do not wage war, that collective violence may not at times appear unrelated to central political organization, or that rebellion may not sometimes occur where regimes have high legitimacy and support. These all may and do occur. But, probabilistically speaking, such patterns are less likely. It is in this probabilistic sense that most of the work in these last three chapters should be considered.

One of the reasons why predictability is not higher for generalizations about social violence is that human beings have the capacity to change their behavior by taking thought. This is true for human groups and organizations as well as for individuals. Because of the expected consequences of a given action, an obviously expected action may sometimes not be forthcoming. This seems to be especially true of those actions, like warfare, which might include strategic violence—where violence is tailored to achieving certain consciously planned goals. To the extent that this is true, we would expect high predictability for our generalizations only for broad statistical trends. On the case-by-case level, we would find considerable variation. The results may therefore give a picture of what would occur (as Lewis Richardson was fond of saying about his equations) if human beings did not stop to think. Viewed in this way, our lack of precise predictability should not disturb us. It may indicate to us something of the room for us to reshape events of this sort by the peculiarly human characteristic of taking thought—including taking thought about what appear to be the primary patterns of the incidence of social violence that others have identified.

Part Four

Strategy in Conflict

9

The Machiavellian Tradition

"It is necessary for a prince, who wishes to maintain himself, to learn how not to be good, and to use this knowledge or not use it, according to the necessity of the case." So was a new ruling prince in Italy once advised by an able but temporarily unemployed diplomat of his state. This advice was justified on the basis that the world of reality is so far removed from the world we like to imagine that "he who abandons what is done for what ought to be done, will rather learn to bring about his own ruin than his preservation. A man who wishes to make a profession of goodness in everything must necessarily come to grief among so many who are not good."[1]

Such is the tone of advice which Niccolo Machiavelli (1469–1527) presents in *The Prince*. This little book was written in 1512, dedicated to Lorenzo de Medici, the new ruler of Florence, and privately presented to him. There is no doubt that Machiavelli hoped, by the impression of worldly wisdom contained in this book, to gain reinstatement in the Florentine diplomatic corps. In this bit of strategy Machiavelli was totally and permanently unsuccessful. He died without ever having a chance again to exercise the political skills that had been so central in his life. But several years after his death *The Prince* was published, and ever since Machiavelli's advice has reverberated through the history of the West.

The Prince is generally seen as a cool and unsentimental analysis of political power. While written in a detached spirit, its approach is also very practical—telling in detail how power may be gained and effectively exercised. It is, in other words, a classic (perhaps *the* classic) work on strategy.

MACHIAVELLI'S ADVICE

Let us dip into Machiavelli's work a bit more to remind our-selves of the nature of his strategic analysis. "The chief foun-dations of all states," according to Machiavelli, can be reduced to two elements: "good laws and good arms." Of the two, he seems to place a stronger emphasis on arms, for "there cannot be good laws where there are not good arms." Therefore, a prince is advised to concentrate his studies on "war and its or-ganization and discipline, for that is the only art that is neces-sary to one who commands." "The chief cause of the loss of states," furthermore, "is the contempt of this art." Machiavelli's book is full of examples of wise and foolish military actions of ancient and contemporary leaders. Something of the same kind of thinking that is applied to military matters is also suggested for dealing with the civilian population. Thus "men must either be caressed or else annihilated; they will revenge themselves for small injuries, but cannot do so for great ones; the injury therefore that we do to a man must be such that we need not fear his vengeance." And "injuries should be done all together, so that being tasted, they will give less offence. Benefits should be granted little by little, so that they may be better enjoyed."[2]

Is Machiavelli's prince to be oblivious to the essential wel-fare of his people? Not at all. The good will of the populace is an extremely important basis of support for the leader. But it must be made clear that their welfare depends on his leader-ship, and not vice versa. "Therefore a wise prince will seek means by which his subjects will always and in every possible condition of things have need of his government, and then they will always be faithful to him." The successful leader thus shows himself to be master of the situation. "And above all, a prince must live with his subjects in such a way that no accident of good or evil fortune can deflect him from his course"; there-fore he will avoid the situation where "the good that you do does not profit, as it is judged to be forced upon you, and you will derive no benefit whatever from it."

Appearances are extremely important to the art of state-craft, according to Machiavelli. "Thus it is well to seem merci-ful, faithful, humane, sincere, religious, and also to be so" and a prince "should seem to be all mercy, faith, integrity, humanity, and religion." And, adds Machiavelli, "nothing is more necessary than to seem to have this last quality." However, one must also be prepared "that when it is needful to be otherwise you may be able to change to the opposite qualities"; for a prince is "often obliged, in order to maintain the state, to act against faith, against charity, against humanity, and against religion." He must therefore "have a mind disposed to adapt itself according to the wind, and as the variations of fortune dictate." It is perfectly possible for a prince to act ruthlessly, though, and still appear a paragon of benevolence to most of his subjects, which of course is to be desired. This is true because:

> Everybody sees what you appear to be, few feel what you are, and those few will not dare to oppose themselves to the many, who have the majesty of the state to defend them; and in the actions of men, and especially of princes, from which there is no appeal, the end justifies the means. Let a prince therefore aim at conquering and maintaining the state, and the means will always be judged honourable and praised by every one, for the vulgar is always taken by appearances and the issue of the event . . . and the few who are not vulgar are isolated when the many have a rallying point in the prince.

We have quoted quite enough to give the flavor of Machiavelli's strategic thinking. But let us include one last famous passage on the attitude of the populace toward the prince. This deals specifically with the question of whether it is better to be loved or feared. Machiavelli's answer:

> . . . one ought to be both feared and loved, but as it is difficult for the two to go together, it is much safer to be feared than loved, if one of the two has to be wanting. For it may be said of men in general that they are ungrateful, voluble, dissemblers, anxious to avoid danger, and covetous of gain; as long as you benefit them, they are entirely yours; they offer you their blood, their goods, their life, and their children, as I have before said, when the necessity is remote; but when it approaches, they revolt. And the prince who has relied solely on their words, without making other preparations, is ruined; for the friendship which is gained by purchase and not

through grandeur and nobility of spirit is bought but not secured, and at a pinch is not to be expended in your service. And men have less scruple in offending one who makes himself loved than one who makes himself feared; for love is held by a chain of obligation which, men being selfish, is broken whenever it serves their purpose; but fear is maintained by a dread of punishment which never fails.

Still, a prince should make himself feared in such a way that if he does not gain love, he at any rate avoids hatred; for fear and the absence of hatred may well go together, and will be always attained by one who abstains from interfering with the property of his citizens and subjects or with their women. And when he is obliged to take the life of any one, let him do so when there is proper justification and manifest reason for it; but above all he must abstain from taking the property of others, for men forget more easily the death of their father than the loss of their patrimony.[3]

MACHIAVELLI'S CONTINUING SIGNIFICANCE

There are a number of reasons why it is fitting that Machiavelli's writings provide the initial topic of discussion for strategy in conflict. These writings well represent some of the central themes of the scientific literature on strategy. Machiavelli bases his analysis on real-world realities; he assumes that means must be considered realistically in relation to ends; that the likely behavior of others must be realistically assessed; and that from these considerations general policies of action may be formulated. These are all central elements in what is generally considered strategic thinking.

We must, if we are to be clear-headed about strategy in conflict, start out with the world as it is, not as we think it ought to be. Machiavelli unambiguously set forth his advice upon this empirical basis. He searched through events of ancient history as well as contemporary Italian politics to give him this empirical base—studying what actually happened under different conditions of action. He did not amass his data quite in the systematic form that a twentieth-century social scientist would use, but there can be no doubt about Machiavelli's empirical spirit. While there are times when the modern literature of strategy stultifies into dogma, the best of the modern work is in the same tradition of realism as that of Machiavelli. Let us look at the real world to observe what actually happens, he advised, as the first step in developing a strategy for action in situations of conflict.

Strategic thinking assumes that we take the interests of an actor as the framework of analysis. That is, we take a particular person, or perhaps a group or nation, as a starting point, assuming certain interests of this party as dominant considerations. This Machiavelli did for his prince. He took the prince as the focal party, assuming further that the primary goals for the prince are the gaining and keeping of power. Treating these ends as given, what must the prince do to most effectively achieve them? This is the central question in *The Prince*. True, we occasionally have suggestions that the welfare of the people must be considered, or that order and political stability must be promoted for the good of society; but the good of the prince, not the good of the people or society, is the central theme. And the means the prince applies to gain and hold power are always evaluated in terms of their success in achieving power for himself, not in terms of some other societal or philosophical end. In modern strategic analyses, the gaining and keeping of power is not the only consideration that may be used, and certainly it is rare today that a monarch's personal interests would be treated as primary. Still, power is usually a central consideration. And the notion that we should be clear-headed about the objectives of our power is certainly a central theme of good strategic thinking.

To act effectively in human affairs, we need not only consider realistically our own interests (or those of the party we take for our point of reference); we must also be careful to consider the interests of others and what they are likely to do about them. We are dealing with, to use a contemporary term, "interdependence." The interests and motivations of others must be analyzed in order to predict their likely actions and reactions. This Machiavelli does at some length. For example, it is because of the attachment of most persons to their property that the prince should be scrupulous in upholding property rights—"for men forget more easily the death of their father than the loss of their patrimony." And it is because people are so fickle in their loyalties (in turn based on their natural selfishness) that a prince is advised not to depend on the love of the populace for continued power. Good strategy, in this view, is always contingent upon a correct understanding of the actions of others.

Strategic thinking is empirically grounded, focused on clearly identified ends, and related to the contingent actions of others. These points all come together in a final general point about strategic thinking: It is generalized in a normative framework.

Heretofore in this book we have basically not assumed a normative structure of thought. We generally think of social science as based on the world as it is and not on how people think it ought to be. Therefore we typically concern ourselves with facts rather than values. And as we put our facts together to derive general principles, the principles we derive are intended to have a descriptive rather than a normative character. That is, they identify what the world is like, not what we are advised to do about it. To be sure, value judgments occasionally intrude into the discussion, but only incidentally and when questions appear to touch naturally upon fundamental human values. This is generally seen as a sidelight in the scientific quest; the basic goal of truth, as viewed by most scientists, is not to be lost in this or that suggestion for practical application. Such has been the main-line theme of science in general, the social sciences in particular, and the vast majority of the works cited in previous chapters of this book.

Now, however, we prepare for a change. We are opening the door in the present chapter to a *normative* social science of conflict. The central principles we seek in a normative science are principles of action, not principles of explanation. We are seeking general guides or rules on how to act, and this is the sense in which we currently open the door to a normative science. The general question for us is: How should a party act in a conflict in order to best achieve his or her (or its) best interests? This is the central question in the strategy of conflict— whatever the nature of the particular conflict may be.

We must be careful to make certain qualifications about the

basis upon which we turn in such a normative direction. We are not starting out with any general ethical principles as given. What is given as a starting point for analysis is the presence of identifiable real-world goals or interests of a certain party. We assume that this occurs in a setting where empirical analysis is relevant to help us know what consequences are most apt to follow from what actions. Based upon such empirical analysis, we derive general rules or policies for action in specified kinds of conditions. This is the approach in a variety of modern disciplines which might broadly be termed "policy sciences"—including organizational cost-benefit analysis, operations research, and various forms of economics and applied sociology. What will distinguish our analysis from these other fields will be our central focus upon social conflict.

Before leaving Machiavelli, it is useful to point out that he not only thought in the general style that we have come to identify as strategic thinking, but also that some of the central ideas in the content of his advice have a very contemporary ring. For example, Machiavelli clearly perceived the principle that power grows out of the dependence of others—a leading idea in contemporary sociological exchange theory.[4] Also, Machiavelli was sure that power was based at least as much upon reputation and appearances as upon any physical reality—which is quite harmonious with attribution theory in present-day social psychology. And some other insights seem quite in line with modern learning theory, such as the advantages of periodic reinforcement for increasing response strength (recall Machiavelli's advice to grant benefits "little by little").

Lest it appear that there is no room to criticize Machiavelli as a master strategist, let us also mention two major flaws in his thinking. Machiavelli probably overdid himself in asserting the selfishness and gullibility of human nature. His view of the nature of humanity may be a useful corrective for the idealistic literature which had previously dominated the discussion of politics, but in providing this corrective Machiavelli probably proved too cynical in his views. As we shall see later in this chapter, good strategy requires taking carefully into account cooperative as well as selfish interests. It is not clear that Machiavelli allowed adequately for this. It is therefore likely that some of his advice—for example, the free use of deceit—might have been, at least in the long run, counterproductive for the Renaissance prince he sought to advise (as well as for a modern political leader). Of course, even though this attitude may not always prove to be good strategy, we do tend to associate a somewhat cynical view of human nature with the whole subject of strategy. Therefore, it may be well to remind ourselves of Machiavelli's cynicism at the outset of our attention to strategy—even if we later will have to qualify such assumptions.

In another respect Machiavelli also appears short-sighted in his analysis; not only does he give too cynical a view of human nature, but he also probably gives too simple a picture of the prince's objectives. Is simply gaining and keeping power enough? Should we not also consider the larger purposes for which power is to be exercised? To do so might complicate the picture, bringing in moral and ethical issues that Machiavelli preferred left aside. But for a full analysis of realistic political strategy, such larger considerations might be necessary.

It can be argued that *The Prince* does indeed include some of these larger purposes, and that its last chapter especially makes this apparent. Machiavelli's final chapter is an impassioned plea to "liberate Italy from the barbarians."[5] The language here is much more emotionally charged than elsewhere in the book. Showing through clearly is Machiavelli's ardent nationalism. And here—also very modern in flavor—is the wider purpose for the prince's strategy: to unify Italy and throw off the yoke of foreign domination. This is apparently the end which justifies the more specific advice on princely power politics. Machiavelli clearly hopes that the prince will use his advice toward the end of Italian unity—but of course, he has no guarantee that this will be the case.

One final note in criticism of Machiavellian strategy: It manifestly did not work for Machiavelli himself. I refer here not only to the fact that Italy was not soon united, and that the prince to whom Machiavelli personally directed this work (Lorenzo de Medici) did little to accomplish this end. I refer even more to the disappointment of Machiavelli's own personal motives. He hoped to get back into the diplomatic service by impressing Prince Lorenzo with his worldly wisdom. But *The*

Prince as a privately circulated manuscript totally failed to bring about this effect. Machiavelli never received the invitation to come back into the service of Florence. Finally, in 1527, the Medici were overthrown. Immediately Machiavelli returned to his city to request reinstatement in the post he had held before the Medicis had come to power, but it was now too late. In particular, too many people had read portions of his privately circulated manuscript for Machiavelli to be trusted in such a post. Almost charitably, Machiavelli died before being informed of this final rejection by his one-time Florentine associates.

CONTEMPORARY MILITARY STRATEGY

The concept of strategy has been associated in particular with military affairs, and traditional military usage has distinguished strategy especially from tactics. In the past, tactics roughly referred to military planning in the context of a given battle, while strategy applied to the overall plan for a campaign. However, with the expansion of military power in the twentieth century, the concept of strategy has also escalated in meaning. For example, we now refer to nuclear weapons with greater power than that which destroyed Hiroshima and which might decisively affect the outcome of a campaign as "tactical," reserving the stronger adjective "strategic" for those which might disable the centers of power and/or population of an enemy nation. Military strategy has thus generally come to mean any planned application of military force in support of the general objectives of national policy.

Whether using the term in either its traditional meaning or its more general contemporary usage, "strategy" in military thinking lies midway between the selection of detailed means ("tactics") and overall objectives ("national policy"). Tactics are selected to be congruent with the larger strategy, and strategy is selected for consistency with the broader objectives of national policy. Only when national objectives call for the use of force does military strategy come under active consideration.

The objectives of traditional military policy, when activated, have most commonly involved the defeat or neutralization of opposing enemy forces. Havoc may be wreaked upon cities and countrysides, and thousands of civilians may lie dead, but these have seldom been prime objectives of military strategy. Rather, these have been incidental casualties of the contest between armies. To defeat or destroy enemy military forces is the primary strategic objective. Another important objective may be the seizure of lands and resources (or defense against seizure of one's own lands and resources). These two general goals of military strategy reflect the larger national goals as they become effective war aims. In service of these general objectives, more particular objectives may be laid out for a given theatre of war. These objectives set the framework for strategy at the operational level.

General doctrines may help guide such military strategy. For example, most military leaders deploy forces with assumptions that military effectiveness is enhanced by being in a position to take the initiative in preference to a purely defensive posture, by having a unity of command structure and avoiding operations with highly complicated coordination, or by being able to mass sufficient combat power quickly for it to be decisive when most needed. Such doctrines of military strategy are of course always conditioned by the particular factors present in a given theatre of war. The common assumption of them all is that military strategy is primarily a contest between military forces. To defeat enemy military forces by destroying them or neutralizing their power is the most common overall objective.

What we have been characterizing as traditional military strategy is still important in contemporary military thinking. However, the nuclear age has drastically changed the emphasis in strategic thinking. Much more emphasis is placed upon the "deterrent" (rather than directly destructive) quality of military forces in their *capacity* for almost total destruction. This theme is not completely new. The threat of destruction *if* forces should be deployed has been of some influence in controlling international relations for many centuries. Also, massive destruction of civilian populations as well as military forces has an ancient and distinguished history. But it is only since World War II that these considerations have become central in discussions of military strategy.

What has fundamentally changed in the nuclear age is the capacity to engage in effective coercion upon an enemy *before* it is defeated. Thomas Schelling has very clearly expressed this point:

> Nuclear weapons make it possible to do monstrous violence to the enemy without first achieving victory. With nuclear weapons and today's means of delivery, one expects to penetrate an enemy homeland without first collapsing his military force. What nuclear weapons have done, or appear to do, is to promote this kind of warfare to first place. Nuclear weapons threaten to make war less military, and are responsible for the lowered status of "military victory" at the present time. *Victory is no longer a prerequisite for hurting the enemy.*[6]

In other words, the ability to disrupt the lives of citizens of another country does not depend on the presence of a conquering army. The launching of a few missiles can accomplish the same purpose. The simplicity of such an action adds enormously to the importance of psychological factors in relationships between nations in conflict. Symbolic military moves may sometimes communicate threats of far greater potency than the achievement of a victory on the battlefield.

That national interests are more directly vulnerable to threats and counterthreats than in the past has left the line between diplomacy and war more and more blurred. Schelling has summarized this new situation as follows:

> Military strategy can no longer be thought of, as it could for some countries in some eras, as the science of military victory. It is now equally, if not more, the art of coercion, of intimidation and deterrence. The instruments of war are more punitive than acquisitive. Military strategy, whether we like it or not, has become the diplomacy of violence.

With this transformation of military strategy to become more and more, in Schelling's words, "the diplomacy of violence," several key consequences follow. Common interests in avoiding mutual destruction more and more unite even the most bitter enemies, and strategy must take into account these common interests—even when they grow primarily out of a "balance of terror" (as Winston Churchill once aptly phrased it). Negotiations—by deed or word—become increasingly important, to be carried on even during fighting to assist in the limitation and control (as well as the termination) of hostilities. Finally, matters of credibility may become more important than capability in the effective use of military might.

Even while modern doctrines of deterrence have emphasized the massive destructive capacity of nuclear weapons, they have also searched for ways to control or limit their potential use. This has come not only in negotiations for arms control or disarmament but also in the development of rationales for the potential use of nuclear weapons. American strategists, for example, have supported a "counterforce" strategy to encourage America and the Soviet Union to recognize a common interest, should there be a nuclear exchange between these two superpowers, of avoiding strikes on cities while both parties seek to neutralize each other's nuclear forces. There are also the common interests of major nations in limiting the sphere of conflict when war does break out. The United States has, for example, fought two major wars since World War II, and in both the Korean and Vietnamese conflicts, despite the tremendous firepower displayed, some restraints were mutually maintained by both sides in limiting the area of conflict and the weapons deployed. Aspirations of victory may be frustrated by such limitations, but the much greater frustrations of a nuclear exchange are at least avoided.

To limit war, it may not be enough to engage in a diplomacy of acts. Systematic diplomacy of a more conventional kind may also be necessary—even between combatants in the midst of war. The effectiveness of limits on the war as well as ways to end it may be enhanced by direct diplomatic contacts between enemy states. Far from war being an occasion to sever diplomatic relations, our age of coercive violence would seem to require that diplomatic channels be more and more used during hostilities—even if only to make clear the credibility of threats.

With the rise of deterrence in strategic thinking, the communication of intent becomes more and more important in influencing other nations. Enormous stockpiles of nuclear weapons create no influence if there is never a possibility for their use. Credibility, and not just capability, becomes the crucial consideration. This, of course, increases the need for communication between potential enemies. It also introduces a tragic dilemma. Deterrence depends on the belief that the weapons involved might be used. There has to be some real possibility that a nation's nuclear weapons may be used in order for them to deter actions of another state. Sooner or later, such weapons will have to be used or they will lose their credibility as deterrents. As Kenneth Boulding has well expressed it in his analysis of threat systems:

> It is easy to prove that stable deterrence is impossible in the long run, for if deterrence were really stable, it would soon cease to deter. That is, if the probability of threats being carried out were zero, their credibility would soon disappear. If, however, there is a positive probability of threats being carried out over a long enough period, they will be carried out.[7]

Obviously, a national security system which rests primarily on the threats of nations to annihilate each other cannot offer much long-range security. A realistic pursuit of national security must therefore include a broader range of international initiatives (political, economic, social, and psychological, as well as military) than have been used in traditional conceptions of military strategy.

VARIATIONS ON A THEME

As we made clear in the previous section, military strategy must always be seen in relation to the national objectives it is meant to serve. We implied that in the nuclear age the idea of maximum destruction through military operations is less and less realistic as a means for obtaining national objectives. How then are national objectives to be pursued? And what are the national objectives we are talking about anyway?

There are many kinds of national objectives which affect international relations. Seldom is "the national interest" so clear and overriding as political leaders seek to claim in their speeches. Nevertheless, the pursuit of wealth, power, and prestige which provides motivation for the individual in society also has its rough counterpart on the national level. A nation does seek to enhance the general wealth of its citizens, the prestige of their way of life, and the power of their state relative to others.

Earlier in this chapter, we characterized strategic thinking in general as based on a realistic assessment of one's own interests, of one's own power to pursue these interests in conflict with other parties, and of the likely effects of the actions others may make. As applied to the actions of nations, this suggests above all the need to be clear in identifying what are the primary national interests and the means by which they can most effectively be pursued in a world of international conflict.

One approach is to assume that power itself is the main purpose of a nation-state. This "realpolitik" view (as nineteenth-century German followers of the Machiavellian tradition termed it) holds that the proper test of success in international relations is whether or not the relative power of one's nation is enhanced. It is assumed that all states seek the enlargement or preservation of their power, and key ingredients in the inevitable power game between them include military action, the threat of military force, and coercive economic measures. War is not necessarily sought, but it is assumed that it is apt to be necessary to resolve important conflicts—and military preparedness is therefore a vital necessity to assure that any results of war will not be to one's own disadvantage. War may be avoided, in this way of thinking, only through a balance of power, which checks the ambitions of the most powerful nations by alliances between other states.

Few political leaders would state the "power politics" assumptions as simply as we have done in the above paragraph, though many use these assumptions in practice. Machiavelli was unusual for his day, not because he thought in terms of power politics but because he failed to disguise it with a rhetoric of idealism. Otto von Bismark, Germany's chancellor in the late nineteenth century, likewise made no apologies for his realpolitick assumptions—which he carried through, incidentally, with considerably greater success than did Machiavelli.

In America, however, the climate of opinion has been quite different. A moralistic tone has generally pervaded the rhetoric of foreign policy and often also the actual operating policies.

Woodrow Wilson and his Fourteen Points for concluding World War I offer a good example. "We dare not turn from the principle that morality and not expediency is the thing that must guide us, and that we will never condone iniquity because it is most convenient to do so," Wilson had said; and his behavior as president was mostly consistent with this philosophy.[8] Likewise we have the example of Cordell Hull, Franklin D. Roosevelt's secretary of state, who flatly rejected balance-of-power thinking in regard to international affairs. Recently, however, there has been a rise in the status of "realistic politics" in discussions of American foreign policy. A leading stimulus has been the writings of the late Hans J. Morganthau. Other scholars who may also be associated with this general point of view include two who have had important roles in helping to shape recent American foreign policy, George F. Kennan and Henry Kissinger. Let us briefly cite some of the views of these three recent proponents of realism.

Morganthau's now classic analysis of international relations, *Politics among Nations,* is explicitly written from the point of view of "political realism," which he characterizes as including the following view:

> This being inherently a world of opposing interests and of conflict among them, moral principles can never be fully realized, but must at best be approximated through the ever temporary balancing of interests and the ever precarious settlement of conflicts. This school, then, sees in a system of checks and balances a universal principle for all pluralist societies. It appeals to historic precedent rather than to abstract principles, and aims at the realization of the lesser evil rather than the absolute good.[9]

Nations *must,* according to Morganthau, be guided by their national interests, whether or not their spokesmen so profess. National interests, furthermore, depend primarily on the structure of political power within the nation. Foreign policies of nations must always take into account the present political and cultural context; this context includes such factors of power as geography, natural resources, industrial capacity, military preparedness, population composition and distribution, national character and morale, and the quality of governmental leadership. It is not inevitable that these factors are always realistically assessed and pragmatically brought to bear on policy decisions. The policy process *may* be short-circuited through legalistic or moralistic formulas, and this tends to reduce the practical effectiveness of policies. But sooner or later the real interests of the nation must be expressed—whether haltingly and vaguely or (as should be usually preferred) realistically and directly. Elsewhere Morganthau states what he calls the "iron law of international politics," which no nation can ever completely avoid, namely that "legal obligations must yield to the national interest."[10]

Political realism, according to Morganthau, considers prudence—"the weighing of the consequences of alternative political actions"—to be "the supreme virtue in politics."[11] Furthermore, the supreme purpose of foreign policy must be to serve the national interest with as much prudence as possible. In this process diplomacy is extremely important, provided it is conducted in a realistic manner. Morganthau sets forth the following as the four fundamental rules of effective diplomacy:

1. Diplomacy must be divested of the crusading spirit.
2. The objectives of foreign policy must be defined in terms of the national interest and must be supported with adequate power.
3. Diplomacy must look at the political scene from the point of view of other nations.
4. Nations must be willing to compromise on all issues that are not vital to them.

The "irreducible minimum that diplomacy must defend with adequate power without compromise" is national security, which in turn may be defined as "integrity of the national territory and its institutions." But today, Morganthau also points out:

> Diplomacy must ever be alive to the radical transformation that national security has undergone under the impact of the nuclear age. Until the advent of that age, a nation could use its diplomacy to purchase its security at the expense of another nation. Today, short of a radical change in the atomic balance of power in favor of a particular nation, diplomacy, in order

to make one nation secure from nuclear destruction, must make them all secure.

Two political theorists whose writings show themes similar to those of Morganthau are George F. Kennan and Henry A. Kissinger. Both Kennan and Kissinger show a strong emphasis upon what they consider to be the realities of national interests. Both also have had opportunities to participate significantly in the formulation of recent American foreign policy.

George Kennan, a distinguished scholar of Soviet-American relations, was with the U.S. Department of State during the administration of Harry S. Truman. He was then a leading architect of the American policy of containment. He has since argued for a more flexible policy toward the Soviet Union than subsequent administrations have shown, and he has been highly critical of the extent to which the United States has expanded its foreign policy commitments throughout the world. He was, for example, dismayed by America's involvement in Vietnam and highly critical of some more recent commitments in the Middle East. These, he holds, tend to be at the expense of the priority interests and obligations of the United States in relation to Western Europe and Japan.[12]

Henry Kissinger first distinguished himself as a scholar of international relations who was especially concerned with policy formulation. In his early books, such as *Nuclear Weapons and Foreign Policy* and *The Necessity for Choice*, he warned against the dangers of dogmatic rigidity and bureaucratic inertia in policy formulation and execution.[13] He emphasized instead the opportunities for a creative shaping of the future through a clear perception of current realities and a determination to find ways of breaking free from the dogmas of the past. During the administrations of Richard Nixon and Gerald Ford, Kissinger found himself with the opportunity to act in just such a role as the chief American foreign policy maker.

Although Kennan and Kissinger have both strongly stressed the importance of a realistic assessment of national interests, the importance of balance-of-power considerations in maintaining peace, and the need for imaginative ventures in foreign policy to relate effectively to current realities—all themes which would be shared with Morganthau and other political realists—they differ in other important ways. Kissinger puts a greater stress on the personal initiatives of men with power, while Kennan emphasizes more the careful coordination of policy. Kissinger envisions for the United States a greater necessity for involvements all over the world than does Kennan, who sees a much more modest role for American influence. Kissinger gives much greater emphasis to military action, while Kennan puts a larger stress on diplomacy. And so forth. On particular policy questions we would also frequently find disagreement among men like Kissinger, Kennan, and Morganthau. But there is a general theme which such men have in common. This is the theme of political realism and the overriding concern for identifying realistic national interests in the formulation of policies for international relations.

◄§

We have come a long way from the time when political realism could be seen primarily in terms of the interests of a prince. Now it is a whole nation whose interests must be considered. But the central Machiavellian tradition lives on. By the central Machiavellian tradition, we refer not to the more cynical judgments about human nature made by the Renaissance diplomat (that is what his name has become primarily known for, but it is not really the core of his thinking). We refer rather to the general way of thinking which may be broadly called strategic: empirically grounded, focused on clearly identified interests to be served, and related to the probable actions of others. Within this broader conception of the Machiavellian tradition there is room for Henry Kissinger and George Kennan as well as Otto von Bismark and Niccolo Machiavelli.

10

The Theory of Games

Strategy, as discussed in the previous chapter, implies a calculated rationality focused on the pursuit of identified interests. It involves a careful consideration of means and ends in conflict-of-interest situations.

In the present chapter, we will explore a particular framework for the analysis of strategy. Game theory is a branch of mathematics created especially to analyze situations involving conflicts of interest. However, exactly where game theory fits into the social sciences is sometimes a bit difficult to explain. This requires a few further comments by way of background.

Persons most conversant with the social sciences generally see two main uses of mathematics. Mathematics is important, first of all, in the measurement of phenomena. Without the quantification made possible by mathematical representation, the problem of describing social reality would be far more difficult. A second use of mathematics, to interpret research, follows closely after the descriptive use. Statistical tools are frequently of great help in assessing the significance of the relationships of variables and identifying broader patterns in the data, as well as in the initial description of data.

Social science professionals will recognize a third important use of mathematics: to build theoretical models. Mathematics may help to refine the theoretical models of social reality by specifying logical and quantitative relationships among variables, making them more precisely identified for purposes of testing against reality. Mathematics is therefore useful in social science for purposes of theory construction as well as for basic description and data analysis.

Game theory, however, fits clearly with none of these three main applications of mathematics to social science. It is not much used for direct description of conflict-of-interest situations or for data interpretation. It is useful for theory building, but (at least in its initial impact) in a manner quite different from the way theory is usually understood. In social science we generally refer to "theory" as an attempt at generalized description—to identify the central and most universal elements in the dynamics of types of social events and processes. In part, game theory helps to do this—but with a peculiar difference. Game theory is, at least in initial appearance, a normative theory. It sets out not so much to describe reality as to identify the best way to change reality. In the end, it may not prove as helpful in this as we might imagine, but we will come back to this subject later. For the present, it is sufficient to identify game theory as a special field of mathematics derived to furnish a *normative* theory for evaluating strategy in conflict-of-interest situations.

Foundations of Game Theory

Game theory has grown out of a more general area known as "decision theory," which gives a mathematical analysis of decision situations. The analysis of probabilities in gambling situations provides an example of decision theory. What is special about game theory is its assumption of an opponent: another decision maker whose likely choices must also be taken into account in the decisions made by oneself.

The "games" analyzed by game theory can include almost any situation of interdependent action involving two or more parties. Parties are usually conceptualized as persons, though a party can be any entity which may be involved in self-conscious action. Groups, organizations, or even nations are sometimes used as game theory "players." Interests of each party are represented by a set of numbers, usually called "utilities," with every possible outcome assigned a value. Usually it is assumed that utility is measured on an interval scale (that is, with real numbers), though sometimes it is not necessary to make this assumption.

We may formally identify the primary assumptions of game theory in its classical form as including the following four:

1. The interdependence assumption: Outcomes resulting from a party's choices depend not only on its own choices but also on those of other parties.
2. The quantification assumption: Outcomes can be represented quantitatively to show the degree of positive or negative interest of each party in each outcome.
3. The exhaustiveness assumption: Every possible outcome which can follow a set of choices or actions is known to each party involved.
4. The maximization assumption: Each party seeks to act in such a way as to maximize its own interests.

While these assumptions may sometimes seem forced, they do have the result of providing a framework in which the analysis of strategy can be most rigorously pursued. Indeed, in game theory the very concept of strategy is transformed to fit this new set of assumptions. Strategy now comes to mean a plan of action that covers all possible contingencies of choice. This includes all the contingencies which result from the choices of all players involved, as the interdependence (point 1) and exhaustiveness (point 3) assumptions help make clear. The other two assumptions (of quantification and maximization) help assure precision in the way strategies may be evaluated.

Simple games are usually represented in matrix form, as illustrated by Game A.

Game A represents a situation in which two parties each have two choices. This is called a "2 × 2" game. The four possible outcomes are represented by cells, and numbers in each cell give the utilities for each party. The row player (R) has two choices, R_1 and R_2, and the column player (C) must choose between C_1 and C_2. The outcome is determined by both choices, assumed here to be made simultaneously. The particular value of each possible outcome for Row is indicated by the first number in each cell (without parentheses); the value for Column is enclosed within parentheses for each case.

Since it usually adds interest to specify some more concrete situation which might be summarized by a game, we will do so

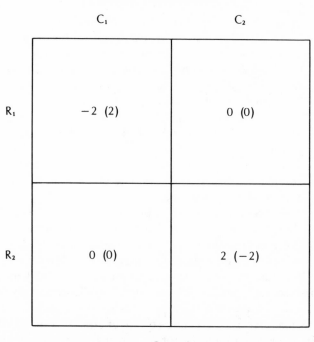

Game A

for Game A. But we should also recognize that game theory as a mathematical form of analysis does not require this. The matrix presented above is quite enough. However, for our own nonmathematical interest, let us assume the following concrete case. It is just after supper. Ralph (the row player) is about to sit down to read the evening paper. His wife Charlene (the column player) looks with some misgivings at the supper dishes. She can either complain to her husband (C_1) or else proceed to do the dishes (C_2). Ralph meanwhile has a choice between paying attention to his wife (R_1) or reading his paper (R_2). We can summarize the outcomes as follows:

1. If Charlene complains while Ralph pays attention to her (C_1 and R_1), his outcomes are doubly unsatisfactory and hers are doubly satisfactory.

2. If Charlene does the dishes while Ralph pays attention to her (C_2 and R_1), neither one gets any significant net gain from the outcome.

3. If Charlene complains while Ralph reads his newspaper (C_1 and R_2), neither gets any significant gain from the outcome.

4. If Charlene does the dishes while Ralph reads his newspaper (C_2 and R_2), his outcomes are doubly satisfactory and hers are doubly unsatisfactory.

Now the game theory question is: What should each do to best realize his or her interests, granted that the possible decision(s) made by the other(s) must also be taken into consideration. In this particular game (Game A), we realize that each has a fairly evident preferred choice. By comparing columns we see that, regardless of what Ralph may choose, Charlene is better off to complain. Likewise, comparing rows, Ralph is better off reading his newspaper than paying attention to his wife, no matter what her choice may be. Each party's interests therefore come together in what game theorists call a "saddle point" or "strictly determined" solution—that is, an outcome which neither party could improve upon by reconsidering only his or her choice. In this particular case, the "best" outcome is where C_1 and R_2 intersect, or the lower left cell: Ralph reads his newspaper while Charlene complains to him, and neither realizes any significant gain as a result.

Suppose our assumed situation was just slightly different, as indicated by Game B. Game B is the same as Game A for three of the four cells. Only in the case of the upper-right cell do we have any change. Both parties now find this outcome moderately satisfactory. So now, how should each player play this new game? Note again, by comparing the numbers in parentheses across columns, that C_1 still dominates C_2, regardless of what the row player chooses. Likewise, comparing the row player's utilities (the first number in each cell), R_2 dominates R_1, regardless of what the column player may choose. By this strategic logic we are led again to the same solution as in Game A: C_1 and R_2 are the strictly determined choices. Now, however, we balk. Would not C_2 and R_1 give a better outcome for both? If we return to Ralph and Charlene, why should he not pay attention to her as she does the dishes, assuming (in Game B) that both get some satisfaction from that state of affairs? Why should they remain with the valueless situation for both, as he reads his newspaper and she complains?

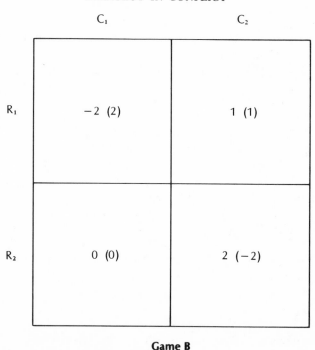

Game B

We can probably argue endlessly with ourselves regarding a proper solution for the players in Game B. In the process, we would put forth one or another criterion for what is a "good" solution. This is precisely the sort of thing done formally by game theory experts.

As earlier indicated, the theory of games is an attempt to give a thoroughly logical analysis of a matrix of outcomes in order to provide rules of action for any or all parties involved. However, we should make clear that the substance of game theory is logical rather than empirical. There is little interest, in game theory proper, in the direct study of real-world situations. Instead we start with a set of numbers. These numbers, whether presented in matrix format as we have done (called the "normal" form) or in some other way, represent the utilities of the parties involved. These numerically represented utilities are the starting point for game theory. From these utilities, game theory proceeds to identify rules for decision making. Since at least one other player or opponent is involved, these rules for decision making also may be considered as defining a strategy. For game theorists, however, it is not enough to give some rule of thumb for decision making. Remember, game theory is a branch of mathematics, and the rules must therefore be logically precise and demonstrable.

Game theory is very much like geometry in its style of thought; both are highly formal analyses of certain features abstracted from reality, and both proceed to demonstrate their conclusions through formal theorems and proofs. This nature of game theory may not be apparent in our brief introduction, but it would be readily apparent to any student who pursues its literature to any significant extent.

As we said before, "strategy" in the context of game theory, has come to mean a specification of choices one is to make *in every possible combination* of circumstances which may follow from choices of others. Note that this requires an exhaustive consideration of the situation—or at least the situation as represented by the matrix of outcomes. Obviously, complicated situations cannot easily be subjected to such a thoroughgoing analysis, so game theory has indeed tended to focus upon rather simple situations. This may limit its usefulness for throwing light on specific real-world situations—which tend to be much more complex than what is possible to analyze in game theory terms. Still, there is a similarity between central patterns of the real world and those which may be subjected to game theory analysis. Frequently there is a shock of recognition as we realize that a given type of game captures in principle the essential structure of some real-world counterpart. At that point, we proceed to follow the game theory analysis with more than purely mathematical interest.

TYPES OF GAMES

We should take note, before proceeding further, of the main distinctions which game theorists have used to distinguish different types of games. These bases for classification include (1) the number of parties involved, (2) the number of choices available to each party, (3) assumptions about the nature of utilities, (4) the degree of conflict of interest built into the matrix of outcomes, (5) the presence or absence of a natural equilibrium, and (6) contextual assumptions. Let us discuss each of these briefly in turn.

1. *The number of parties involved.* Game theorists usually distinguish between "two-person games" (involving two parties or players) and "*N*-person games" (involving three or more parties). Obviously, *N*-person games involve much more complex analysis. All the examples of games we will present in this chapter represent two-person games.

2. *The number of choices* or actions available to each party. While not as fundamental a distinction as that between two-person and *N*-person games, the number of choices available also affects the degree of complexity of analysis.[1] Obviously, the simplest possible game is that involving two parties who each have only two choices—generally known as the "2 × 2" game. Even this most simple game is the subject of an extensive game theory literature.[2]

3. Assumptions about *the nature of utilities.* Most of the game theory literature has assumed that the values in the outcome matrix represent true interval-scale measures for each player, but that a common comparison between players may not be possible. It is not assumed that utilities have the same meaning for both (or all) players. It is also commonly assumed that utilities are neither conservative nor transferable. That is, they cannot be saved up or given to someone else. Changing these assumptions would usually change the nature of the game. For example, the most liberal set of assumptions would be that utilities represent not only a true interval scale but also one with a standard set of meanings for all parties, with utilities both conservative and transferable. With these assumptions, it would be easy to anticipate side payments being made to help derive a strategic solution. With any of these assumptions lacking, such side payments could not be easily included in a recommended strategy.

4. *The degree of conflict of interest* built into the outcome matrix. Some games (generally known as "zero-sum" or "constant-sum" games) are games of pure opposition.[3] In each of these

games, one player's positive utilities are exactly balanced by another's negative utilities. All other games may be classified into the two further categories: games of pure cooperation, and mixed-motive games. In a game of pure cooperation, the utilities of any particular outcome are similar for all parties involved. In other words, there is no significant difference in interests. In this extreme case, conflict completely vanishes. All other games (that is, all games which fit neither the "pure opposition" nor the "pure cooperation" category) are mixed-motive games, which embody some combination of opposition and common interests.

5. *The presence or absence of a natural equilibrium* among the outcomes in a matrix. Some games have a joint outcome which is the result of each player choosing his option which dominates all others (it dominates in the sense of being at least as good as any alternative for all conditions of choice of the other player(s), and better than any alternative for at least one condition). When this occurs, the game may be said to have a natural outcome, usually called a "saddle point." Such an outcome is also an equilibrium point, in the sense that no person can improve upon it by unilaterally changing his choice.[4]

6. *Contextual assumptions,* or broader aspects of the situation. Other variations which may be important in identifying types of games are: whether or not complete information is assumed, whether or not communication between parties can occur before choices, whether or not choices are made simultaneously, and whether or not agreements made between parties are fully enforceable. Most game theory has used assumptions of perfect information (that is, that every party perfectly understands everyone's outcome matrix), simultaneous choices, an absence of communication before choices, and no reliable means of enforcing norms or agreements which might be brought to the situation. For games of pure opposition, these additional assumptions may not make much difference—so long as all parties understand the pure-opposition nature of the game. For other games, however (especially for mixed-motive games), nuances of knowledge, communication, and norm enforcement may be crucial for what might be the most logically defensible strategy.[5]

SOLUTIONS

We will not here go into the formal reasoning—the theorems and proofs—by which game theorists derive their solutions for different types of games. We may, however, summarize what strategic solutions are generally recommended for a few of the possible types of games.

For all two-person games of pure opposition with an equilibrium point, each party is advised to stay with the choice leading to this equilibrium. The "minimax" principle (which probably should be called the "maximin" principle, since it encourages seeking the least bad outcome) is persuasive here. One looks for the worst that can happen with each choice, then picks his "best worst" among choices. In Game A, for example, C_1 provides a better worst outcome for Column that C_2, and R_2 for Row has a better worst outcome than R_1. If both follow this minimax principle, they are led to a C_1 and R_2 outcome—and neither can do better unless his opponent chooses irrationally.

All other two-person games of pure opposition can also be "solved" in terms of the same minimax rationale. That is, a particular strategy can be recommended which will be the best a party can achieve against a fully rational opponent. It turns out that this usually involves a strategy mix (that is, a specified probability with which each choice is to be made) rather than a single choice.

Game C, for instance, is a game of pure opposition, but without a saddle point. The reader should examine this game to be convinced that there is no natural equilibrium. Nevertheless, the saddle point philosophy can be applied here to a mixture of choices which would assure each party of his "best least." The general method of doing this involves selecting a choice with a frequency which is inversely proportional to the degree of variability of outcomes which might be experienced with that choice. In the specific case of Game C, the precise recommendations for Column would be to choose C_1 with a probability of $\frac{2}{3}$ and C_2 with a probability of $\frac{1}{3}$. Row is recommended to stay with a probability mixture of $\frac{1}{2}$ for each choice. If the game is played repeatedly, any player varying from these

	C_1	C_2
R_1	−1 (1)	2 (−2)
R_2	1 (−1)	−2 (2)

Game C

proportions would tend to be vulnerable to be taken advantage of by his opponent.[6]

So long as we assume the game to be one of pure opposition, some of the other distinctions between types of games are not particularly meaningful. For instance, pure opposition implies just two parties; an N-person game does not seem to fit unless it can be simplified into coalitions forming two sides—thus producing a two-person game. Utilities in pure-opposition games need not be transferable, interpersonally comparable, or conservative, though the strategy-mix calculations usually suggested require that the outcomes for a given player be measurable on an interval scale. Aspects of the larger situation are not too important either. Complete information is a convenient assumption, though it can be relaxed without changing the strategic situation, so long as each party assumes his informa-

	C_1	C_2
R_1	2 (2)	1 (1)
R_2	1 (1)	0 (0)

Game D

tion is shared by the other. Approximate simultaneity of choices is necessary, though other aspects regarding the nature of the game situation do not seem to matter much. Communication, for example, is irrelevant once the game is thoroughly understood.

Much different is the case with games of pure cooperation or mixed-motive games. In games of pure cooperation, for instance, the presence of effective communication between players may be of the most cruical importance. In fact, the mathematical structure of the game may recede to become almost of no interest. The solution is so obvious that little mathematical reasoning is necessary—if only the players can coordinate their actions. In simple games, such coordination may not pose a significant problem, though in more complex games it may be more difficult.

Consider, for example, Game D. To imagine a concrete example, suppose the players are two brothers, Jim and Joe, who enjoy mutual insults. Their choices are to insult (R_1 or C_1) or not insult (R_2 or C_2). If they both insult (R_1 and C_1), each is doubly happy. If neither insults (R_2 and C_2), each feels quite neutral about the outcome. Both are only moderately pleased when insults are not reciprocated (lower-left or upper-right cells), for they would much prefer the stimulation of mutual insults.

In the above game, clearly the interests of both parties converge in the first choice for each. So, each should simply take this action. The resulting (upper left) outcome clearly fulfills the interests of both. So long as they both see the game in the same terms, there is little question that this is the solution for each.

Let us take another example of a game in which the interests of the players are in complete harmony. In Game E we

	C_1	C_2
R_1	2 (2)	0 (0)
R_2	0 (0)	2 (2)

Game E

have two solutions—either R_1 and C_1 or R_2 and C_2. But which one is to be chosen? It doesn't really matter, so long as the choices are coordinated to match. The problem here is not that of conflict of interest; rather, it is a matter of communication and coordination. In game theory terms, either joint outcome with mutual reward constitutes a solution. In real life there may still be a problem of reaching a solution if the parties are unable to communicate in advance of their choices.

Let us consider a concrete example of this type of situation. For this we will greatly (almost infinitely) expand the choices of each player. Imagine that a friend has left a message that you are to meet her in Washington, D.C., next Friday. You have no way of getting more information before then. Assuming that you both have only this information as to day and place, where will you go to try to meet her? And when? [7]

Obviously the number of possible places in the city of Washington is almost endless, so how is a particular location selected? If you know the other person well, the problem may appear to solve itself almost automatically. For example, you may have a close mutual friend who lives in Washington, or you may belong to an organization with headquarters in that city. In either case, it might be easy to coordinate actions as to place, and just staying there until the other shows up might take care of the time question. But if neither of you has important associates in Washington, then what? Is coordination impossible? Perhaps not, though it is clear that the more shared understanding through communication exists, the easier it is to solve such a game of pure cooperation.

Finally, we consider the matter of mixed-motive games. Does game theory provide us with clear solutions for strategy in such games? Before considering the answer to this question, it is well to remind ourselves that the great majority of real-life conflicts are of this type. Except for parlor or playing-field games, pure opposition is relatively rare. Even war is something less than pure opposition; otherwise war would always end with a total destruction of one of the parties. Almost always, some aspect of common interest is mixed with elements of conflict; and that is essentially what the mixed-motive game represents.

In simple mixed-motive games there sometimes appears to be a natural equilibrium. That is, self-interest choices tend to converge in an outcome which neither party can improve upon. Such an equilibrium point appeared to be present in Game B. However, a careful examination of this game yields another insight: Sometimes the natural equilibrium may not be the best outcome. In Game B the lower-left square satisfied the minimax principle for identifying a saddle point. Also, neither player has any advantage in moving unilaterally from this convergence of choices; it therefore appears to be a stable equilibrium. Still, however, if both can be induced to change their choices at the same time, the result (in the upper-right cell) is clearly better for both than the "equilibrium" solution of 0 for each (in the lower left). This mutually preferred outcome (of 1 for each), however, is difficult to obtain. It requires coordination and agreement. Once it is agreed to, each party is strongly tempted to defect from the agreement; it is to the interest of each to renege on the agreement—provided the other does not.

With games of this sort, game theory comes to an impasse.[8] It can give us no good and simple solution as a guide for strategy. Or more correctly, it gives us diverse solutions that appear to be mutually contradictory. For this we should not blame game theorists. It is to their credit that they have identified formally just how far certain solutions appear to apply and precisely where diverse criteria for a rational solution contradict each other.

Given this impasse, those who have been caught up in the excitement and promise of game theory have several possible approaches open to them. One is to continue to develop game theory as classically conceived. Ever more esoteric questions within the traditional framework of individual rationality may be raised, and more complicated variations can be devised. Elegant solutions can be identified in the more manageable regions of game theory (especially in games of pure opposition). In other areas one can continue to grind out the consequences of different assumptions, even though they may yield diverse solutions. In the present chapter, we have only sketched a very brief introduction to some of the key elements of game theory and applied them to the very simplest of games. The reader who is interested in pursuing this field further will find an ample intellectual challenge in it.[9]

Another approach is to turn away from the quest for a normative science of strategy in favor of the descriptive study of how people actually behave in strategic decision making. Instead of pursuing the full logic of game theory assumptions, we may content ourselves with studying how people actually choose in certain general types of situations which are of special interest to us. This approach will be pursued further in the following chapter.

A third approach to the impasse we find in mixed-motive games is to change our basic assumptions about rational behavior. Purely individual rationality may be supplemented with another kind of rationality based on mutual interests. In the following section, we will pursue this approach further.

CONTENDING COOPERATIVELY

Most of our discussion in the present chapter has assumed a framework of individual rationality. Each party attempts to maximize his values individually. This, however, has led us to rather odd results in certain situations, such as in Game B. There individual rationality led us to a solution which was clearly less than both could obtain if each made the opposite choice. Situations such as this lead us to recognize the limits of using simply an immediate individual rationality as our guide.

In the present section, we will consider an alternative conception of rationality. We will be searching to maximize the interests of all, and not just those of each player individually. We will adopt the overall perspective of a cooperative approach, and only in a secondary manner consider the role of interest conflicts. This contending within an overall cooperative framework is precisely the opposite of the approach we have previously used (namely, that of pursuing directly individual interests in conflict and only secondarily concerning ourselves with possibilities for cooperation).

A key distinction which we will find useful in this more cooperative reformulation of game theory (or, as it is sometimes called in the game theory literature, the "theory of the cooperative game") is between Pareto-optimal and Pareto-deficient outcomes. The Italian social scientist Vilfredo Pareto has given us several tools for formal analysis, and this one has continued to bear his name. A "Pareto-optimal" outcome is a set of joint outcomes which cannot be improved on by any party without someone being disadvantaged. A "Pareto-deficient" outcome is a set of joint outcomes which can be improved on by at least one party without anyone suffering a loss. To illustrate, consider again Game B. The R_2-C_1 solution we considered before is not Pareto-optimal because both players could do better with R_1-C_2. Three cells, in fact, have outcomes which are Pareto-optimal: R_1-C_1, R_1-C_2, and R_2-C_2; in none of these cases could the players find an alternative which would be better for one and no worse for the other.

The first principle for a theory of cooperative games can now be stated: Only Pareto-optimal outcomes can be considered as solutions. Cells which are Pareto-deficient are automatically excluded because they can always be improved upon. But sometimes there are several Pareto-optimal cells, as is the case with Game B; which of these, if any, is to be designated as the solution?

To help us consider the problem of Game B further, let us display it in the form of a graph. We will plot Row's values on the x-axis (or horizontally) and Column's values on the y-axis (vertically). The four combinations of outcomes give us the four points shown in Figure 10.1. Lines are drawn to connect these points; the resulting triangle gives the space within which any mixtures of the various outcomes (if we conceive of averages from the game being repeated a large number of times) would fall. Since the interests of Row are pushing horizontally toward the right and those of Column are pushing upward, their combined interests are pushing toward the upper-right ("northeast") part of the triangle.

Previously we identified R_1-C_1, R_1-C_2, and R_2-C_2 as all Pareto-optimal solutions, viewing the game as a one-shot exercise. If we consider the game as one which may be repeated a large

Figure 10.1 Graphic representation of Game B.

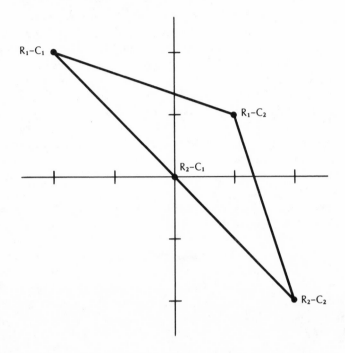

number of times, yielding possibilities of a strategy mix, then we could consider as a Pareto-optimal mixture any point on the two lines connecting R_1-C_1 and R_2-C_2 to R_1-C_2.

But could we not do better and identify a single solution for this game? If so, we need something more than the Pareto-optimum guide. What more might we use?

If we assume that utilities are both conservative and transferable (that is, that they can be saved and exchanged) and that interpersonal comparisons are meaningful (that is, that different players have the same scale of values), then our problem becomes far simpler. We simply go for the outcome with the highest total value. Unless there is some reason why one player should get more than the other, they then make side payments to divide the total reward equally. In Game B this would dictate the choices of R_1-C_2 yielding +1 for each. Since both players already have the same amount of reward, there is no need for any side payment for them to share equally.

It makes little difference for Game B whether we assume that the game is repeated or is played only once. R_1-C_2 remains the cooperative solution in either case. We therefore don't need to bother with the problem of calculating a mixed strategy. Even if we change some of our initial assumptions about the nature of utilities, the R_1-C_2 outcome can still be defended as a solution.[10]

But not all games are so simply analyzed as Game B. Consider, for example, Game F. This can also be expressed graphically, as in Figure 10.2. Here we have two Pareto-optimal outcomes: R_1-C_1 and R_1-C_2. This narrows down the search for a solution to these two possibilities (or to a mixture of them). But which one is the best (or which unique strategy mixture of these two possibilities is recommended)?

	C_1	C_2
R_1	0 (2)	3 (−1)
R_2	−2 (−2)	1 (0)

Game F

Figure 10.2 Graphic representation of Game F.

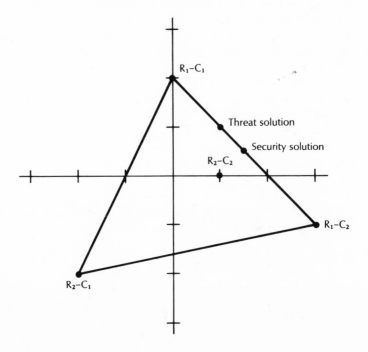

Even if we assume that both players for Game F have the same scale of values for measuring utilities, our search for a solution is not much helped. For both R_1-C_1 and R_1-C_2 have the same total (net) value. And given the fact that the two players now have somewhat different positions, is the assumption that they must share equally in any final value still tenable?

More than one approach has been suggested for resolving these issues in determining a unique solution for coordinating the choices of players in a mixed-motive game. Without going into technical detail any more than necessary, we will now outline the procedures suggested by one mathematician, John Nash. There are other approaches besides that of Nash, and we will mention at least one alternative later; but at present, Nash's approach seems more generally accepted than any alternative.[11]

There are two main steps in obtaining Nash's unique solution: (1) identifying a status-quo point which takes into account the relative positions of the two players, and (2) determining the unique Pareto-optimal point which maximizes the increases in values from the status-quo point. Let us take up each of these in turn.

1. *Identifying a status-quo point.* Nash assumes that differentials in the bargaining power of the two players should be reflected in the status-quo point. This may be done by transforming the game into a new one which represents the difference in interests between players with each outcome, then solving this as a zero-sum game. The solution to the zero-sum game is then used to establish a status-quo point in the original game.[12] For Game F this status-quo point turns out to be R_2-C_1.

2. *Determining a unique Pareto-optimal solution, given a status-quo point.* This is done by moving in the direction of the interests of both players (up and to the right, or "northeast," if graphed as in Figure 10.2) until the Pareto-optimal line is reached. For Game F, this turns out to yield +1 for each player. This point is labeled the "threat solution" in Figure 10.2.[13] It could be obtained by a strategy mix of R_1-C_1 and R_1-C_2 with a ratio of 2:1.

The procedures we have just outlined do give us a unique solution for any mixed-motive game which we may choose to analyze in this way. Essentially, this gives us a single solution cooperatively obtained (by the coordinated actions of players) but which also takes account of the interest conflicts inherent in the game. It allows for the possibility of greater consideration for the player with strategic advantages in the interest conflicts contained within the game. It may be viewed as a "threat point" notion of the status quo—where we should start from if we view the players as already having struggled for maximum advantage.

But is it necessary to start out with such an initial struggle to find a status-quo point? No, it is not necessary. There are alternative procedures. Instead of a threat point, we may identify a "security point" based on the minimum each player can assure himself. To do this, simply let each player identify his choice which contains the "least worst" (that is, the choice for which the worst outcome is better than the worst for any other choice). Then let the least worst value for each player constitute the status-quo point. Then follow the same procedures previously outlined for finding a unique Pareto-optimal point from a given status-quo point. For Game F this procedure identifies a status-quo point at 0 for Row and -1 for Column, which produces a Pareto-optimal solution of 1½ for Row and ½ for Column. This point is labeled in Figure 10.2 the "security solution."[14] It can be obtained (for this particular example) by a strategy mix which equally combines R_1-C_1 and R_1-C_2.

It may be readily seen that of the two solutions we have identified, the security solution is more to Row's interest and the threat solution is more to Column's interest. This is simply a function of the relative positions of the two parties at the status-quo point. Generally the threat status-quo point will be lower for both players than will the security status-quo point, but their relative positions will vary with the particular game structures involved.

Do the procedures which we have just outlined constitute a satisfactory resolution of the problems of the mixed-motive game? Our affirmative answer to this question must be qualified. We have not produced just one general solution. There are instead several solutions, each reflecting a slightly different way of assessing the relative positions of the players. Players will therefore have different interests as to which procedure is used, which may produce a new game of choosing between different approaches to a coordinated solution. Nevertheless, we have shown that reasonable procedures can at least be devised to provide a general approach to solving such games.

We should point out again that our general approach has assumed that the players would, in the end, play the game co-operatively. That is, they would coordinate their actions according to some agreed upon plan. This, in turn, assumes communication between them, and perhaps also a mechanism for enforcing the agreements they reach. They might jockey for relative position, but they would end up working together. In this respect, we have moved a considerable distance from the image of pure conflict and minimal social structure generally associated with game theory. We now assume a social structure which provides the possibility of coordinated action. And the meaning of strategy now becomes less that of acting against another party than that of acting together to resolve a conflict. In keeping with this new perspective on strategy in conflict, we will return to the subject of the present section later in our more general discussion of conflict resolution.

11

A Science of Strategy?

In Chapter 9 we reviewed the Machiavellian tradition, which has been so influential in the political thought of the modern world. The focus was upon a strategic mode of thought which is grounded in a realistic analysis of available opportunities. In Chapter 10 the focus was again on strategy, but within a very different framework. There we dealt primarily not with real-world decision making, but rather with logical and mathematical abstractions as set forth in the theory of games. In the present chapter, the attempt will be to see if these two traditions can be successfully combined. Can we combine real-world strategic thinking with the abstractions of game theory to give us a bona fide science of strategy? That is the question now before us.

IS GAME THEORY APPLICABLE?

In Chapter 10 we introduced and illustrated some of the main ideas of game theory. Our illustrations were not really applications, just examples to help show the operations of game theory concepts. Now the question must be faced: Are these concepts helpful in the real world of human decision making?

First, let us consider the possibility of direct applications. They are few. Planning a security system for an apartment complex or an inspection system for international arms control, calculating the likely consequences of different strategies in games like chess or poker, planning military moves in war games or perhaps in an actual military campaign—these are a few of the situations in which we can imagine direct applications of game theory. Pure conflict can be assumed (at least within the framework used for strategic planning), main alternatives for action can be identified, and possible outcomes can be objectively assessed. Some simplification of the situation will still ordinarily be necessary, for to consider literally all outcomes for all alternatives may still be too ambitious. But we can nevertheless imagine game theory being used as a tool by decision makers in such situations as mentioned above. For the much more common mixed-motive situations (for example, strategy in labor-management negotiations), there are probably too many ambiguities (both in the concrete situations and in the theory of games) for decision makers to make direct applications from game theory.

All in all, it is a rare practical problem that fits nicely into a game theory matrix. There are just too many complications in most situations of the real world. This does not mean that game theory is of no possible value for decision makers in such situations. It may still be a helpful intellectual tool as they sort out some of their main alternatives, but they cannot hope to get their decisions directly from the results of game theory analysis.

Although direct applications of game theory to practical decision making are limited, indirect applications may be more promising. Even for situations which cannot be translated directly into a game theory matrix, the attempt to do so may still be fruitful. Game theory may here serve as a model to guide the decision maker to more rigorous thinking about the interests at stake and the possibilities for realizing them. It can help decision makers recognize certain types of situations in which good decisions are especially difficult, thus cautioning them against too high expectations. This may help to moderate the emotional reactions which might otherwise result in impulsive and short-sighted actions.

Despite these possible applications of game theory to assist decision makers, we must still look elsewhere for the most important applications of game theory. I refer now not to decision makers themselves but to those who systematically analyze decisions in retrospect. These are the social scientists who look at behavior and try to make sense of the patterns of human actions they observe.

An excellent example of this application of game theory is provided by Glenn Snyder and Paul Diesing in their book, *Conflict among Nations*.[1] They select a dozen major international crises (such as the Berlin blockade of 1948–49 and the Cuban missile crisis of 1962) and attempt to study them in terms of game theory (as well as other models of decision making). The result is a considerable clarification of the nature of these crises, their outcomes, and some of their main similarities and differences. This does not require any assumption that the national decision makers involved in these crises were planning their actions in terms of game theory, only that in broad outline the results of their decisions fit into patterns which may be modeled in game theory terms.

Applications may also be made to situations in which we would least expect persons to behave in terms of strategic rationality. Richard Berk, for example, has had some success in applying game theory models to crowd behavior. From this he concludes that crowds are not so irrational as we usually think.[2] This may well be true. However, the retrospective success of a game theory model for clarifying a set of behaviors does not necessarily mean that strategic rationality was used by those behaving. The same result might occur through a process of trial-and-error learning as certain individuals stumble on a solution that others around them find satisfying. Indeed, game theory has even been applied to the apparently blind processes of biological evolution. In a paper on "The Logic of Animal Conflict," J. Maynard Smith and G. R. Price attempt to explain why restraints on violence have evolved in the behavior of most powerful species of animals. By a computer simulation of different contest styles, they have demonstrated a superior long-run survival advantage for a species pursuing a "strategy" for within-species conflict which they characterize as "limited war"—that is, being prepared to fight but without fighting to the death.[3]

NEW DIRECTIONS

In our previous treatment of game theory, we discussed as simply as possible the theory of games which results from certain basic assumptions about interdependent decision making. We may call this "classical game theory" to distinguish it from some variations which we will soon mention.[4] Classical game theory, while satisfying from a mathematical point of view, has some very serious limitations imposed by its primary assumptions. Relaxing any of these assumptions tends to bring complications for our logical analysis. But perhaps some of these complications are necessary in order to bring game theory models closer to action in the real world. In the present section, we will mention several fairly recent developments in game theory which stem from some relaxation of the classical assumptions. Each of these developments gives promise for an increased flexibility in relating game theory to situations of the empirical world.

Among the assumptions which we mentioned at the outset of our discussion of game theory, only the interdependence assumption (that outcomes resulting from a party's choices depend not only on its own choices but also on these of other parties) seems reasonably beyond question. That is, we assume almost by definition that interdependence is involved when there are interest conflicts. Without this assumption, the analysis of strategy would lose most of its meaning.

The exhaustiveness assumption (that every possible outcome which can follow a set of choices or actions is known to each party involved) is clearly more questionable. It serves as a convenient simplification to allow game theorists to get on with the task of mathematical analysis, but it seldom applies completely to any real situation. However, it is possible to relax this assumption. John Harsanyi has made an important beginning in the formal analysis of such "games with incomplete information"; so far, however, there has not been much work to follow up on his lead.[5]

The quantification assumption (that outcomes can be represented quantitatively to show the degree of positive or negative interest of each party in each outcome) has been more commonly relaxed. Game theory has at least increasingly sought only a rank-order assessment of outcomes for a given player, rather than measurement on an interval scale (as is typically assumed in classical game theory). Examples of this trend can be seen in recent work by Anatol Rapoport, Nigel Howard, and Steven Brams.[6] This is probably a step in the direction of realism for representing most situations; seldom do parties in conflict think of their interests as measured by real numbers, but they often compare them in terms of better or worse.

The maximization assumption (that each party seeks to act in such a way as to maximize its own interests) seems generally reasonable. However, this too can be questioned. As Herbert Simon has suggested, much behavior of individuals and organizations seems more geared to assessing whether or not outcomes are "satisficing" than whether they are "maximizing." That is, they seem to respond more to the crude distinction between satisfactory and unsatisfactory outcomes than to the fine gradations necessary to assess maximization.[7] This suggests the need for a new formulation of game theory in which outcomes may be identified as either satisfactory or unsatisfactory, rather than to use either real numbers or rank orders for labeling outcomes.[8]

In addition to these four primary assumptions of classical game theory, two others which are usually made may cause serious difficulties when we try to relate game theory to concrete reality. One of these is the assumption of contemporaneous choice. The other is that interpersonal comparisons of utility typically are excluded.

On the matter of contemporaneous choice, it is true that sequences of choice (what game theorists call "extensive form") can usually be reduced to a matrix pattern (or "normal form"), but to do so leaves out patterns of sequential reasoning which may be critically important. Persons respond not only to an immediate set of opportunities but also to what their eventual opportunities might be after the series of present moves by themselves and their opponents. Game theory needs to consider more seriously how such conditional forms of decision making may be included (though Nigel Howard has certainly made a significant contribution in this direction in his theory of "metagames").*

---

*A "metagame," as Howard uses the term, is a new game derived from the original game by allowing one of the players to choose his strategy after, and with knowledge of, the choices of the other(s); higher-order metagames can deal with questions like "What should I choose if the other chooses that after I have chosen this?"[9]

Interpersonal comparisons are another problem which the classical theory of games has generally tried to avoid. But in the real world, outcomes may be viewed very often within the framework of an interpersonal comparison of utilities. That is, the utility scales of players are affected by each other, and particular outcomes may change in value simply through knowledge of the values which others attach to them. Complications of this sort have been generally ignored in game theory,[10] though this has had its cost in terms of empirical relevance.

It seems to this author that alternative forms must be developed if game theory is to be applied more fully to the great variety of conflicts in our empirical world. I have elsewhere suggested that this might begin with a relaxation of the maximization and quantification assumptions to create a theory of "primitive games" (that is, games for which outcomes are indicated in only positive, negative, and neutral categories).[11] With this simplified mathematical structure, it should be more easy to bring in variations in information conditions, interpersonal contexts, and sequential arrangements and to study more directly the patterns of strategic behavior which result. We might conceive of a basic science of strategy being built in this fashion, a science which would be organized by theoretical constructs but whose main task would be to explain the observed regularities of strategic interaction in the real world. Game theory does not yet (in the writer's view, at least) provide such a science.

Nigel Howard is among the game theorists who have consciously moved away from some of the limitations of classical game theory, especially by taking more into account the conditional nature of choice sequences (in his theory of metagames) and by relaxing the quantitative assumption. He justifies such departures as being in the direction of creating an empirical science. He comments:

> . . . in the early stages of its development nearly every scientific theory has tried do three things at once: it has tried to be *logically necessary* (deducible from logic alone), *normative* (productive by itself of recommendations or guidance as to what we should do), and *empirical*. After much mental effort and revolutionary reconceptualization, each mature science has fi-

nally decided that it can only be the third of these three things. Astronomy, physics, evolutionary theory, economics—each has followed this course; and I believe that the theory of human conflict and cooperation must follow it too.[12]

Can game theory serve as the core theory for such an empirical science of human conflict and cooperation? Perhaps it can, but as Howard implies, this requires a game theory somewhat revised from its classical form. As he also implies, we do not yet have such a comprehensive theory of strategic conflict.

FURTHER COMPLICATIONS

Game theory assumes that all alternatives are laid out for rational assessment by a decision maker. But in the real world of decision making, seldom can *all* the alternatives be identified, let along assessed rationally. To make decisions in these situations, individuals (and organizations) must find ways of selecting what they consider to be the most practical alternatives, then focusing attention on them. This process of selection is one of the most important aspects of decision making in situations of social conflict, and it is made more difficult because conflict tends to heighten some of the potentialities for biased selection.

Decisions are frequently made by a group rather than an individual. When facing the pressures of external conflict, a group often becomes more cohesive. Even with individuals something similar occurs, for, as George Simmel once observed, "The fighter must 'pull himself together.' "[13] The pressures toward unity, however, may have their casualties in decision-making effectiveness. One of the chief casualties is a biased scanning of alternatives for action, selecting only those for attention that are anticipated to have high acceptance by others in the group. The result may well be a group-induced tendency to omit consideration of unusual possibilities of action.

Irving Janis has identified what he calls the "groupthink syndrome," which he sees as especially likely to occur in highly cohesive decision-making groups. He identifies eight symptoms of this syndrome, which may be summarized as follows:

1. An illusion of invulnerability, which makes members of the decision-making group overly optimistic;
2. Collective rationalization, which avoids the reconsideration of policy assumptions;
3. A stance of self-righteousness, which avoids considering possible ethical problems of their decisions;
4. A stereotyped view of the enemy, which neglects to consider how the opposing side might realistically respond;
5. Pressures toward group conformity, which make clear that dissent is not welcome;
6. Self-censorship, which minimizes the doubts and resistances of individual members;
7. A shared illusion of unanimity, which results from the above factors and leads to a sense of consensus; and
8. The emergence of self-appointed "mindguards," which protect the group from information which might oppose their consensus.[14]

The general effect of such features is to reduce the quality of decision making. In his book *Victims of Groupthink,* Janis explores several recent cases in the making of American foreign policy in which the operation of these tendencies by policy-making groups seemed to be especially important factors (such as the Bay of Pigs invasion and escalation in the Vietnam War).[15]

If group forces are often important factors in poor decisions, would we not be better off to rely more on individuals? Probably not. Committees are a part of policy formation in organizations for very good reasons. They usually help to give a more critical analysis of the alternatives than would be the case with a single decision maker. And individual decision makers also have additional shortcomings.

Recent work in the psychology of decision making has made us much more aware that the basic psychological processes involved are fraught with possibilities of error. There are, first of all, the effects of stress, so often present in a conflict situation. The "hot" cognitive processes aroused by stress frequently short-circuit a thorough search of policy alternatives, as we saw in Holsti's analysis of the onset of World War I (in Chapter 8).[16] But there are also the "cool" processes which occur when no particular stress is present; here too human judgment is easily liable to err. And such errors follow some clearly identifiable patterns. Two of these have been called the "representativeness bias" and the "availability bias", respectively. We are indebted to Amos Tversky and Daniel Kahneman for clarifying how these two sources of error operate in everyday processes of judgment.[17]

Much everyday judgment involves an implicit estimation of probabilities. In doing so, we are especially prone to take account of resemblances to what we imagine to be typical. A strikingly beautiful woman on the street may be thought of as a fashion model because of our association of models with beauty, even though she is much more likely to be a housewife. If we have been robbed by a Pakistani, we are apt to think of people from Pakistan as thieves—despite all available evidence to the contrary. If we expect rain at least once a week in April and we approach the final days of the month without any rain for eight days, we may feel sure it will rain within the next day or two—in spite of contrary reports from the weather forecaster. All of these are examples of what Tversky and Kahneman call the "representativeness heuristic." This process of analytic simplification makes judgments easier by ignoring base rate probabilities (such as the small relative number of fashion models in the population), limited sample sizes (for example, having been robbed only once), and by other misconceptions of chance (such as that the weather must follow a law of averages regardless of meteorological conditions).

Somewhat similar is the availability bias. This leads us to judge the plausibility of an idea by the ease with which it can be brought to mind. Having once seen a fire in an office building, it is easier to imagine another fire in the office where we work than the restaurant where we eat. Having known dozens of Americans of Japanese ancestry who were Protestant Christians, it may be hard for us to think of a new acquaintance as a Buddhist. If we know someone who was injured in a traffic accident recently, we are apt to consider the rate of accidents as unusually high although it has actually remained constant.

In all of these cases, the availability of evidence leads us to-overestimate its significance.[18]

We do not mean to imply that such analytical shortcuts as we have just mentioned necessarily incline us to judgmental errors. We find both the representativeness heuristic and that of availability generally useful. The problem comes when we use these tools of thought habitually and uncritically—as we often do.

Let us return now to the decision maker involved in a complex instance of social conflict. Imagine, for example, the foreign minister of a nation which is locked in a dispute with a neighboring country. His thinking is apt to be biased by overuse of common heuristics of judgment. Emotionally laden pressures—of himself, his prime minister, or from the press and the people—tend to lower his ability for reflective analysis. His policy advisors may in addition be suffering from groupthink, giving him a very incomplete assessment of the policy options available. Finally, there are the imponderables about what the decision makers of the other country will soon do—and what they might do eventually, depending upon all the varieties of intervening contingencies. Can we really imagine a science of strategy which would be useful to such a decision maker?

Before we too quickly answer no, let us clear up some possible misconceptions. The phrase "science of strategy" may bring to mind some scheme of precise prediction and complete certainty which can be concretely applied. But this is not necessarily the case. The generalizations of science cannot always be translated into precise predictions. Nor can they necessarily always be concretely applied—at least not to every problem we may have at hand. And complete certainty is by definition outside the range of empirical science (which always, and by definition, must be satisfied with tentative generalizations that are subject to disconfirmation by further evidence).

Once we recognize the more modest implications of the phrase "science of strategy," we begin to see some of its bits and pieces already in existence. Significant scientific contributions are available to the decision maker, such as the foreign minister mentioned above. The systematic study of international behavior has been developed by political scientists. Sociological and anthropological studies may point to important societal and cultural dimensions to consider. The social psychology of groups (and the systematic study of public opinion) points out some of the limitations which social factors impose upon effective decision making, and such areas of knowledge may be taken into account in planning for decisions—as well as knowledge gained from the psychology of human judgment and decision making. All of these scientific fields are relevant for our decision maker's consideration of strategy. But of course, none of them simply dictates any decision. Rather, they point to factors to consider, along with the decision maker's empirical assessment of present realities.

And what about the theory of games? At present it is mainly a logical tool, which may be used to help think through some central aspect of a problem. In the future it might develop into a more generally applicable and empirically based study of conflict behavior (or, if you will, a true general science of strategy), but this is not yet an achievement. Sitll, the logical clarification that can be provided by game theory formulations is at least a useful tool for the decision maker's thinking.

Suppose that twenty years from now all the scientific fields mentioned above will have shown continued development, and that game theory in particular has evolved into a general empirical science of interdependent decision making. Would this fundamentally change the task of a major national decision maker? The writer would think not. There is still the concrete situation of choice to be faced. The necessity of responsible choice is not eliminated by sharpening the intellectual tools which may be applied; even if these tools may be used to reduce some of the ambiguities of the decision-making situation, significant imponderables will always remain. The actual making of decisions will therefore remain more of an art than a science; scientific tools may help it become a more fully rational art, but an art it nevertheless will remain.

Part Five

The Resolution of Conflict

12

The Dynamics of Bargaining

Bargaining may be said to occur when (1) two parties face each other in a mixed-motive situation (that is, with significant potential common interests as well as conflicts of interest); (2) both parties consider it possible that some agreement or understanding might be reached which would leave them better off than if such an agreement is not reached; and (3) they enter into a process of discussion, including the consideration of proposals and counterproposals, in search of some commonly agreed upon solution.

As we use the terms, "negotiation" and "bargaining" are roughly synonymous. Both emphasize a process of discussion between parties in search of an agreed upon solution. Although the connotation of "negotiation" puts more emphasis on the process of conferring and "bargaining" connotes more attention to the underlying structure of interests and how it may be modified through agreement, we will not quibble over these differences in emphasis. We do need to recognize, however, that not everything of importance in the bargaining process goes on in the face-to-face negotiations between parties. There must also be recognition of the role of actions that may be taken away from the bargaining table. Such implicit or tacit bargaining is not well suggested by the term "negotiations" (which implies an explicit attention to discussing proposals and counterproposals), though important real-world negotiations are rare without some degree of such side action. It is of course also possible that the forms of negotiation will be used without any real bargaining. This occurs when one of the parties privately decides that there are really no advantages to be gained by an agreement. In such a case, we do not really have all the requirements previously mentioned (in particular, that both parties consider an agreement possible which might improve their situation). There still, however, may be legal or public-relations purposes to be served through negotiations—though at the risk of accusations of "bad faith bargaining."

Bargaining in Real-World Settings

Systematic studies of negotiations in real-world settings have been done primarily in the areas of labor-management relations and international negotiations. Of these two areas, the patterns observed in labor-management relations appear more clearly established (perhaps because the issues in international negotiations vary more from case to case). We will therefore attempt to summarize the basic patterns observed in labor-management negotiations for our initial understandings of the dynamics of bargaining.

In this section, we shall draw especially on books by Ann Douglas and by Richard Walton and Robert McKersie.[1] Douglas presents a systematic analysis of a series of directly observed labor-management negotiations, pointing to basic regularities which may be therein discovered. Walton and McKersie take a more analytical approach, incorporating the evidence from many sources into their behavioral theory framework. Both of these works draw primarily on industrial relations in the United States. This may give a certain emphasis to our discussion which may not fit precisely other forms of negotiations or even industrial relations in other parts of the world.[2]

The typical pattern of American labor-management negotiations falls into three stages which can be identified as (1) establishing the positions, (2) exploring the strengths and weaknesses of positions, and (3) reaching a conclusion. Although there are usually no clear-cut markers to separate these phases, most bargaining sessions do fit one or another of these categories. And the order for these phases is always the same.

The first stage of negotiations is apt to involve some long and rather formal speechmaking as both sides lay out in detail their well-planned positions. Positions are stated with strong conviction, as though the contrasting arguments of the other side are not worth serious attention. Both sides know that there will have to be some retreat from these carefully prepared positions, but both appear to believe that the retreat will have to be made entirely by the other party. As the positions are stated, there are obvious differences which appear irreconcilable; and a spirit of antagonism often tends to emerge. Sometimes the antagonism presents itself in direct attacks upon the positions of each other, and occasionally it grows into apparent personal animosity (we say "apparent" because skilled negotiators must be able to use bitter language at one point in negotiations and still be able to smile happily with each other before the cameras when an agreement is announced).

If they could be present to witness the events of early bargaining sessions, casual neutral observers would be dismayed at the gulf between positions and the apparent lack of any spirit of compromise. They would question whether such sessions really can serve the purposes of conflict resolution. But experienced negotiators understand that an essential function is being fulfilled. In stating their positions, the parties are establishing the framework for bargaining. In more technical terms, they are establishing the "negotiating range"—all that area which includes and lies between their stated positions—within which any settlement must be found. It is an unwritten law that a position, once initially set forth, will not be changed in the direction away from the other party (such a move would generally be considered "bad faith" bargaining). So, by establishing their positions, both parties know the area within which to search for an agreement. And the more strongly these positions are presented, the more clearly the parties understand the range of potential solutions.

The second stage or phase of negotiations occurs as the parties probe for weaknesses in the positions of each other. This is a rather delicate business, and there is a great deal of subtle communication necessary. Both parties stoutly claim to hold to their original positions, but through critical questioning each begins to sense which elements in the adversary's proposal offer most room for compromise. Considerable skepticism is expressed about the opponent's proposals in order to search for possible weaknesses. There is a great deal of indirect communication in the nuances of tone and phrasing. Then at last there is the indication that one side is "willing to discuss" some hypothetical point even though it may contradict the stated position. This is the signal that here may be a place for some compromise—even though it is maintained that it is just a hypothetical discussion. One must be careful here, though. To enter too early or easily into hypothetical discussions which suggest some possible concessions may not always be productive. As Douglas points out:

> With the parties working simultaneously in two directions, both to give and to obtain cues, concessions ahead of schedule benefit no one, not even the receiving party. Not only does a party tantalize and mislead the opponent if it relaxes its firmness too quickly, but the parties also need the opportunity to experience exhaustion of their demands before they can be satisfied that they have drained what was there to be had. Premature movement robs them of this experience.[3]

Great patience is necessary, as the probing may go on for session after session with little sense of overall movement. Nevertheless, there are cues which accumulate to show the parties where movement may be most likely. Furthermore, through the sparring between parties, an impression is gained of their relative strengths and thus a basis for assessing how far the other side might be pushed in a showdown.

Finally, there comes a time for bringing the negotiations to a head. Sometimes this occurs when one side presents a new "compromise" proposal, perhaps including in one package a number of the points discussed earlier in hypothetical fashion; this might be followed by a counterproposal from the other side and some hard bargaining to reduce the differences (such as, "if we yield some ground on Section B, will you be willing to accept our Section D?"). Sometimes the proposals and counterproposals had been presented earlier but were not then considered seriously. At any rate, sooner or later there comes the sense that further sparring would be redundant, that all important issues have been exhaustively discussed, and that one understands the opponent's strengths and weaknesses as much as would be possible through further discussion. When both parties have come to this point of view, then it is time to bring the negotiations to a conclusion. The parties now focus systematically on how they can reduce the bargaining range which divides them and still protect the interests of their side. Activity around the bargaining table increases, as does the intensity of contacts each group carries on with leaders of its constituency who are not represented around the table. If a deadline has been imposed for negotiations, the approach of this time may signal a special need for a conclusion, bringing the negotiators into all-night sessions just before this deadline.

Sometimes the conclusion must be that the parties cannot reach an agreement. If such an impasse becomes clear, there is usually little reason to continue with negotiations. They are simply broken off, allowing the consequences (such as a strike or an indefinite extension of the old contract) to occur as they may. This may only delay the time for reaching an agreement, which sooner or later must be concluded; however, it may be more possible to reach an agreement after, say, a strike of six weeks than had been possible before the strike was called. Except in instances where the parties represented at the bargaining table are not really the critical parties for resolving the dispute (for example, a school board's restraint in raising teachers' salaries may simply reflect voter resistance to local tax increases which teachers may hope to change through a strike), both parties typically have more to gain from a settlement than no settlement at all. The problem is to work through to a compromise which both in the end will find acceptable—despite its distance from the positions forcefully presented at the start of negotiations.

Our previous discussion has emphasized the process of compromise between two initially opposing positions. However, one must guard against too simple a characterization of the dynamics of bargaining, recognizing that what we have examined is only a commonly observed pattern and not necessarily an inevitable series of distinct stages. A framework suggested by Walton and McKersie reveals more clearly some of the further complications which are typically part of the bargaining process. Walton and McKersie use a behavioral theory with four central models to sum up the essential features of bargaining. These models, which are all assumed to be relevant to bargaining at any stage in negotiations (though some, of course, may be more dominant at one phase than at others), are identified as those of (1) distributive bargaining, (2) integrative bargaining, (3) attitudinal structuring, and (4) intraorganizational bargaining.[4]

"Distributive bargaining" is probably the most obvious aspect of negotiations. It refers to the process of resolving the differences between the bargaining positions of the two parties. It is distributive in the sense that the closer a solution is to one party, the greater must be the sacrifice of the other party. There is here, in other words, a direct conflict of interests. Each party attempts to manipulate the negotiations so that the conclusion will come as close as possible to its own preferred position—leaving the other side to make most of the concessions. At the same time, each must resist the pressures which come from the opposing side. Both do this by presenting forcefully and with conviction their own positions, responding with considerable skepticism to the position of the other side, and by pointing to numerous facts which support the needs of one's own case and undermine those of the other side. Tactics of commitment are also important features of distributive bargaining. Public commitments to the rank and file by the union or to the stockholders by management may effectively make certain parts of the opponent's position impossible to accept; if so, the opponent may be left with no choice but to yield—if an impasse is to be avoided. A general reluctance to yield may be another important tactic for distributive bargaining, for the side which can resist making concessions most stubbornly will have its views most successfully represented in the final agreement, if there is a final agreement.

"Integrative bargaining" refers to the process of resolving problems of mutual interest. On some specific issues the two sides may have common or complementary interests, and negotiations may help the parties decide how these can best be pursued. Product quality, market position, and worker morale offer examples of areas where union and management interests may often be similar. In terms of the negotiations themselves, there is a common interest that they proceed in some reasonable fashion and that some agreement is finally concluded. Of course, there may be sharp differences over the specific terms of the agreement, but that there should be an agreement will at least give some structure for the common interests of both sides. One of the key dilemmas for negotiators is how far to push for integrative (cooperative) bargaining at the expense of distributive (competitive) bargaining. To neglect hard-nosed distributive bargaining may lead to a loss for one's own interests in the ultimate conclusion, but to neglect integrative bargaining may well result in no agreement at all. A frequent response to this dilemma is to engage in a large amount of tacit communication. Understandings may be implied by the selective focus on issues, or by gestures or intonation in discussing certain points; such understandings may serve to carry the bargaining forward along integrative lines without formally relinquishing any of one's own positions.

"Attitudinal structuring" refers to the influence negotiators exert on the thinking of each other. With all the expressions of resistance which may be observed in negotiation sessions, it is sometimes not obvious how much the parties may be influencing each other. Nevertheless, the facts and opinions presented are selected at least in part for their power to persuade, and some of the intended messages do get through. This is necessary for both effective distributive bargaining and integrative bargaining. Without being able to convince the other side of the importance of one's own needs, it is difficult to get a favorable settlement. And unless there is an effective process of mutual learning on matters of common interest, there may be no agreement at all.

Not only may the parties influence the thinking of each other about particular items under discussion, but there are also fundamental attitudes about their general relationship which may be critically altered through negotiations. Such general attitude structuring may not always create understanding in a positive sense; it may also include a growth of antagonism and a conclusion that the other side cannot be trusted to negotiate in good faith for common objectives. Whatever the outcome, however, there is mutual influence going on. Perceptions the parties have of each other and of the salient issues are shaped by both what is said in negotiations and the way it is said.

Finally, there is "intraorganizational bargaining." This refers to the process by which each side comes to its own set of proposals initially, as well as the process by which new positions are accepted during the course of negotiations. In the three previous models of negotiations, we have treated each of the two parties as if it were a single actor. In truth, of course, each side represents a diverse set of interests, and to present a united front for negotiations is often a very difficult task. Nevertheless, a consensus must be obtained and presented if bargaining is to get effectively under way. Furthermore, each side must continually touch base with its constituency as negotiations continue. This is necessary to avoid impossible expectations, to explore the feasibility of various possible compromises, and to prepare other members of one's organization for the form of agreement which appears most likely to result. As the period for reaching a conclusion approaches, negotiations typically become more intense both at the bargaining table and in intraorganizational bargaining. A rationalization must be given for discrepancies between the original position presented and the kind of compromise currently considered. There must be some assessment of support for the possible agreement, and efforts made to convince those who hesitate to join the consensus. This is typically more of a problem on the side of labor than with management, because management usually negotiates as a more tightly organized group. Management negotiators may therefore need to clear positions with only one or two persons not present at the table, while the union may have concerns about ratification by the rank and file as well as the support of a dozen or so key leaders.

Although these four models of the negotiation process (distributive bargaining, integrative bargaining, attitudinal structuring, and intraorganizational bargaining) are derived primarily from industrial studies, they can be applied to the analysis of almost any kind of bargaining. They are especially useful in classifying the major forms of activity in real-world bargaining behavior. As we move from this world to the laboratory, however, our sights typically become focused on more specific aspects of bargaining, as we will directly see.

BARGAINING IN THE LABORATORY

Distributive bargaining is the focus of some of the most important experimental work on bargaining behavior. How do bargainers "divide the pie" under different bargaining conditions? An early example of how this question might be addressed experimentally was done by Sidney Siegel and Lawrence Fouraker in simulations of economic factors of bargaining. They rigidly limited the form of social contact of bargainers in their laboratory studies; indeed, negotiators did not even know with which other individuals they were bargaining (all communications were by written notes conveyed by the experimenter, and only messages about the quantitative aspects of a possible agreement had any real purpose). The investigators gave central attention to the quantitative properties of agreements which negotiators would reach under different experimental conditions.

In an initial series of experiments, Siegel and Fouraker explored the case of bilateral monopoly with equal bargaining strength. That is, the two parties negotiating (one in the role of buyer and one as seller) had equal power to suggest deals which combined price and quantity figures. Negotiations were usually allowed to continue until an agreement was concluded. The most commonly obtained pattern of agreements specified a quantity which would maximize joint interests and a price which would provide an equal split between buyer and seller. An equal division was most likely, furthermore, the more complete were the conditions of information.[5]

Another series of experiments simulated the unequal-strength case. In this series, price leadership was created by having the seller set the price and the buyer choose the quantity. This creates a situation of special theoretical interest in that there is a built-in incentive for the seller to maximize his share of the profits by suggesting a price which allows less than the maximum possible joint return. In technical terms, there is an equilibrium solution which is less than a Pareto optimum. In basic structure, therefore, this case raises interesting questions about the conditions under which bargainers will be able to raise themselves above the equilibrium solution. In most of their experiments, Fouraker and Siegel found bargainers preferring the equilibrium solution. However, their series of experiments demonstrated that three variables could strengthen the tendency toward higher joint profits than the equilibrium. The strongest variable was that of the form of bidding; an opportunity for repeated bidding on a series of contracts moved the parties further toward higher joint profits than when only a single bid was allowed. The amount of information given also affected the results; in particular, if parties had complete information about each other's rates of return, they were more apt to move to a joint maximum than if they had tables which gave only their own returns. Finally, if the joint maximum allowed an equal division of profits, it was more likely to be selected than if such an equal division were not possible. In fact, the only experimental condition in which most subjects moved to agreements near the joint maximum was one which combined all three of these variables to provide repeated bids, complete information about each other's profit tables, *and* the possibility of an equal split of joint profits.[6]

Fouraker and Siegel also report on a series of experiments simulating conditions of oligopoly by having either two or three sellers. As is not surprising, an increase in the number of sellers also increases the tendency toward competition or rivalry. It is not necessary to characterize the rather complex results of these oligopolistic experiments, since our interest in negotiations is more directed to the two-party (or "bilateral monopoly") case. However, we may note that one secondary theme was present in the interpretation of these experiments which the same authors also indicated in their discussion of bilateral monopoly results. This is the importance of the level-of-aspiration concept. Although it was not directly manipulated experimentally, the authors found a level-of-aspiration interpretation useful in searching for consistent patterns in their data. According to a level-of-aspiration theory of bargaining, parties start negotiations with a certain expectation level in mind. They will show cooperative behavior in negotiations so long as they consider it likely that their expectations will eventually be realized. Should, however, the other party behave in such a way as to negate these expectations, two results are apt to follow: The first party will become more competitive in behavior, and expectations about the level or timing of an ultimate agreement will be reconsidered.

Among recent laboratory experiments of negotiations, those by Otomar Bartos are of special interest. Rather than use a simulation of economic transactions as the basic model for experimentation, Bartos used international negotiations. In one series of negotiations, for example, he had subjects play the roles of the Soviet Union, Great Britain, France, the United States, and the People's Republic of China, giving each information about a number of possible issues on which they might reach agreement. Each also was given a value (translated into real money consequences for participants) for any possible agreement. Behavior was then observed for up to two hours as the parties sought to negotiate a common agreement or package of agreements; outcomes for all parties were zero if no agreement could be negotiated within the two-hour period.[7]

Bartos goes to great lengths to test the adequacy of various mathematical models. He derives a negotiation model from the arms race conceptualizations of Lewis Richardson (see Chapter 6), substituting negotiation demands for armaments spending and slightly changing the form of Richardson's equations. This model turns out to describe the *process* of bargaining moves in Bartos' experiments surprisingly well. As to the *point* at which the parties are most apt to come to an agreement, Bartos compares a number of models. Among them, that derived from the work of Nash (which we discussed in Chapter 10) seems to approximate most closely the agreements actually obtained. Agreements tended toward a point which would be proportional to what each would have as the maximum possible when the other received nothing. In a later summary model of the negotiation process, Bartos uses the Nash model as a definition of fairness, and suggests that it might be realized in practice as follows:

> The theory proposes that each negotiator should search for a proposal that is favorable to him but barely acceptable to the opponent. Once a pair of such proposals is found, the negotiation can start and the two proposals are viewed as opening bids. Moreover, if there is a series of bids before an agreement is reached, each negotiator ought to view his opponent's last bid as fair if (and only if) it does not alter his expectations about what the ultimate agreement will be.[8]

Note that each party identifies an expected solution on the basis of a "fair" division, given opening positions. The assumption of fairness borrowed from Nash is essentially that of an even split of the difference between opening positions. So long as bids are not inconsistent with progress toward this expected solution, negotiations may proceed with effective progress. This suggests that when negotiations break down, it is either because the opening presentations had misrepresented the real bargaining positions of the parties or because one or both sides had misjudged the point for an equitable compromise.

Bartos obviously gives a central place to level-of-aspiration concepts. In his formulation, the levels of aspiration for negotiating parties are derived primarily from their opening positions. Another scholar of negotiations who has emphasized the importance of expectation levels is John Cross, who has made some notable refinements in his analysis of the bargaining process. However, he puts less emphasis than Bartos on the initial positions presented. Cross basically views negotiations as a learning process in which parties gradually adapt their expectations until an agreement becomes feasible.[9]

Although the particular theoretical formulations and results of the work just reviewed show important variations from author to author, there is a clear general interpretation of the negotiating process suggested by this experimental work. This interpretation emphasizes a gradual rapprochement of the conflicting parties. This rapprochement is guided by the aspirations set in motion by the initial positions (stated to maximize the self-interest of each), but it is also affected by changes in expectations which may be created by the negotiations. As they respond to their own interests and to the actions of each other, the parties gradually converge on a compromise consistent with the expectations created through the negotiation process.

FURTHER CONSIDERATIONS

The laboratory studies cited in the last section do not begin to exhaust the experimental literature of bargaining behavior.[10] Our interest was in choosing a few studies focused on the essential nature of a bargaining relationship which could be reviewed with minimal technical detail. These studies provide a central general interpretation of the bargaining process which is reasonably consistent with our earlier discussion of bargaining in real-world settings.

So far, things seem to fit together quite nicely. There are, however, further considerations which keep the bargaining process from fitting perfectly into the mold we have just described. One problem concerns the identification of initial positions. Our early characterization of labor-management negotiations emphasized that these initial positions constitute the framework for bargaining, and our interpretation of experimental work (especially that following from Bartos) saw the outcome of negotiations as largely determined by these positions. If, however, initial positions are this critical, they cannot be so simple to develop and present as we have implied. For if the outcome depends on one's initial position, surely it is important to present an initial position which maximizes one's advantage. This means that a realistic consideration of the situation and one's own interests may not be all that is important; strategic considerations for subsequent bargaining may also enter into the presentation of initial positions. This helps us to understand not only that strategic care must be taken in presenting one's own position, but also why skepticism and resistance may be needed in receiving the initial position of the other party. Initial positions cannot be simply accepted at face value; they must also, in a real sense, be negotiated. That is, a position must be fully established not just by an initial presentation but also by surviving the critical objections of the other party. Each side must be able to pierce through the exaggerations and outright deceptions of the other party to perceive what in fact is the realistic position (which is often different from the officially presented position) of the other side. This must be done if effective bargaining is to follow.

If initial positions cannot be taken at face value, but rather themselves come to be defined through early negotiations, then surely expectations about an equitable solution are not easy to identify either. Part of the problem is the difficulty of clearly identifying suitable initial positions (especially those that meet the standard of being barely acceptable to the other and serving the best advantage for oneself). Another part of the problem is that there is more than a single definition of equity possible. Insofar as different conceptions of equity may be possible, expectations regarding a proper solution may well be influenced by the degree to which a given definition of equity facilitates one's own interests. Equity too may therefore be a matter for some negotiation (usually implicit and indirect) before the expectations of the two parties can converge on a solution.

It is true that one particular model of equity (identified as the Nash solution) received the strongest support in experiments by Bartos. We must, however, remain open to the possibility that different models of equity may be applicable in different bargaining contexts, if only because assumptions about "other things being equal" may not always be appropriate. For example, we generally assume an equality between the parties in two-party bargaining, but this may not always be true. This may help explain why at least one attempt to test the predictions of the Nash model in real-world collective bargaining failed to find substantial support (in this study by Daniel Hamermesh, management received more and unions less than the Nash model of equity would appear to predict).[11]

Another limitation of the picture of bargaining previously presented is that the positions of parties may be changed through the bargaining process. Certain strategic moves may actually change the reality perceived by both parties and thus the positions each may realistically take. Bargaining commitments and threats may have such an effect. For example, a public pledge by union negotiators to recommend a strike if a certain wage level is not attained may make it impossible for negotiators to consider wages below that level. The framework for negotiations may therefore be effectively changed through events that grow out of bargaining.

Finally, we need to recognize that some negotiations are on much more complex issues than others. Studies of negotiations we have examined have generally sought a simplification of issues in order to bring a greater precision to the analysis. The focus has been mostly on economic issues, and the conditions of negotiations (especially in the laboratory studies we have included) have been quite standardized. When the issues become more varied and less easily subject to quantification and when the parties have a less well-established pattern for negotiations, then we might find less clear support for predictions such as we have examined.

William Zartman characterizes the approach toward bargaining which we presented in the last section as the "concession/convergence approach." He suggests that for many instances of real-world bargaining this represents a misleading model. After briefly examining recent international negotiations (including the 1962 Cuban missile crisis, the Paris negotiations to end the war in Vietnam, and Henry Kissinger's role in Middle East peace talks), Zartman concludes that a more useful general model would be what he calls a "formula/detail approach." As he summarizes this model:

> Rather than a matter of convergence through incremental concessions from specific initial positions, negotiation is a matter of finding the proper *formula* and implementing *detail*. Above all, negotiators seek a general definition of the items under discussion, conceived and grouped in such a way as to be susceptible of joint agreement under a common notion of justice. Once agreement on a formula is achieved, it is possible to turn to the specifics of items and to exchange proposals, concessions, and agreements. Even then, details are resolved most frequently in terms of the referents which justify them and give them value rather than in their own intrinsic values. This means that convergence does not take place by inching

from fixed positions toward a middle, but rather by establishing a referent principle from which the value of the detailed item will be derived.[12]

Henry Kissinger's description of his own negotiating style is somewhat similar to Zartman's characterization of a formula/ detail approach. While discussing negotiations to end the Vietnam War, Kissinger records in his memoirs:

> In the negotiations that I conducted I always tried to determine the most reasonable outcome and then get there rapidly in one or two moves. This was derided as a strategy of "preemptive concession" by those who like to make their moves in driblets and at the last moment. But I consider that strategy useful primarily for placating bureaucracies and salving consciences. It impresses novices as a demonstration of toughness. Usually it proves to be self-defeating; shaving the salami encourages the other side to hold on to see what the next concession is likely to be, never sure that one has really reached the rock-bottom position. Thus, in the many negotiations I undertook—with the Vietnamese and others—I favored big steps taken when they were least expected, when there was a minimum of pressure, and creating the presumption that we would stick to that position. I almost always opposed modifications of our negotiating position under duress.[13]

An even broader view of negotiations is presented by Anselm Strauss in his book *Negotiations*. Strauss considers not only explicit negotiations in formal bargaining sessions but also a wide variety of implicit negotiations which take place in everyday interaction. He emphasizes that all social orders are to some degree "negotiated orders"—that negotiation in the sense of an agreement derived through the interaction of contending parties is to some degree present in all social relationships. Furthermore, Strauss emphasizes that the forms that negotiations take depend fundamentally on the nature of the larger social context. To focus upon the explicit bargaining over, say, wages and hours in an industrial contract dispute may lead us to neglect the more basic aspects of negotiation going on, such as the fundamental relationship assumed for the nature of labor-management cooperation.[14]

Writings such as those of Zartman and Strauss should help us guard against a too neatly limiting conceptualization of the process of bargaining in the resolution of conflicts. Given a conflict of interests between two parties which may be clearly defined in quantifiable terms and where the pattern of relationships between the parties is well established, under these conditions we may derive from laboratory studies some well-founded generalizations about the process toward agreement and the most likely outcome of negotiations. Often, however, the conditions are more complex. Then the negotiation process does not simply take place within the assumed constraints but may function at least partly to redefine these very constraints. The result may be a new pattern for the relationship between parties which goes far beyond a simple division of interests on a single commonly agreed upon dimension. Bargaining, in this perspective, becomes much more creative than a first look at a typical labor-management bargaining session would suggest.

13

Varieties of Resolution

Popular discussions of conflict resolution often suggest that there are just two alternatives: negotiations or physical force. We generally think first of negotiations as a vehicle for resolving conflict; force is seen as a last resort, to be applied when negotiations fail to produce effective results.

We have followed this popular framework by presenting first (in the preceding chapter) an examination of negotiations and bargaining. Later in the present chapter, we will consider conflict resolution by physical force. Before we do so, however, we should point out the simplistic nature of much popular thinking in this area. We think of negotiations and force as though they are quite distinct approaches; in reality, however, they may merge into one another. In the previous chapter, we touched briefly on the role of threats and other unilateral actions in changing the framework for negotiations, and we must not neglect the possibility that forceful actions by either party (such as a strike or lockout threat, or even some implication of direct physical punishment) may enter into considerations weighed around a negotiating table. Particularly is this true in international negotiations, where the rule of law is more uncertain than in most domestic disputes. And even when there is no negotiating table, the forceful actions of parties may be seen as a form of implicit bargaining, as we will consider later in the present chapter.[1]

Another popular simplification is in the limited recognition of the wide variety of forms of conflict resolution which have been actually used in human affairs. We will review numerous examples in the next section of this chapter. We should, however, bear in mind that most of these are not mutually exclusive patterns; any concrete case may well have a mixture of forms of conflict resolution.

To expand on this last point, we may briefly consider assimilation (fusion into a common identity) and segregation (mutual avoidance and a delineation of separate spheres). These two sociological processes will be treated in the next section as though they provided opposite forms of conflict resolution. It is, however, not uncommon to find mixtures of these patterns. For example, two craft unions may join together in a common labor organization for general purposes but still draw a sharp boundary line between their spheres in resolving jurisdictional disputes. Or two large oil companies may join forces for certain international operations and still remain competitors for domestic distribution. Political organizations also show similar combinations of opposite patterns. Under a parliamentary system, a coalition government may be formed without eliminating the separate identities of the parties involved. And nation-states may help to reduce some of their conflicts through formation of a larger body such as the United Nations or the Organization of American States, and at the same time this larger body may help the nations define and protect their separate identities and "sovereign" interests.

In sum, any concrete case may carry the legacy of a rich mixture of forms of conflict resolution. Some of the theoretically possible forms will be outlined in the following brief detour into local American politics.

GRASS ROOTS PACIFICATION

Hundreds of times in America's past, localities have vied with each other for the honor of being established as the seat of county government. This writer has investigated dozens of such cases which developed to the point of a violent confrontation between towns; these cases, especially common in states of the Midwest, are known to local and regional historians as "county seat wars." Considerable energy has been expended in these little local "wars," and numerous tales of high (and low) strategy could be recounted. At present, however, we are on the subject of conflict resolution, and it is in this context that we here wish to examine the county seat wars. These struggles illustrate a wide variety of approaches to conflict resolution.[2]

Most states have laws providing for local elections to decide issues of county seat location. The central issue of a county seat war has therefore usually been decided by a vote of local citizens. But these elections were themselves often contested, leading to numerous court cases. In the normal pattern of resolution of a county seat dispute, the battle was waged first by the ballot box and then, when necessary, through the courts. Resolution therefore occurred most commonly by popular vote, with adjudication providing settlement for cases of extreme controversy. There were some cases, however, in which elections and adjudication were not sufficient to provide resolution. Or at least these normal means of resolution have not been the only ones applied for settling a county seat war. In the process of examining other approaches toward settlement of these disputes, we may remind ourselves of some of the richly varied ways that human conflicts may be resolved.

Negotiations have occasionally been a primary route toward resolution of a county seat war. Grant County, in northeastern South Dakota, offers such an example; an agreement was formally drawn up and signed in 1883 by representatives of the warring towns of Milbank and Big Stone City. Similar formal negotiations between leaders of Crete and Wilber brought their dispute over the location of the Saline (Nebraska) county seat to an end in the present century.

Adjoining Grant County, South Dakota, is Roberts County. The original county seat of Roberts County was at a place (since deceased) known as Travare. When the railroad came through the area and missed Travare, another town named Wilmot, located securely on the railroad, challenged Travare for county seat honors. In the ensuing election, however, Travare was victorious. Undaunted, the citizens of Wilmot took the law into their own hands. One night in December, 1884, two armed groups from Wilmot came to Travare on sleighs, seized the county records and safes, and sailed over the snow with them to Wilmot. Having taken the county seat by force, the

Wilmot partisans refused to relinquish their prize. Given this situation, the legislature of Dakota Territory passed a special act to recognize the change. Roberts County thus gives us one of several examples in which resolution by conquest occurred in a county seat war.[3]

The assimilation of parties is in theory another route toward conflict resolution, and this approach has also been attempted in ending county seat controversies. Grant County, Kansas, offers an example. Originally there was a three-way contest for county seat honors between townsites (just beginning their settlement) known as Surprise, Cincinnati, and Ulysses. Surprise and Cincinnati then consolidated into a new town named Appomattox, which began its struggle with Ulysses for the county seat. Hoping to avoid a controversy which might continue indefinitely (as well as to guard against personal financial ruin), the primary investors in the two towns in 1888 negotiated a secret pact. Whichever group won the upcoming election was to provide partial reimbursement for the losses of the other group, which would then join in boosting the winning town. Although the conflict was not quite that neatly resolved (news of the secret pact became known as returns showed Ulysses winning the election, and Appomattox supporters nearly lynched their own leaders), it is true that most Appomattox residents soon moved and Ulysses remained as the county seat.

Another form of assimilation is shown in the case of Potter County, Texas. The town of Amarillo was established and the county seat there located, but Henry B. Sanborn, wealthy owner of the nearby Frying Pan Ranch, wanted the county seat located on his own property. Mr. Sanborn proceeded to buy important buildings in the old town to move to his new townsite. Soon the courthouse was the only important building left in the old town, since Texas law prohibited removal of the county seat within five years of its establishment. But after five years the county seat too was moved, and Amarillo was safely established on Sanborn's site as the capital of Potter County. "Assimilation through purchase" might be the label applied to this Texas example of resolving a county seat controversy.

The separation or segregation of parties is another approach which has been applied in resolving county seat wars.

One instance occurred in the early 1820s over Albion's selection as the county seat for Edwards County, Illinois. Only an agreement to divide the county into two (forming Wabash County out of its eastern part) brought peace to this area. An even more unusual case of division occurred in 1888 when no less a body than the United States Congress acted to separate Latah County from Nez Perce County in Idaho Territory, thus giving the towns of both Lewiston and Moscow an opportunity to serve as county seats.

Another conceivable way of resolving a conflict is through a tournament between champions of rival groups. In one sense this is what occurs in court cases, as lawyers champion the cases of their clients in a legal joust. This has been the means of resolution for many of the most bitterly contested county seat wars. That the tournament might take a direct physical form as well as an electoral contest or court case is barely credible, but one Iowa county seat war has been described in Homer Croy's *Corn Country* as having been settled in this fashion. In a wrestling match held in the town square of Homer, a man named Maxwell defended the local honor against a Mr. Duncombe for Fort Dodge.[4] This is such a good story that we are tempted to resist the evidence of local sources that this public wrestling match (which did occur) was actually not decisive for determining the movement of the county seat of Webster County (Iowa) from Homer to Fort Dodge.

"Acts of God" is a category we sometimes use to identify events that cannot adequately be explained through normal human causation. This writer is not aware of any American town seriously claiming the county seat by divine right, though natural disasters have occasionally been decisive. Such was the case, for example, in Tom Green County, Texas. In an initial contest, San Angelo lost out to a town with the unlikely name of Ben Ficklin. However, when Ben Ficklin was destroyed by a flood in 1882, there was no good alternative but to move the county seat to San Angelo.

Finally, we must consider the possibility of a conflict continuing without resolution. Although all the county seat conflicts were eventually resolved, in some cases the process of resolution required several decades. Such protracted conflict (that is, conflict without any near-term resolution) must be seen as another possible pattern for a dispute. Cass County, Illinois, offers an example of such a case. The towns of Beardstown and Virginia opposed each other through four bitterly disputed elections between 1837 (when the county was organized) and 1876 (when a decision of the state supreme court finally awarded the prize to Virginia). The conflict in Saline County, Nebraska, had lasted even longer (a full half-century) when Crete and Wilber negotiated a truce in 1927.

Such examples of the uncertainties of conflict resolution in American county seat wars should remind us of the difficulties in resolving even some of the most petty of our human quarrels. But they also serve to enlighten our imagination concerning the variety of forms that the pursuit of peace may take.

CAN RESOLUTION BE FORCED?

Because of the importance sometimes attached to force as an approach to conflict resolution, we will devote the rest of the chapter to this topic.

Physical force is often used as a method of carrying on a conflict, but can it also be an effective means for resolving it? This question immediately invokes strong ideological reactions and, for most individuals, personal ambivalence. We have a deep distaste for the use of physical force in human affairs, but most of us still carry the conviction that force must sometimes be used as the ultimate persuader. It takes only a modest acquaintance with human history to recognize that physical coercion has been frequently used to resolve conflicts. The question therefore is not so much whether physical force ever resolves human conflicts, but rather *when* it may effectively do so.

We have no precise scientific evidence to present in answer to this question. Physical force is not something that we can freely use in laboratory studies, though there are some interesting experimental studies of the effects of threats upon bargaining.[5] Quantitative studies of international relations (such as the correlates-of-war project we discussed in Chapter 8) do support a positive relationship between military power and international influence, but the precise conditions which make military force effective are not clear in this literature.[6] And in domestic matters, there is evidence that social protest groups which use violence are more likely to be successful than those which do not, though such violence may be more a result of increased power and success than a cause of it.[7] Given both the obvious importance of our central question (that is, under what conditions may a conflict be effectively resolved by physical force?) and also the absence of clear empirical data to answer it, we will content ourselves with a largely conceptual analysis of physical force and coercion.

First, let us point to an important distinction between coercion and physical force. "Force," as we here use the term, suggests either the presence of physical violence (that is, its active use) or a direct threat to use it (its potential use). "Violence," in turn, refers to physical injury to persons or destruction of their property. "Coercion," though close to force in its connotations, is somewhat different in its locus of action. Force emphasizes the agent of influence and the means of bringing its influence to bear; coercion emphasizes the effect, the process of being impelled regardless of one's own will. This opens up the possibility of coercion occurring without force or violence as well as force without coercion. We may in fact identify the following three basic types of situations: (1) coercion with force and violence, (2) force and violence without coercion, and (3) coercion without physical force and violence.

Coercion with force and violence is probably the easiest of the three conditions to imagine. Here physical force, backed by violence, has coercive effect. A superior military force, for example, may conquer a neighboring territory and impose its own laws on a newly subject population. Or the power of a community's police may be applied to quell forcibly a riot of its citizens. Or a rebel group may overpower the established government. All of these cases raise clear images of bloody coercion. It is not pleasant to imagine this kind of reality, but we know it exists and that it has existed with considerable frequency since the dawn of recorded history.

Force and violence without coercion also has a rich history. There are, in fact, three distinct subtypes of violence without coercion, each with consequences which may be devastatingly real. First of all, we may note that violence may sometimes be more an end in itself than a means to an end. To some people at some times, violence can be fun, a break from a boring routine, and perhaps even an experience of exhilarating personal meaning. Gary Marx has pointed to the possibility of what he calls "issueless riots," exemplified by San Francisco's wild and violent celebration of the end of World War II.[8] In a slightly different context, Franz Fanon has suggested that violence may give pride and dignity to persons suffering from oppression—even when the violence may not be strategically effective.[9]

Another form of violence without coercion may occur when force is exerted ineffectively. In contrast to the issueless riot or violence to retrieve a lost sense of manhood, this form emphasizes the deliberate use of force. However, though the intent is coercive, the effect may not be. Thus a dying regime may order its troops out to disperse with violence a protesting crowd, only to find the protest gathering strength from its martyrs. Or an army may go on the march to seize a neighboring piece of territory, only to find itself forcibly thrown back. Violence does not always succeed in its purposes, even when systematically and energetically pursued.

Then too it is possible to conceive of violence without coercion when force is both deliberately and successfully used, for a total destruction of an enemy may leave nothing to coerce. Such an "ultimate solution" has not been common in human affairs, but it has been frequently imagined and occasionally even achieved. When Joshua fought at Jericho, for instance, we are told that "they utterly destroyed all in the city, both men and women, young and old, oxen, sheep, and asses, with the edge of the sword."[10] After such a feat there is really no room for coercion—not even over oxen, sheep, and asses!

Finally, we must conceive of the possibility of coercion without physical force or violence. Force which threatens violence may be used without actually requiring any violence. Or violence may not be threatened at all, though its shadow may still be present in the authority used for coercive purposes. Then again, there may not even be a hint of possible violence, though coercion may still take place. We have therefore three subtypes of coercion without violence: (1) with force, but keeping actual violence in reserve, (2) with the shadow of force continuing to give indirect support without being directly suggested, and (3) with coercion, but without any use of force or violence.

It is not too difficult to imagine coercion with the indirect support of force or violence. The police do not usually require violence in making an arrest, though the possibility of physical force is well communicated by their manner and by the equipment they keep, literally, close at hand. Much less direct is the force that helps convince citizens to pay their taxes; no policemen with billy clubs or guns need be at the door for citizens to recognize that the state has means to back up its authority to tax. It is, however, more difficult for us to grasp the possibility of coercion with no threat of physical force. Still, it is important to recognize that such coercive persuasion does exist and that its reality is far broader than most of us realize.

A few years ago, Stanley Milgram surprised his fellow social psychologists by demonstrating how obedient experimental subjects might be. They were asked by the experimenter to send what they believed to be near-fatal shocks to another subject—and most subjects complied with such requests.[11] Some popular commentaries on Milgram's studies have seen in them a dark message about human nature. Most of us clods, it is implied, naturally tend to do automatically whatever we are told. This, however, misses Milgram's main point, which in turn leads to the point we wish to make by citing this research. Milgram's thesis was that obedience can be treated as a dependent variable in experimental research, thus allowing us to study variations in conditions affecting the amount of obedience. In the particular conditions he first explored, there was indeed a surprising amount of obedience. What surprised many readers was that this obedience was forthcoming with quite minor powers of reward or punishment on the part of the experimenter. In particular (and what is centrally important for our present discussion), there was no suggestion of physical force to back up the commands of the experimenter. But close examination of the conditions involved reveals other compelling reasons for subjects to follow the commands of the experimenter. The whole experimental setup was strange to them, though the experimenter appeared to understand it perfectly. Furthermore, he was supremely sure about what must be done. It was also clear that the study was for a noble scientific purpose—that of a better understanding of the role of punishment in learning and memory (subjects were instructed to send shocks in response to wrong answers from fellow subjects identified as "learners," though these were actually confederates of the experimenter). Presumably some discomfort of the subjects might be necessary to prove how ineffective such procedures were. Certainly it was being conducted under the sponsorship of a most reputable organization (Yale University) and in a location which emphasized its scientific nature. After starting to follow the orders of the experimenter, most subjects felt that they had no choice but to continue with the next requests, disagreeable though their task might be.

The point we wish to make here is a very modest one—which, once made, seems quite obvious. Yet many people neglect this point in their assumptions about the role of force in the resolution of conflict. The point is simply that coercive persuasion does not necessarily require either force or violence or even an implied threat of force. Effective authority can rest upon other bases. Coercion can occur through simple obedience to authority, especially if the persons involved see no other choice as effectively available.

As Max Weber has persuasively pointed out, systems of power do not rest their claims of command simply on physical force.[12] Naked power, power without legitimation, is a rare feature in human society. Much more common is authority that has become accepted and thereby legitimated. This, in Weber's view, is the basis of most social order, and he saw three main types of legitimate authority: (1) legal, (2) traditional, and (3) charismatic. Holding an office which requires setting forth rules for others to follow would be an example of legal authority; following past precedents in assuming a position of leadership illustrates traditional authority; and highly personalistic claims to authority, supported primarily by the emotional attachment of followers to their leader, represent charismatic authority. Weber, of course, considered these types as usually combined in reality, but their separate analysis helps to clarify the different theoretical bases (rational, traditional, and emotional) from which legitimate authority may derive.

Physical force, we must conclude, is not the only factor which might lead people to act against their wills or desires. There is also the power of moral force, operating in the guise of some form of legitimate authority. Because of the acceptance of legal authority, persons hating school have nevertheless attended year after year; a priest, using traditional authority, may still persuade a couple to continue an unwanted pregnancy; and some individuals have even been known to commit suicide at the request of a cult leader with a strong personal appeal (or charismatic authority).

So far, our analysis has prepared us to see coercion as possible both with and without physical force. We have not yet examined systematically the conditions under which physical force would or would not be effective in providing conflict resolution. Although we will not presume to identify such conditions in detail, some discussion of the concepts of capability, credibility, relevance, and legitimacy may prove helpful.

Force, to be used effectively, must be sufficient to overcome opposing forces. It must, in other words, have sufficient *capability*. Speaking in military terms, we see manpower and firepower as especially important. We must not, however, neglect attention to mechanisms for supplying front-line troops or the organization of the command structure. All of these are vital factors in military capability. As we move to nonmilitary matters (such as the role of force in the control of crime), we recognize even more clearly the importance of being at the right place at the right time. Total firepower available counts for little in comparison to the mobility of police forces, which in turn depends more on factors of human organization and skill than on the number of policemen or the size of their guns. There must be force sufficient to make an arrest, but greater force does not necessarily increase capability. In either a military or a nonmilitary context, capability must be seen as indicating both the presence of sufficient force and the ability to apply and control it with sufficient skill to achieve whatever objectives are sought.

The concept of capability focuses on the party which may use force; *credibility,* in contrast, focuses on the party which may receive the force. Force is effective not just in being exercised but also (and more importantly) in the threat of its use. It is the belief that force would in fact be used unless certain conditions are met which makes it most persuasive. Force may in this manner become most effective in coercion without being used at all. Rather, it is used as a form of implicit bargaining with an adversary. What coerces (or *deters,* to use the more popular term for the negative case) is the belief that it might be used. This leads to a curious paradox: To be credible, there must be some evidence that force would in fact be used; but if force is actually used, it loses efficiency. The most efficient coercion occurs where credibility can somehow be achieved without actually having to resort to force. Sometimes this can be achieved by a careful show of force combined with an irrevocable act of commitment to use that force in certain contingencies.[13]

Another quality which must apply to force if it is to be effective is *relevance.* Force must be relevant in two chief ways. It must be relevant in the sense that it can drastically affect, in a negative way, persons with real power. And it must also be relevant in the sense that it helps these persons make the associations and draw the conclusions necessary to be coerced.

Force expended in punishing, or threatening to punish, those not really responsible for decision making suffers from irrelevance. The more directly persons with central decision-making powers are affected, the more relevant the force becomes as an instrument of persuasion. One of the reasons, among others, that war has traditionally been such a colossal waste is that firepower has mostly been spent punishing people who are not responsible for important decisions. Even battlefield generals are usually protected well to the rear of the battle, and these generals, in turn, are pledged simply to follow the orders of their commanders. The major decision makers of warfare on either side are affected only indirectly (such as through loss of troop strength or territory held) and only after massive carnage has occurred. Such, at any rate, has been the dominant historical pattern. The nuclear age brings the possi-

bility of an important change, however, for missiles with nuclear warheads may now be delivered directly to the power centers of an enemy nation. This force is thus more dangerous for
the stability of international relations, but it also becomes more
relevant (in the sense that threats can be made with a greater
likelihood of directly affecting persons with central influence).

Relevance also has its cognitive side. Not only must force
have a potential for affecting central decision makers, but it
should be in a form which helps them draw correct inferences.
Sometimes messages accompanying an operation of force are
crucial in its interpretation, though the form of force selected
may also be critical. In this regard, it is instructive to compare
American actions in the Cuban missile crisis of 1962 with the Bay
of Pigs invasion of the previous year. The 1961 invasion gave
little opportunity for Cuba's government to think of anything
except resistance. Lacking the air support and combat strength
to be a successful conventional attack, the invasion nevertheless
had just enough of both to discredit it as an authentic Cuban
home-grown revolt, and therefore served to drive most Cubans
further into Castro's fold. The attack thus proved irrelevant
and counter-productive in its aim: to weaken or displace the
Castro regime. On the other hand, in the Cuban missile crisis
of 1962, the threat of force by the United States was directed
(and accompanied by clear communications of intent) against
ships and missile sites known to be under the direct command
of Russian leaders. American force made ready was clearly relevant to a particular set of objectives: preventing the Russians
from arming offensive nuclear missiles in Cuba and persuading
the Soviets to remove them. This carefully measured and applied resort to force proved in the end to be much more effective in limiting Cuba's threat to the United States than the Bay
of Pigs invasion. The specific nature of the force selected, the
verbal messages accompanying the commitment of force, and
the degree to which enemy decision makers were directly con-
fronted were all elements making for the greater relevance of
the force used in the 1962 crisis than in the previous year.

Finally, there is the matter of the *legitimacy* of force. This,
in turn, has three aspects: (1) legitimacy in the eyes of those
who may exercise physical force, (2) according to those upon

whom the force is used, or threatened to be used, and (3) in the view of others who may observe the events.

The coordination of actions usually necessary in a successful recourse to force requires a certain acceptance of the legitimacy of that force. This may take the form of a suspension of individual judgment, so that anything that is commanded is considered legitimate (an objective of much military discipline); or it may take the form of explicit approval of the means being exercised. In either case, at least some minimal sense of legitimacy is necessary to overcome the aversion persons feel toward the use of force. Soldiers must be given at least some explanation of how their actions will defend their country, or their morale will deteriorate in battle; police must believe that a forceful arrest will help to reduce crime, or they will simply look the other way; and parents must believe a spanking is really for their child's good, or they will not so lift a hand (or they might swat only in ineffective anger). Without a sense that forceful action is legitimate, perpetrators of force are seldom able to use it effectively.

When the threat of force is raised, its response is strongly affected by whether or not it is seen as legitimate by those who may receive it. When our government threatens us with jail if we fail to pay our income taxes, our readiness to pay increases as we consider these taxes as legitimate. But suppose that we were threatened with jail for not going to church on Sunday; that would be a different matter. Most of us no longer consider this to be a legitimate concern of the state; an edict of this sort would therefore be widely ignored as illegitimate. When force (or the threat of force) is perceived by its recipients as illegitimate, it more frequently also sets in motion the appeal to counterforce; much greater force is therefore necessary for forceful persuasion than when its legitimacy is more accepted.

Third parties may also be important. Nations can no longer threaten other nations with force without at least some concern as to how this may be viewed by other members of the international community. The police will hesitate to use force (although they personally believe it is warranted and could be effectively employed) if they anticipate a negative popular response to their actions. And even terrorists have occasionally shown a shrewd respect for public opinion in releasing hostages and moderating their demands. Although the larger human community may appear unconcerned in a particular resort to force, a general form of third party consciousness of legitimacy may still be instilled. Many persons see their actions as ultimately accountable to God, raising the possibility of at least some external judgment of legitimacy. Others want their actions justified by "history"—leading at least to the consideration of what may or may not be considered legitimate in very broad human retrospect.

Our extended conceptual analysis of coercion and the conditions for its effective use leads us to two general conclusions. The first is that physical force can most effectively be applied to resolve a conflict when one party has a clearly superior capability to use such force *and* when such force also clearly has the attributes of credibility, relevance, and legitimacy. A second conclusion is that where the claim to legitimate authority can be asserted most persuasively, the use of physical force is often redundant.

So, force and violence must be recognized as important parts of the social fabric of power. They are not, however, the only ingredients in human power. Force functions most effectively in bringing an end to conflicts when it is firmly supported by other forms of power (that is, when it is encased in fully legitimate authority). Naked force (that is, force separated from legitimate channels of social power) can resolve little or nothing. Like a terrorist hijacking, it can at best win temporary acceptance. On the other hand, when clearly legitimate authority obtains, effective coercion may be possible without the use of force.

Most problematic are those cases in which legitimacy is unclear or divided; force then may prove a tempting resource with which to buttress other claims to power, and it is in such cases that we most often find force and violence applied—but with very mixed and uncertain results so far as conflict resolution is concerned.

14

Resolution through Reason

Reason in the sense of intelligent action does not constitute a
distinct approach to conflict resolution. Intelligence, even a
highly reflective and carefully considered intelligence, can be
applied within any of the frameworks discussed in the last two
chapters. True, we are more likely to associate resolution
through reason with negotiations than with other forms. But
negotiations have their nonrational elements too, and there is
no reason why reflective intelligence may not be applied in
other forms of resolution. The use of physical force, for example, may be the result of a carefully considered plan of action just as clearly as may negotiations.

There is, however, one possible meaning of "resolution
through reason" that leads us to have a separate chapter with
this as a title. "Reason" also may be held to mean a set of standards for thought and action which grow out of general human
experience, reflectively considered. This is the meaning we intend to use in the present chapter. Our basic search is for a
framework which goes beyond the short-term objectives of parties locked in conflict, a framework which, when applied to
these parties, may help them see beyond their immediate case.
Our search, then, is for principles and procedures of wider
support and more general validity which may be fairly applied
to both parties in a particular dispute.

The search for a more general and rational perspective to
resolve a conflict sometimes comes through procedures which
invite the assistance of neutral parties. Before considering some
of the more philosophical issues of justice and equity, let us
note briefly some of these procedural forms.

THIRD PARTY INVOLVEMENT

A third party may be used as a direct and explicit aid to negotiations between two parties. The most commonly discussed form of explicit third party involvement is that of mediation; however, it is important to see that this is only one of a range of possible roles for third parties. This range may be represented by contrasting four possible patterns: (1) good offices, (2) mediation, (3) arbitration, and (4) adjudication. In the good offices case, a third party provides a setting where negotiators may meet, also sometimes serving as a go-between to facilitate communication between the parties. In mediation, the third party communicates more actively in seeking to help the opposing parties reduce their differences and arrive at a solution. In the case of arbitration, the third party has actual authority, delegated by previous commitments from both parties, to decide how a dispute is to be resolved. With adjudication, the legal structure of the state is brought to bear on the dispute, deciding it in line with whatever is established as law.

In practice, the distinctions between the forms of third party involvement are not always clear. For example, a group of public employees may find many conditions of their work regulated by law and thus subject to adjudication; in addition, local lawmakers may make themselves available in a good offices capacity when a contract dispute is brewing, and a state labor agency may also be available for informal mediation and "fact finding" (a formal process of mediation designed to bring the sides together through a suggested solution); and parts of the last contract may call for compulsory arbitration of grievances. In such a case, it is possible to imagine all of these forms of third party involvement accompanying each other in attempts to resolve a dispute.

Explicit third party involvement occurs primarily as an adjunct to bilateral negotiations. Only with adjudication is it usually unnecessary to assume some ongoing process of negotiations (even arbitration occurs through the past agreement of parties, which could be changed through new negotiations). Although negotiations may not be required with adjudication, frequently negotiations for an outside-of-court settlement (or a settlement which might later be formally recognized by the court) proceed side-by-side with taking a dispute to court.

Even when there is no direct third party involvement, a third party may still largely determine the process of conflict resolution. This is most clear in considering the role of the state in settling disputes between its citizens. The law is called into play not only by cases which are taken to court but also by more numerous disputes which never show up on a court docket. The knowledge of what the law is, and how it would be apt to be applied in a court case, is sufficient to guide parties (with the help of their lawyers) to their own resolution of the issue in dispute.[1]

ANCIENT APPROACHES TO JUSTICE

So far, we have considered primarily the procedural forms which may encourage broader considerations to enter into the rational settlement of disputes. We have now to consider the content or principles which may be applied. Are there some general principles of justice grounded in the common experience of humanity which can be brought to bear upon a wide variety of particular conflicts? If so, how do we discover and identify such principles?

The search for rational principles of justice is far older than modern social science. Social scientists have recently rediscovered the centrality of issues of justice and equity for understanding human behavior, and it is amazing how closely parallel some of the contemporary questions are to those posed many centuries ago. Before we turn to the contemporary literature, it would be well to remind ourselves of some of the most relevant contributions from this early legacy. For this we turn briefly to review the contributions of the two most famous philosophers of ancient Athens, Plato and Aristotle.[2]

The human being, in Plato's view, is a compound of three main elements: the senses or appetites, the spirit or will, and intelligence or reason. Though all of these are necessary, a person can be truly effective only when the intelligence or reason plays its role of central coordination. Closely parallel to his view of human personality was Plato's view of society. As Plato interpreted the past, society emerged and developed largely through an increased division of labor; and the members of the resulting society may be classified into three main groups: those who live primarily by activities of sensual gratification, those who live for honor and prestige, and those who live in pursuit of reason and truth. In the first class are the artisans; in the second are the police and soldiers; and in the third are the intellectuals.

Just as the intellect should govern the life of the individual, Plato held, so should the intellectuals govern the life of the community. In *The Republic* Plato goes on to argue that the proper system of governance must be personally disinterested, with the intellectual guardians of society carefully selected and subjected to the most rigorous education possible. He was quite specific about the kind of education necessary for such guardians, and he saw an especially crucial place in it for mathematics (particularly geometry). Mathematics, he held, provides critical training of the mind for reasoned discourse and for the perception of fundamental forms which are to serve as the framework of analysis.

For Plato there was a world to be grasped by the intellect which is more fundamentally real than the world we know through the senses. This reality of "ideas" or "forms" is the fundamental basis on which human justice must be ordered. That is, persons with intellect must be able to perceive the underlying principles which should apply to a particular case. They should be able to do this partly because of their own skill with abstract reason and their long training to think in terms of fundamental abstractions. This assumes that the intellectual training of these guardians will have been long and arduous, with many, many hours spent in the study of higher mathematics. It also assumes that they will be able to analyze matters from a disinterested position, that their long training would also be geared to overcoming petty self-interest, to see beyond the limited interests of particular groups to the universal requirements of human justice.

Disinterested intelligence is the means, for Plato, for discovering the requirements of justice, but what is the *content* of such justice? Here Plato gives us no precise formula, but instead a general framework for its perception. Just as the effective person must have a well-integrated combination of the senses, the spirit, and intellect—with intellect the final master—so must the good society have a proper combination of its constituents and functions. Artisans, soldiers, and intellectuals—each group must have its place and contribute to the working whole. The just society is one in which each person and group will play its proper role, guided by the considered judgment of the intellectuals about what constitutes the most rational order. The proof of the achievement of justice is found in the extent to which the various segments actually work together as a unified whole. Such at least was the image of justice presented by Plato.

Aristotle, like his teacher Plato, viewed the conception of the good society as more important than the detailed empirical study of society. He had, however, somewhat different ideas on the nature of the good society. He was repelled by many of Plato's particular recommendations, especially the communistic system Plato envisioned to keep his intellectual guardians of society from becoming selfish in their motivation. In Aristotle's view, self-interest was not something to be avoided, but rather something to be supplemented with the cultivation of a broader public interest. Similarly, Aristotle's whole approach to society and politics was not (as was Plato's) to search in a world beyond experience for the fundamental principles of the good society; rather, Aristotle sought out the good as something already inherent in our experience of nature. It is in man's nature and in the nature of society (which cannot be really separated, for man is by nature a social animal) that the good society must be found.

Justice, however, requires a balance. Sometimes the expressions of human nature are one-sided or extreme; these cannot be called truly good or just. The good life, for Aristotle, is always a balanced life, bringing together external goods (wealth), goods of the body (health), and goods of the soul (personal character, including intelligence). As with the happiness of its individuals, so too the welfare of society depends on a proper mix of material prosperity, a physically sound population, and persons of effective character. Furthermore, the overall organization of society is best which promotes the fullest development of all of these foundations of personal and social happiness. Generally, as Aristotle saw it, this would depend on a predominant political role for the middle classes (in terms of material resources), for the "golden mean" of the best balanced political system would be unlikely to emerge if led by either men of great wealth or the masses who had little or no property.

Aristotle was of a more empirical cast of mind than was Plato, but neither of these ancient Greeks approached the world with the objective spirit of modern science. Both saw no need to separate what is from what ought to be, thus neglecting the first requirement for an objective science. To Aristotle, as to Plato, nature is infused with purpose (inherent in the essential nature of things in the real world for Aristotle, inherent in a world of forms beyond the real world for Plato). This sense of inherent purpose made it impossible for either to adopt a fully objective frame of reference. Both insisted on merging questions of social reality with those of social ethics, making it difficult for us to see either as presenting scientific contributions to an analysis of human conflict.

That the theories of both Plato and Aristotle were so profoundly normative limits our use of them for most purposes of a modern science of conflict. In one area, however, that of conflict resolution, their normative orientation may be a definite asset. Here they may serve as fundamental models of how human reason may be applied to obtain standards for conflict resolution.

To the extent that parties to a conflict search for a just solution, to that extent they are seeking some rational standard that may guide their conduct to resolve the conflict. Plato and Aristotle give us two basically different models of the nature of a rational standard for conflict resolution. For Plato, the answer must come through the identification of some abstract rational principle; the principle, once identified, can then be used as a basis of restructuring the relationship between the conflicting parties. Some overriding principle is necessary to refocus the situation of conflict, allowing the particular interests of the parties to be transcended. For Aristotle, in contrast, conflict resolution must be based upon the real interests of the contending parties. It is in the very mix of the contending interests that resolution must take place—through a proper balancing of these interests, and not in some abstract rule which ignores them.

CONTEMPORARY CONCEPTIONS OF JUSTICE

We have not considered the ancient views of Plato and Aristotle out of any special concern for antiquity. Quite to the contrary, our interest is primarily in understanding the conceptions of equity which are at the cutting edge of modern social science theory and research. It just so happens, however, that these modern conceptions have a surprising degree of similarity to issues laid out long ago by the philosophers of ancient Athens, and that a reminder of the views of Plato and Aristotle may help to prepare us for examining these contemporary ideas.

One of the most influential contributions to social science theory in the 1970s is contained in the book *A Theory of Justice* by John Rawls. It is a bit ironic to find sociologists and political scientists paying so much attention to the work of Rawls, for it represents such a contrast to their main theoretical traditions. The dominant pattern in these fields of social science is to derive theory from empirical data; the concept of a normative theory is quite foreign to their recent traditions. Nevertheless, a variety of factors (including increasing attention to policy questions and disenchantment with the more mundane forms of empiricism) have combined to provide a respectful reception for this new theory of justice. An additional factor in this positive reception of *A Theory of Justice* is the care and sophistication with which Rawls has formulated his theory.[3]

It would be misleading to label Rawls' theory as Platonic. In most respects there is little similarity between the content of Plato's philosophy and that of Rawls. Still, however, we wish to point out one very basic similarity between Rawls and Plato. Both are searching for a general theory of justice which can be founded upon rational principles of universal validity. Furthermore, both intend that these principles, once identified, be used for the criticism and reconstruction of existing societies.

Before deriving his fundamental principles of justice, Rawls found it necessary first to build a foundation of basic assumptions. Individual autonomy and rationality are key themes in these assumptions. Individuals are not assumed to enter into relationships with others unless they have something to gain by so doing. Furthermore, such relationships should be based on a rational perception of interests. Such considerations lead Rawls to borrow heavily from the social contract tradition of political theory. In contrast to earlier social contract theorists such as Hobbes, Locke, and Rousseau, Rawls is not primarily interested in formulating a theory of the origin of the state or the nature of sovereignty. His purpose, more sociological than political, is to derive central rational norms for social organization. He takes up the social contract model because this permits him to imagine an "original position" from which persons might rationally proceed to construct a society. The basic question is: What are the limits which reason must be expected to impose upon the framework of that society?

Persons in the original position are not, for Rawls, stripped of their basic humanity. They are hypothesized to be rational and intelligent creatures; however, they are conceived to be without any knowledge of what their own positions might come to be in any future set of organized relationships. This "veil of ignorance" is assumed so that any rational principles guiding the organization of a just society will necessarily transcend the particular interests of its individual members.

Reasoning from these assumptions, Rawls derives two fundamental principles of justice, which he states as follows:

> First: each person is to have an equal right to the most basic liberty compatible with a similar liberty for others. Second: social and economic inequalities are to be arranged so that they are both (a) reasonably expected to be to everyone's advantage, and (b) attached to positions and offices open to all.[4]

In his further discussion, Rawls makes it clear that the first principle (that basic liberties should be equally distributed) takes priority over the second. Furthermore, within the second principle (allowing for inequalities), part (b) has priority over (a); that is, equality of opportunity has a rational precedence over considerations of results. These priorities give a generally egalitarian cast to Rawls' basic conception of justice. Note, however, that there is room for some inequality. Inequalities in outcomes for different persons can be justified so long as they are to the benefit of everyone. Rawls gives special attention here to those persons least advantaged by proposed social arrangements; if they will become better off through these arrangements, the criteria of justice may be satisfied—even if someone else may reap greater benefits.

Although his central principles of justice are derived from a hypothetical situation ("persons in an original position"), Rawls clearly intends that they may be applied to criticize contemporary institutions. Is a given arrangement of society just? To answer this question, we have only to apply to our detailed examination of society the further questions: Are basic liberties provided for all? Is there a fundamental equality of opportunity? And are inequalities in outcomes associated with at least some gains for those least advantaged? If these questions can be answered affirmatively, the basic criteria of justice are met.

Rawls understands that justice is not the only basis on which a given arrangement of society may be judged. Productive efficiency, for example, may sometimes be higher in societies where there is little justice than under just arrangements. Furthermore, much social organization may be seen as growing without explicit human choice; and to the extent that human choice is not involved, an evaluation in terms of justice may not be appropriate. Nevertheless, Rawls stresses the importance of the criteria of justice, giving justice priority over other considerations in evaluating those arrangements of society which flow from conscious human action.

Rawls' theory of justice can be criticized on various grounds. Reviewers have raised questions concerning assumptions about the original position, the logical derivation of certain presumed consequences, and the way applications are made for evaluating contemporary society.[5] We do not here need to get into a detailed evaluation of Rawls in order to recognize that (1) *A Theory of Justice* is a very carefully reasoned work, and (2) it makes some basic assumptions which are open to question. For example, different assumptions about the nature of persons in the original position could easily lead to a rather different theory of justice. Nevertheless, this book remains one of the most persuasive contemporary theories of justice.

The implications of Rawls' theory for conflict resolution are fairly clear. His is a theory which suggests certain fundamental principles of rational justice. Parties in conflict can use these principles as a general basis for resolving their conflict, perhaps with the assistance of a scholar trained in ethical philosophy. Although the content would come out rather differently from the more elitist principles of Plato, Rawls is very much in the same tradition as the ancient Athenian so far as his basic philosophical procedure is concerned. Plato would probably be pleased.

If Plato would be pleased by the way self-interests are rationalistically transcended in Rawls' theory of justice, Aristotle would no doubt be happier with a theory associated with sociologist George C. Homans.[6] "Equity theory" is the name usually applied to a recent development in social psychology which originated largely in George Homans' formulation of exchange theory. It is in his conception of distributive justice that Homans raises the issue of equity, and here he explicitly uses the ideas of Aristotle as his point of departure. Aristotle had identified justice as a matter of balance and proportion; a relationship between persons should give them rewards in proportion to their proper deserts, for, as Aristotle put it, "it is when equals possess or are allotted unequal shares, or persons not equal, equal shares, that quarrels and complaints arise." Homans proceeds to formulate this into his central principle of distributive justice, namely, that rewards among a group of persons must be proportional to the investments or contributions of each. He goes to considerable pains to argue that this is not just an ideal rule about how people ought to behave, but that persons actually tend to order their behavior in accordance with this notion of equity.

Although the basic idea is the same, other social psychologists have formulated equity theory in slightly different terms. Stacy Adams, for example, expresses the principle of equity as a relationship between "inputs" and "outcomes," and Elaine Walster and associates use the same terms as Adams but a slightly different formula for combining them to define equity.[7] Regardless of the precise terminology, all equity theorists would agree that groups tend to develop equitable systems for rewarding their members (equitable in the sense that those with greater contributions get greater rewards), that individuals tend to internalize these standards for evaluating their own behavior and the behavior of others, and that persons experiencing what they feel is an inequitable relationship will tend to act in such a way as to restore equity.

This sounds almost too simple—as though with a few generalizations like those just stated we could sum up the operational principles of achieving justice in society. The simplicity, however, vanishes when we approach an empirical problem for analysis. Then come the complicating questions: What constitutes reward and what constitutes input or investment? How is each measured or assessed? To which others are comparisons made—to other persons directly participating, to other persons of similar position, or to whom? And what are the available actions which may affect the balance of equity? As we raise such questions the principles of equity, which stood out so clearly at our first theoretical glance, begin to recede into a morass of relativity. Equity, we finally conclude, is in the eye of the beholder, and each participant in a relationship may have his own perception of what is equitable.

If we concern ourselves only with the subjective judgments of individuals, many issues about equity evaporate. By focusing on the individual, we are less bothered by the fact that equity judgments may vary from person to person. But such a psychological approach does not necessarily contribute to the resolution of *social* conflict. We can use concepts of equity as a basis for resolving social conflicts only when the parties share a common frame of reference. For this there must be consensus on at least a rough scale on which inputs and outcomes of different individuals may be compared. This leads us to very difficult assumptions about measurement, especially when we assess inputs.[8]

Some of the problems of equity theory could be greatly reduced by introducing certain simplifications. One simplification would be to limit ourselves to comparisons between parties involved in direct interaction. Another would be to forget inputs, limiting our attention to the (usually) more straightforward task of comparing outcomes. The problem of equity then becomes reduced to a matter of the just distribution of outcomes among those involved in an interdependent relationship. By accepting these two simplifications, we transform equity theory into what turns out to be a special class of game theory. Equity theory with these restrictions becomes equivalent to the theory of cooperative games for mixed-motive bargaining (which we discussed in Chapter 10). The problem therefore becomes that of finding a reasonable standard of dividing the rewards in cases where (1) the parties may increase their rewards by coordinating their actions, but (2) the parties have different interests in which particular actions are to be selected to coordinate.

We have already treated this problem in our previous discussion of the theory of games. Here all we need to add is that the various rational solutions to the theory of cooperative games may also be considered as theoretical answers to the age-old problem of justice. Two of the most commonly discussed solutions are those which we earlier (in Chapter 10) called the "threat" and "security" solutions, respectively, to cooperatively resolving mixed-motive games. They differ primarily in the basis for comparisons among outcomes. The security solution uses as a basis for comparative evaluations the minimum that each can guarantee for himself. The threat solution uses the range of threats that the parties can direct to each other as a basis for comparing relative positions.[9]

◄§

In the present chapter, we have seen that there are various possible rational approaches to the problem of justice. Plato and Aristotle presented their perspectives long ago; and in recent years we have seen the blossoming of somewhat parallel approaches in the works of John Rawls and the social psychological equity theorists. Finally, we have seen how a species of game theory can be used as still another formulation of equity theory. In all of this, our central search has been to identify basic standards of social justice. But justice, which seems to be such a simple idea when we first hear it invoked, turns out to be not quite so simple when we examine it more carefully.

Justice is, furthermore, not the only consideration in resolving a conflict. An effective solution must be understandable and mutually enforceable as well as just. But the perception of what is just is one of the most critical elements present in conflict resolution; and the science of conflict has only just begun to delve into the theoretical and empirical questions which follow a full recognition of this point.

15

The Search for Peace

In popular thought, peace is often viewed as the absence of conflict. Further, it is often seen as a more natural or normal condition than conflict. This suggests that it is only as a result of special circumstances that humans come to be pitted against each other. Conflict, in this view, is abnormal; the normal state for human beings is that of peace.

Such a view, however, ignores the real and very natural existence of interest conflicts throughout practically all human social life. If we wishfully imagine the absence of conflict as the normal state of the world, we are apt to feel overwhelmed with indignation when the forces of conflict at last confront our attention. "This should not be," we tell ourselves; "surely there is something very wrong that somebody has done somewhere." And so, we set ourselves on a quest to extirpate the evil—or the evildoer—which has so disrupted our sense of equilibrium. The result is often a much more heated conflict than would have occurred with a more realistic acceptance of its existence.

However, to say that conflict exists in practically all social life is far from asserting the ubiquity of violent conflict. Life is not fundamentally a war of all against all. Most conflicts are regulated and controlled, so violent conflict is actually only a very small proportion of all human conflict.

In one way or another, people usually resolve their conflicts short of violent confrontation. It is this fact that offers special hope for our quest to make the conditions of peace more widespread. Peace, in this view, is not an absence of conflict. Rather, it is a way of dealing with conflicts so that, if they may not be resolved, they are at least controlled. In the remainder of the present chapter, we will seek to identify some general factors which are commonly part of such a peace process.[1]

THE DREAM OF REASON

In the preceding chapter, we examined two main ways that reason may enter into the process of conflict resolution. Reason, in both cases, was understood as a set of standards for thought and action which grow out of general human experience, reflectively considered. We were first concerned with procedures by which the experience of other parties may be brought to bear on those locked in a dispute. Here our concern was to see how third parties may assist the protagonists to resolve the issues that divide them. Secondly, we were concerned with deriving a standard which might be persuasively applied to settle an issue. Here we sought a rational basis for identifying an appropriate or just solution for conflicts.

Judicial proceedings well illustrate both of these forms of reason. The judge is the third party who brings a broader framework of human experience to bear on the dispute. The law, by which he is guided, provides the standards which give a rational basis for settling the issue. Sometimes these legal standards come through as matters of fixed general principles, presenting justice in the form of careful applications of firm dogmas. Sometimes more empirically derived equities are sought and applied to give a balanced decision. In most court cases, both the general principles and the particular considerations of fairness have a part in the outcome.

But are we equating human reason with judicial proceedings? There are good arguments to refrain from doing so. We have heard of too many cases in which judgments appear arbitrary or the law itself may seem unreasonable. Surely we cannot claim that all justice as dispensed through the courts is truly rational justice. And if we start making exceptions, what are the rational grounds we use to judge them differently?

It is possible to appeal to a law higher than that which the courts use to dispense justice. But the trouble here is that more than one higher law is possible. There are many possibilities.

And where do we come out if each disputant is to be allowed his own higher law to support his own side of the case?

One possible answer is that the last word is simply a matter of power. As Thrasymachus argued against Socrates many centuries ago, justice may be seen as simply the interest of the stronger party. We accept the claims of parties in accordance with standards which are in turn set by whoever holds power. Those in power, in this view, naturally use their own interests in defining these standards.

Viewed narrowly, this approach is clearly unsatisfactory. Reason and justice cannot so simply be seen as servants of whoever holds political power. Viewed more broadly, however, this argument is more persuasive. Power may be viewed not simply as that of the political authorities or the ruling class but as the *total persuasive power* residing in symbolic value systems as well as concrete political and economic systems. In this broader view, reason represents those who are able to argue most persuasively, all things considered. Persuasiveness may indeed partly reflect the interests of those with political and economic power; but it depends more directly on the power of words and the legacy of common human values which may be thereby conveyed.

But the broadening of the power argument leads us back to the same problem mentioned before. There is no longer a single standard possible. Reason turns out to have many able voices of persuasion.

Will not one voice inevitably prove most persuasive in the end? This, we suggest, is the dream of reason; and we further suggest that it is indeed usually an illusion. A struggle for persuasive power through words may be less physically destructive, but it is no more likely to arrive at a clear conclusion than is a struggle using physical means. We are still left with the likelihood of multiple claims to what can be called the dictates of reason.

Our illusions, nevertheless, recede only slowly. We still often dream of fixed principles of Reason or Divine Justice which will provide an ultimate resolution for our conflicts, if we will but listen and apply the higher truths. But how rarely can we agree in seeing these higher truths come shining through when a strong conflict of interests is at stake!

Even if reason fails to give us an ultimate single solution for a social conflict, it can frequently help in providing effective resolution. As it helps us identify the most relevant facts, interests, and values, a framework for conflict resolution may be encouraged to emerge. This point will be pursued further in the following section.

Not all conflict control, however, is the result of a conscious search for resolution. Peace (at least in the sense of conflict regulation and the control of violence) is probably more commonly produced indirectly than as a result of its conscious pursuit. Parties typically pursue their own interests in a given direction only so long as it is profitable to do so. In market systems, where the search is for mutually beneficial exchanges, conflict is often automatically regulated by the parties' self-interests. Even in threat systems, where mutual harm may be considered, the self-interests of parties usually counsel restraint. The resulting balance of power may not be what we immediately think of when we speak of "peace" (and certainly there are enormous dangers in relying upon systems of mutual deterrence for long-run security or stability); still, it must be recognized as an important factor in the practical limitation and control of conflict.

The Habit of Truth

In the full flowering of the Age of Enlightenment, wars were seen as relics of barbarism which would gradually vanish from the civilized world. Writing at the close of the American Revolution, Thomas Paine considered that "there is now left scarcely anything to quarrel about"; and when France was in the throes of its revolution, the Marquis de Condorcet could look forward confidently to the time when "nothing will remain to encourage or even to arouse the fury of war."[2] Such optimism was based on the growth of science and reason. The great discoveries of natural science were being applied to improve the physical conditions of human life, and a similar spirit of human reason was fostering the reconstruction of social institutions. As Condorcet expressed it:

> Just as the mathematical and physical sciences tend to improve the arts that we use to satisfy our simplest needs, is it not also part of the necessary order of nature that the moral and political sciences should exercise a similar influence upon the motives that direct our feelings and our actions?[3]

Although Condorcet's faith in the power of human reason was overdone, we wish to argue in the present section that it was not without *some* substance. A sometimes grossly idealized picture of the fruits of science and reason should not deter us from seeing in the scientific enterprise at least a substantial set of general tools for the construction of peace.

But first we must recognize the folly of expecting that somehow perpetual peace will be established directly by the forces of reason. Especially is it misplaced faith to assume, with Condorcet, that this is somehow "part of the necessary order of nature" which will assert itself if only we will let it. This view grew in part out of an image of science that saw a few central principles determining the detailed operation of the physical universe. This Newtonian world machine captured the imagination of eighteenth-century intellectuals, inspiring them to think in similar terms about their social world. If only we can recognize through reason the central principles of human society, we can then remake our institutions to fit this natural pattern. We will then be able to see a gradual withering away of war and conflict.

Alas, it is not so simple. Not even the physical universe is conceived simply in terms of the unitary order of Newton's laws. And we have still failed to establish through reason what is the "natural" order to be embodied in our reconstructed social institutions. As we argued in the last section, such an achievement of human reason can only be a dream. Nature—especially the human social natures of individuals and groups in conflict—does not present itself to us in such a unitary pattern.

But if hopes fade for the establishment of universal brotherhood through the unitary dictates of reason, this should not lead to a rejection of reason and science. The scientific attitude, carefully reasoned analysis, and the collective reduction of error by the community of scientists are among the most useful tools which can be applied to the building of a peaceful world. Their effective use, however, requires us to see the world as one of multiple and diverse truths, not as embodying some simple ultimate truth.

The scientific attitude is one prepared to learn from experience. Ideas are held in tentative form. Indeed, we systematically seek out the facts that might lead to their revision. This same empirical spirit is frequently helpful in defusing the passions aroused by social conflict. Issues of conflict are not automatically eliminated, but careful attention to their reality (usually less fearsome than the emotional images people conjure up) may make them more manageable.

Carefully reasoned analysis is also no guarantee of satisfactory conclusions. The facts and assumptions with which one starts may be false, leading to false conclusions. But we can at least assure ourselves of the correctness of the inference process, thus using questionable conclusions to lead us back to question our initial facts and assumptions. In facing issues of social conflict, we are also not sure that carefully reasoned analysis will lead to a resolution. But more often than not, a resolution becomes enhanced when the parties carefully reason out the possible consequences of their clash in interests.

The community of scientists provides a means for the gradual reduction of error through practices of critical review, publication, and replication. Although individual scientists are as selfish and vain as anyone else, the collective results of their work provide a self-correcting character to the search for truth. Sooner or later, mistaken assumptions or faulty observations are replaced, and our knowledge is gradually enhanced. Such an institutionalization of critical review of facts and ideas is not often associated with social conflict. If it were, however, it would be harder to arouse the passions in support of violent ventures. And complexities involved in a conflict would be better understood and more fully taken into account in any resolution which may be achieved.

The title of this section, "The Habit of Truth," has been

borrowed from that of a lecture by Jacob Bronowski in which he argues that the empirical spirit of modern science has helped greatly to humanize the values of the modern world. His point is not that the *applications* of modern science and technology have marvelously improved our world (the most commonly advanced, though sometimes questioned, justification for science). Rather, he claims that the thoughtways of science have themselves helped us discover and confirm our humanity. He refers to "the habit of testing and correcting the concept by its consequences in experience" as "the spring within the movement" of modern Western civilization.[4] He sees such a "habit of truth" as leading us ultimately to transcend most of our parochial conflicts by a broader view of humanity. He concludes:

> The dilemma of today is not that the human values cannot control a mechanical science. It is the other way about! The scientific spirit is more human than the machinery of governments. We have not let either the tolerance or the empiricism of science enter the parochial rules by which we still try to prescribe the behavior of nations.

The point expressed by Bronowski can well be broadened to apply to human conflicts generally. An empirical spirit dissolves the rigidities of thought which so often fuel the flames of violent confrontation. By cultivating the habit of truth (through the patient accumulation of facts and their interpretation through rational debate among persons most fully informed), we cultivate as well a means for keeping our petty quarrels in proper perspective. We do not thereby eliminate our conflicts, but we reduce the likelihood of their escalation into hostile confrontations.

A QUESTION OF IDENTITY

In the quotation most recently cited, Bronowski suggests that the habit of truth leads naturally to a broadening of the sense of identity. But is this necessarily so? We may argue that a disciplined empiricism and an expansion of identity do not inevitably go together. A careful experimental scientist, for example, is not always more dedicated to humanity than a butcher or baker. Nevertheless, there is a sense in which the institutions of science bring these two features (a disciplined empiricism and an expansion of identity) together. It is, in the final analysis, the *community* of scientists with an interest in a particular area of knowledge which together determines what constitutes truth; that is, it is the combined judgment of that community which gives the provisional assent to a particular generalization from the available evidence. The scientist must therefore organize and interpret his work within the framework of this community. In so doing, his own sense of identity is at least partly and temporarily expanded to give countenance to the concerns of this broader community.

Something similar is present in judicial proceedings. Established practices of courts seek both to support the habit of truth and to broaden the context of identity within which parties consider their acts. That witnesses may be compelled to testify to "the truth, the whole truth, and nothing but the truth" indicates how seriously the courts regard the gathering of relevant evidence. That the major parties involved must present their cases in terms of the broader interests of the community (represented by the judge and the law which he interprets) demands that they assume, at least temporarily, a perspective beyond their own selfish interests.

The main point we are making in this section should by now be apparent: The control of conflict and its resolution is often assisted by a broadening of the identities of the parties. To the extent that they can transcend their identities as parties in conflict, the conflict becomes less acute. And when a broader perspective can be shared by the parties, a resolution of the conflict becomes much more likely.

This does not mean that conflicts can be resolved only if the parties in some way merge their identities, taking ultimate refuge in the notion of a common humanity. Such a radical transcendence is rarely practical—especially for parties involved in a bitter conflict. But there still may be steps which may be taken in the direction of a broadening of identities. Appeals to general ethical principles sometimes point in this direction. So too may self-interest, when a violent confrontation appears a likely alternative. Institutionalized pressures and appeals from other parties can assist to broaden the perspectives from which the parties act, particularly when they may be called on to justify their actions in some wider forum (such as a court of law, a meeting of the United Nations, or even something so nebulous as the "judgment of history"). Finally, the parties themselves may manipulate their relationship to create positive interdependence as well as conflict.

Some very instructive experiments in intergroup conflict and cooperation have been reported by Muzafer Sherif. Actual camp settings for young boys were manipulated to divide the campers into two competitive groups. This appeared to be fairly easily accomplished. It proved more difficult to build cooperative relations between the boys in the two groups once the lines of opposition and antagonism had been drawn. A number of approaches to this were tried. Contact was encouraged between boys of the two groups, but this often only allowed for additional expressions of hostility. Sunday religious services were encouraged to emphasize brotherly love and cooperation, but this had little, if any, effect upon intergroup behavior. More promising was the introduction of what Sherif calls "superordinate goals." For example, a managed disruption of the water supply system brought the two groups together to solve the problem; or a large truck "broke down" which was going to bring them food for an outing, and boys of both groups were required to push the truck to get it started. Reports Sherif: "Joint efforts in situations such as these did not *immediately* dispel hostility. But gradually, the series of activities requiring interdependent action reduced conflict and hostility between the groups."[5]

What happened to Sherif's campers was that a variety of everyday experiences made their group conflict recede before their wider identity as members of the camp. Sherif is not hesitant to suggest a broader lesson. "Intergroup conflicts," he asserts, "are never resolved so long as the conflicting parties appraise and orient their actions within the confines of their own interests and standards." The sense of a larger "common predicament" is important for creating a broader framework for their actions.

Sherif has probably overstated his conclusions. Conflicts can sometimes be regulated or resolved even though the parties proceed from limited self-interest perspectives. But certainly the chances of a genuine resolution of a conflict are much enhanced when the parties are able (and are encouraged by their social institutions) to broaden the perspective from which they view their conflict.

THE RELATIVITY OF CONFLICTS

An invasion from outer space is sometimes imagined as a solution for purely earthly conflicts. Faced with such an external threat, would not Americans and Russians forget their rivalry, or at least lower their estimate of its importance? And would not Jews and Arabs—as well as Greeks and Turks—band together to face a new common enemy? So may run our fertile imaginations, based on the recognition that a common threat often does in fact bring previous opponents together. Whatever may be the science fiction value of such an idea, it helps us now raise the theme of the relativity of conflicts.

In this book we have frequently used a frame of reference which allowed us to view conflicts in a one-at-a-time manner. In reality, however, we must recognize that one conflict is seldom isolated from others. Conflicts occur in dynamic relationship to each other. The pursuit of a major conflict may require the resolution or suspension of numerous others. Thus the pursuit of World War II led the United States and the Soviet Union to put aside temporarily their ideological differences, reduced the friction in America between the interests of capital and labor, and weakened patterns of racial segregation as well. As old movies on television may remind us, many other conflicts were resolved—and new conflicts engendered—in towns and households throughout America in the face of World War II. And the resolution of that major conflict led, in turn, to the raising of numerous others. Previous allies now found themselves facing each other in a new cold war, with the means of resolving the previous conflict (for example, the terms of the Yalta agreement and the occupation by Soviet forces of Eastern Europe) now providing key issues in the new conflict. And once again throughout Western Europe the political cleavage between left and right became more sharply marked.

To recognize the relativity of conflicts leads us to recognize the larger truth that both conflict and its resolution are woven into the complex fabric of human society. Conflict is a part of the ongoing social process wherever humans interact—and so is the resolution of conflict. Generally the forces of conflict management and resolution (in all their variety, including many which operate with little conscious attention to conflict resolution in the minds of participants) are sufficient to contain violence. Sometimes, though, they are not; and at still other times, the strain of a conflict becomes so severe that special means are sought to bring about a resolution. It is then that the search for peace becomes a fully conscious objective.

Effective peacemaking requires, above all, that a conflict be resolved in the context in which it occurs. An idealistic rhetoric of peacemaking counts for little unless it can be accompanied by a recognition of the real interests at stake and how these may be accommodated. It also needs to be recognized that resolving one conflict, important though that may be, does not resolve conflict in general; other conflicts may in fact be increased. There is no broad avenue which leads to peace in general, only a crooked and often uncertain path that leads us through and around some conflicts, only to find others down the road.

๏ৡ

Although we may not be able to resolve conflict in general, particular conflicts can be resolved, and most conflicts (whether resolved or not) can be controlled so that violence is avoided. How this may be done has been the subject of these last few chapters, and we will not attempt to review them here. We do, however, wish to point out that it is on a world scale that our most serious and violent conflicts now occur. It is therefore necessary to conceive and develop effective mechanisms of resolution and regulation on a world scale if major wars are to be avoided or quickly contained and terminated.

This is probably the most important single task now facing mankind.

While the detailed examination of the problem of world order is beyond the framework of the present book,[6] the main points of this final chapter may give a helpful general perspective for facing this issue. We must recognize, first of all, that there is no ultimate natural state of world peace directly dictated by human reason. Rather, a world order must be constructed from the forces actually existing. A critical and empirical spirit in studying the forces of conflict and the possibilities for their resolution is of the highest importance in seeking to build a world order. So is a broadening of identities, so that the narrow interests of race, class, and nation may be transcended. Finally, we must recognize that conflicts are often highly intertwined, that order in one place may be at the cost of disorder somewhere else.

There is no magic by which *all* conflicts can be resolved. Nevertheless, there certainly can be a more tolerable order than that which now exists among the nations of the world. Dealing with this issue of world order by a new generation of peace researchers may well be the most important activity to be pursued on earth in the final years of the twentieth century.

Notes

CHAPTER 1. A NEW SCIENCE?

1. For the reader's convenience, bibliographic citations will ordinarily be found in these notes rather than the main text. For the writer's convenience, citations will usually be brief, with further information about each book found in the References (following these notes). Richardson's books thus may be cited as Richardson (1960a) and Richardson (1960b), with the publication details in References. For a relatively nontechnical introduction to some of Richardson's ideas, see the first five chapters of Rapoport (1960).

2. "Peace is artificial; war is natural" is the way Quincy Wright (1965, p. 1518) expressed the idea that conflict is a more general condition than is peace.

3. Boulding (1978), p. 343.

CHAPTER 2. OVERVIEW

1. We take this opportunity to mention some excellent sources for readers in pursuit of additional general materials on social conflict. Good theoretical works which are interdisciplinary in character include Boulding (1962), Rapoport (1960), and Rapoport (1974). McNeil (1965) also offers a wide variety of perspectives. A good review of sociological conflict theories is Duke (1976); other important books with strong sociological content include Himes (1980), Kriesberg (1973), and Oberschall (1973). Collections of readings broadly selected from the conflict literature include Brickman (1974) and Smith (1971).

2. One can also make the case that not all violence involves very significant conflict. For an interesting case study which attempts to demonstrate both conflict without violence and violence without conflict, see Schwartz (1972).

CHAPTER 3. CHARLES DARWIN AND THE BIOLOGY
OF HUMAN AGGRESSION

1. Darwin (1959), p. 120.

2. Darwin (1927), p. 4. The following quotation is from p. 525. In the next paragraph is a quotation from p. 524.

3. Darwin (1898), p. 628. The following quotation is from p. 629.

4. Quotations in this paragraph are from Darwin (1898), p. 126 and p. 625. The quotation about Spencer in the following paragraph is from p. 125.

5. Quoted by Barnes and Becker (1938), v. 1, p. 667.

6. Quoted by Barnes and Becker (1938), v. 1, p. 715. Other sources for Gumplowicz include Barnes (1948) and Gumplowicz (1980), the latter with excellent introductory material by Irving Louis Horowitz.

7. Quoted by Ellwood (1938), pp. 481–482. The following two quotations are from the same source, p. 483 and p. 488.

8. LaBarre (1954), pp. 89–90.

9. Appropriate citations for this paragraph include Ardrey (1961, 1966), Lorenz (1966), Morris (1967), and Wilson (1975). See also Eibl-Eibesfeldt (1970, 1971).

10. The above quotation is from Lorenz (1966), p. 42. Lorenz further argues that "if in the Greylag Goose and in man, highly complex norms of behavior, such as falling in love, strife for ranking order, jealousy, grieving, etc., are not only similar but down to the most absurd details the same, we can be sure that every one of these instincts has a very special survival value, in each case almost or quite the same in the Greylag and in man. Only in this way can the conformity of behavior have developed" (p. 218).

11. Scott (1975), p. 62. Useful books on the physiological nature of aggression include Delgado (1969) and Moyer (1971).

12. Aversive stimuli such as shock or intense heat have been demonstrated to produce fighting behavior in animals, apparently in the absense of learning (Ulrich and Azrin, 1962; Azrin et al., 1964; Azrin et al., 1965). Also, a fighting response has been produced by stimuli which have been systematically paired with pain (Vernon and Ulrich, 1966). Frustration, the blocking of goal-directed behavior, has also been proposed as a near-universal cause of aggression (Dollard et al., 1939; Miller, 1941). However, human studies have usually shown that whether or not pain or frustration leads to aggression depends on how the situation is interpreted more than the physical situation as such. Probably representative of current scientific thinking is the conclusion of Berkowitz (1969), p. 18): "The emotional state arising from the encounter with the aversive stimulus may in itself contain distinctive stimuli which can instigate the aggressive reaction, particularly if the emotion is strong enough; but the presence of appropriate aggressive cues (in the external environment or represented internally

in thoughts) increases the probability that an overt aggressive response will actually take place."

13. Wilson (1975), p. 247. The quotation in the above paragraph is from p. 248. The quotations in the following materials are from p. 242, p. 254, and pp. 254–255, respectively.

14. These ideas are further developed in Wilson (1978). For a rebuttal of the sociobiologists' view of human culture, see Sahlins (1976).

15. Wilson (1975), p. 574; Montagu (1976), p. 274.

16. Divale et al. (1976).

17. Harris (1974), pp. 79–80.

18. The phrase is that of Alfred Lord Tennyson in his poem, "In the Valley of Cauteretz." Such an image, according to Tennyson, opposes "Creation's final law" of love.

19. Darwin (1898), p. 633.

CHAPTER 4. ADAM SMITH AND THE SOCIAL PSYCHOLOGY OF INTEREST CONFLICTS

1. Despite the rather misleading dates indicated, Smith's two main works may be found in our References as Smith (1910) and Smith (1976). The quotations in the following four paragraphs are from Smith (1910), v. 1, p. 12; v. 2, p. 155; v. 2, p. 181; and v. 1. p. 436, respectively.

2. Smith (1910), v. 1, p. 13. Subsequent quotations are from v. 1, p. 400, and v. 2, p. 180.

3. Smith (1976), p. 87. Subsequent quotations in this section are from p. 216, p. 82, p. 83, p. 319, p. 83, p. 20, p. 13, pp. 110–111 (the extended quotation), p. 215, p. 134, p. 294, p. 230, p. 50, pp. 50–51, p. 51, p. 50, p. 88, pp. 233–234, and p. 234, respectively.

4. Relevant passages of Smith (1910) for this paragraph are from v. 2, p. 187; v. 1, pp. 436–441; and v. 2, p. 430. Those of Smith (1976) are from pp. 227–230 and pp. 154–155. Also see Smith (1970), pp. 281–335.

5. This is in fact the basis for his choice of title for *The Wealth of Nations.* A passage in which the nation is considered an analogous to the individual is Smith (1976), pp. 154–155.

6. Coser (1967), p. 29.

7. Smith (1910), v. 1, p. 12.

8. Smith (1910), v. 2, p. 180. This seems to be Smith's preferred phrase for referring to his system of thought.

9. Quotations in this paragraph are from Smith (1976), p. 86 and p. 316.

CHAPTER 5. KARL MARX AND THE SOCIOLOGY OF CONFLICT

1. As included in Tucker (1978), p. 109. This quotation is from the sixth of Marx's *Theses on Feuerbach.*

2. Tucker (1978), pp. 473–500. The quotation is from p. 473.

3. As quoted by Ellwood (1938), p. 330.

4. As quoted by Payne (1968), pp. 111–112.

5. The quotation gives, of course, the closing words of the *Communist Manifesto* (Tucker, p. 500).

6. "Audacity, audacity, and still more audacity!" Quoted by Barnes and Becker (1938), v. 1, p. 646.

7. A good overview of conflict theory as well as sociological theories which explain conflict is provided by Duke (1976).

8. Dahrendorf (1979), p. 54.

9. Dahrendorf (1959), p. 121. The quotation in the following paragraph is from p. 126.

10. Tucker (1978), p. 297.

11. Both of the above sets of propositions are quoted from Dahrendorf (1964), p. 103. Dahrendorf there disclaims a priority for either of the two models, though in his later writings (especially in Dahrendorf, 1968), he gives priority to the conflict and change model.

12. Dahrendorf (1964), p. 105.

13. Cited by Angell (1965).

14. Quoted by Dahrendorf (1968), p. 131. His essay, "In Praise of Thrasymachus," pp. 129–150, is the main source for this section.

15. The quotations here are from Dahrendorf (1959), p. 302.

16. Dahrendorf (1968), p. 145.

17. Quoted by Duke (1976), p. 40. Duke's review of Weber is contained in pp. 37–72. The quotation which closes this chapter is from pp. 69–70.

CHAPTER 6. THREE PIONEERS

1. The preceding data are from Richardson (1948).

2. Richardson (1960b). The following discussion of arms races is based on Richardson (1960a) and Rapoport (1960), pp. 15–46.

3. Following citations will be from the second edition (Wright, 1965), published as a single volume.

4. Wright (1965), p. 248.

5. Wright (1965), p. 1350.

6. Brinton (1965), p. 247.

CHAPTER 7. FURTHER STUDIES OF STRIFE

1. Tocqueville (1955), pp. 176–177.

2. Davies (1962, 1971). The quotation is from Davies (1971), p. 136.

3. Feierabend and Feierabend (1966).

4. Gurr (1970).

5. Gurr (1972). This is also the primary source for the following paragraphs.

6. Gurr (1969).

7. Gurr (1972), p. 141.

8. Smelser (1963), especially p. 8. The six factors mentioned in the following paragraph are summarized by Smelser on pp. 15–18.

9. Hoffer (1951); Fromm (1941).

10. Levy (1969). The data summarized in the accompanying figure are found especially on p. 88.

11. This and the following paragraphs are based mostly on Spilerman (1970). See also Spilerman (1971).

12. Spilerman (1970), p. 645.

13. McPhail (1971) is the basis of this discussion, with a later quotation from p. 1070.

14. Portes (1971a, 1971b); Isaac et al. (1980).

15. Tilly (1978); Tilly et al. (1975).

16. Tilly et al. (1975); Snyder and Tilly (1972). The quotations in the following two paragraphs are both from Tilly et al., 1975, p. 248.

17. The primary source for the following section is Clark (1979).

CHAPTER 8. RECENT RESEARCH ON WAR

1. The issue was that of December 1970.

2. Singer and Small (1972), p. 201.

3. Three exceptions are worth at least a brief comment. Turkey and China, though frequent participants, were seldom on the winning side. This should be seen against the pattern of their general decline as powers during the period in question, with most of their wars involving a rearguard action to maintain their territory or major power status. The United States also is an exception, but in another way. Without ever being defeated (the Korean War was counted as a stalemate), the United States still had only a moderate frequency of war participation (five international wars plus the Philippine pacification of 1899–1902). This may be interpreted in part against the background of the relative isolation geographically of the United States from other great powers.

4. These no-war nations include many recently independent states, such as most of those of Africa. But they also include some long-time members of the international system, such as Sweden, Switzerland, and Venezuela.

5. Singer and Small (1972), p. 345.

6. P. 370.

7. Singer (1972). The following quotations are from p. 266, p. 267, and p. 267, respectively. For recent collections of articles on the correlates-of-war project, see Singer (1979a, 1979b, 1980).

8. Choucri and North (1975), p. 14.

9. The one exception is that military capability was strongly and universally predicted by the military capability of the previous year. But this involves such a close conceptual correspondence between pre-

dictor and predicted variables that not much should be claimed for this regularity.

10. Choucri and North (1975), p. 244. The following quotations are from p. 254, p. 278, and p. 235 (italics in original), respectively.

11. Holsti (1972), p. 9 (italics in original). Later quotations from Holsti are from p. 141 and p. 82 (italics in original), respectively. Materials for Tables 8.4 and 8.5 are from p. 86 and p. 93, respectively.

12. Gamson (1975).

13. The problem here is not primarily time and energy, for modern computers are magnificent slaves to help in such work. The problem rather is that mathematical operations for handling complex causal models require simplifications in order to represent the whole system in a set of soluble equations.

CHAPTER 9 THE MACHIAVELLIAN TRADITION

1. Machiavelli (1950), p. 56.

2. Quotations in the above paragraph are from p. 44, p. 44, p. 53. p. 53, p. 9, and p. 35, respectively. Quotations in the following two paragraphs are from p. 39, p. 35, p. 65, p. 65, and p. 66, respectively.

3. Machiavelli (1950), pp. 61–62.

4. "A wise prince will seek means by which his subjects will always and in every possible condition of things have need of his government, and then they will always be faithful to him" (Machiavelli, 1950), p. 39). Other passages relevant to this paragraph have also been quoted in the preceding section of this chapter.

5. Machiavelli (1950), p. 94 and following pages.

6. Schelling (1966), p. 22 (italics in original). The following quotation is from p. 34.

7. Boulding (1973), p. 96.

8. Quoted by Morganthau (1951), p. 24. In the same source we have Cordell Hull quoted as commenting: "I was not, and am not, a believer in the idea of balance of power or spheres of influence as a means of keeping the peace" (p. 30).

9. Morganthau (1973), pp. 3–4.

10. Morganthau (1951), p. 144.

11. Morganthau (1973), p. 10. The later listing of rules of diplomacy is derived from pp. 539–542. The final two quotations in this paragraph are both from p. 541.

12. See especially Kennan (1977).

13. Kissinger (1957, 1961).

CHAPTER 10. THE THEORY OF GAMES

1. One might here also recognize that some games appear to represent a series of moves over time, while others represent a single point in time. It is possible, however, to reduce the former to the latter

by representing each possible sequence of moves as a single move. That is, a set of conditional moves can be treated as a finite number of distinct possibilities initially anticipated in a matrix of choices. This can quickly make an enormous number of possible choices, but in theory it is always possible thus to transform a game into its "normal" form.

2. See, for example, Rapoport et al. (1976). In our simplified introduction to game theory, we naturally limit our illustrations almost completely to this most simple kind of game.

3. Technically, there is a distinction which can be made between zero-sum games and other constant-sum games. In a zero-sum game the utilities of all parties for each joint outcome or cell must sum to zero. In a constant-sum game the sum of utilities for each joint outcome must be the same (allowing some extraneous force, such as "Nature," to affect all outcomes alike). All zero-sum games are therefore constant-sum games, but not all constant-sum games are zero-sum. Also, one could imagine a case in which a constant-sum game could be transformed into a non-constant-sum game (for example, by some extraneous force causing all utilities to be multiplied by a constant factor) without the game losing its pure conflict-of-interest character. However, for an initial understanding of game theory, these distinctions are not very important. For simplicity, all our examples of pure opposition will take the form of zero-sum games.

4. The terms "natural outcome," "saddle point," and "equilibrium outcome" are not quite synonymous in the game theory literature. Although usage may vary slightly from writer to writer, a natural outcome is generally viewed as we have described it, namely, the result of choice dominance for each player. There are, however, gradations of choice dominance which may be given recognition. The term "saddle point" is used mainly with games of pure opposition—in which rider and saddle may metaphorically meet while pushing in opposite directions. A natural outcome or saddle point is always an equilibrium, in the sense that no party can improve upon it by unilaterally changing his choice. But not all points of equilibrium are necessarily natural outcomes. Complex games often have several points of equilibrium; more rarely is there more than one natural outcome or saddle point (which would indicate that the game has no unique solution). Sometimes a game is without a natural outcome or saddle point, but an equilibrium point may still be identified.

5. It is for this reason that mixed-motive games have recently become of great interest to social psychologists. See for examples the review of Pruitt and Kimmel (1977).

6. For the 2×2 zero-sum game, we can give some simple formulas to derive the best strategy mix for either player. For simplicity, let us first ignore Column's outcomes (remembering that they will always be the reverse of Row's) and represent the outcomes for Row as follows:

$$C_1 \quad C_2$$

$$R_1 \quad a \quad b$$

$$R_2 \quad c \quad d$$

Given this indication of utilities, Row should make choices with probabilities derived from the following formulas:

$$p(R_1) = \frac{d-c}{a+d-b-c}$$

$$p(R_2) = \frac{a-b}{a+d-b-c}$$

Meanwhile, Column should choose with the following probabilities:

$$p(C_1) = \frac{d-b}{a+d-b-c}$$

$$p(C_2) = \frac{a-c}{a+d-b-c}$$

We can also indicate the expected value of the game (that is, what players would on, the average, be able to assure for themselves) for Row and Column, respectively, as:

$$V_r = \frac{ad-bc}{a+d-b-c}$$

$$V_c = 0 - V_r$$

7. This example has been suggested by Schelling (1963), pp. 55–56. Schelling conducted an informal poll regarding a similar problem posed for New York City. Most respondents solved this problem by selecting Grand Central Station at 12 noon.

8. Some readers may recognize Game B as the special type referred to in the literature as the Prisoner's Dilemma. That this type of game has such an extensive literature (see, for example, Rapoport and Chammah, 1965) is due to the fact that it very simply embodies key issues regarding strategic rationality.

9. Good nontechnical introductions to game theory may be found in Rapoport (1960), pp. 107–242; McNeil (1965), pp. 195–226; and Brams (1975), pp. 1–50. More advanced general works include Luce and Raiffa (1957), Rapoport (1966), Rapoport (1970), and of course the classic which initially established the theory of games: von Neumann and Morgenstern (1944).

10. Though there remains a problem concerning interpersonal comparisons. If we really assume that there is no basis for interpersonal comparisons, we cannot conceive of a total value for both players. Then the whole approach to a combined cooperative solution fal-

ters, and we're back to the framework of individual rationality (including the possibility of multiple rationalities).

11. See Nash (1950, 1953). Discussions of the Nash approach may be found in Luce and Raiffa (1957), Rapoport (1966), Rapoport (1970), and Rapoport et al. (1976).

12. More precisely, we can specify the procedures for finding the unique status-quo point as follows:

a. "Normalize" the original game to correct for the possibility of different value frameworks for the two players. This may be done by multiplying all payoffs of one player by a constant (or for both players, using different constants) until the slope of the Pareto-optimal line on a graph shows an equal increase for each player. For Game F this normalization is not necessary because the Pareto-optimal line connecting R_1-C_1 and R_1-C_2 already has this slope.

b. Transform the *differences* between payoffs of players in this normalized game into a new zero-sum game. Then solve this as a zero-sum game to show how the parties would come out if only their conflicting interests are considered. For Game F, the appropriate zero-sum game (representing differences between players) becomes:

$$
\begin{array}{ccc}
 & C_1 & C_2 \\
R_1 & -2(2) & 4(-4) \\
R_2 & 0(0) & 1(-1)
\end{array}
$$

For this, we have a saddle point at R_2-C_1, which is the solution for the zero-sum game.

c. Use the solution of the zero-sum game to establish the status-quo point for the original game. For Game F this is therefore R_2-C_1.

13. Mathematical terms and formulas which can be applied generally to two-person games, once the Pareto-optimal line is identified, are:

a. Using the slope of the Pareto-optimal line as $y = -ax + b$, let $b =$ the distance from 0 where the line crosses the Y – axis and b/a the corresponding change in the value of X (that is, the distance at which the line would meet the X – axis).

b. Let Xo and Yo equal the respective values for Row and Column at the status-quo point.

c. Let X^* and Y^* equal the respective values for Row and Column at the solution point on the Pareto-optimal line.

d. Solve for X^* and Y^* in the following equations:

$$ X^* = \frac{b}{2a} - \frac{Yo}{2a} + \frac{Xo}{2} $$

$$ Y^* = -aX^* + b $$

In the case of Game F, we get the following values:
$$b = 2, a = \tfrac{1}{2}, X_0 = -2, Y_0 = -2, X* = 1, Y* = 1.$$
The author is indebted to his colleague, Michael Harsh, for guiding him through the mathematics of the above procedures (though the present notation and example are his own).

14. Other approaches have also been suggested for determining a status-quo point. See Rapoport (1966), pp. 108–122, for a discussion of several alternatives. See also Heckathorn (1978) for arguments and evidence to support alternatives to the Nash procedure.

CHAPTER 11. A SCIENCE OF STRATEGY?

1. Snyder and Diesing (1977).

2. Berk (1974). See also Berk (1972).

3. Smith and Price (1973).

4. We consider von Neumann and Morgenstern (1944) and Luce and Raiffa (1957) to be the primary statements of classical game theory.

5. Harsanyi (1967–68).

6. Rapoport et al. (1976); Howard (1971); Brams (1975) and Brams (1977).

7. Simon (1957).

8. Kelley and Thibaut (1978) have discussed analyses of this sort.

9. See Howard (1971). Another important example of work in this direction of emphasizing conditional strategies is a recent paper by Brams and Wittman (1980) on "nonmyopic equilibria."

10. A notable exception is Brams (1977).

11. Schellenberg (1980).

12. Howard (1970), p. 316.

13. Simmel (1955), p. 87. Coser (1956) also considers this a key generalization about the consequences of conflict.

14. Janis (1972); the above points are adapted and summarized from pp. 197–198.

15. Janis (1972) also gives notable examples where the tendencies toward groupthink were controlled, and he presents detailed recommendations for avoiding such tendencies.

16. For a thorough analysis of such psychological processes, see Janis and Mann (1977).

17. Tversky and Kahneman (1974).

18. For a further discussion of such sources of judgmental error, see Nisbett and Ross (1980).

CHAPTER 12. THE DYNAMICS OF BARGAINING

1. Douglas (1962); Walton and McKersie (1965).

2. For example, in Western Europe there is usually less concern than in America upon local bargaining and more upon industry-wide

planning. In the United States there is generally less governmental involvement than elsewhere in regulating economic conditions, including conditions of wages and hours. Perhaps as a result of such differences, strikes tend to be more frequent in the United States than in most other industrialized nations. To put the matter another way, conflict on economic issues tends to be more clearly focused on direct two-party negotiations in the United States than in other parts of the world. Although the American pattern therefore may not simply and fully represent the world, it does exhibit the essential dynamics of bargaining, and with an especially sharp focus.

3. Douglas (1962), p. 42.
4. Walton and McKersie (1965).
5. Siegel and Fouraker (1960).
6. Fouraker and Siegal (1963). This is also the source for the following paragraph.
7. Bartos (1974). Other experiments of a somewhat more abstract character were also reported.
8. Bartos (1977), p. 576.
9. Cross (1969, 1977).
10. An excellent review is provided by Rubin and Brown (1975).
11. Hamermesh (1973).
12. Zartman (1977), pp. 628–629.
13. Kissinger (1979), p. 437.
14. Strauss (1978).

CHAPTER 13. VARIETIES OF RESOLUTION

1. For a stimulating discussion of the role of force in diplomatic negotiations, see Schelling (1966).
2. Schellenberg (1974). See also Schellenberg (1970, 1973).
3. See Schellenberg (1973) for other examples of such successful use of force.
4. Croy (1947), pp. 62–63.
5. With largely inconclusive results so far as our present question is concerned. See Oskamp (1971), Deutsch (1973), or Rubin and Brown (1975).
6. For example, it is still not clear whether peace between nations is most often correlated with large power discrepancies between them or with conditions of relative equality. For some of the complications of this issue, see Singer, Bremer and Stuckey (1972), Ferris (1973), Garnham (1976), and Stoll and Champion (1977).
7. Gamson (1975).
8. Marx (1970).
9. Fanon (1966).
10. Joshua 6:21, *The Holy Bible,* Revised Standard Version.
11. Milgram (1974).
12. See Weber (1947, 1968).

13. See especially Schelling's essay on "The Art of Commitment" (Schelling, 1966, pp. 35–91).

CHAPTER 14. RESOLUTION THROUGH REASON

1. Somewhat similar to this indirect role of the law in settling disputes is the impact of other external forces. We may consider here not only clearly identified persons and organizations but also generalized agencies, such as custom or tradition, religious directives, distinctive natural events, or the economic interplay of market forces. Although these represent impersonal forces, their impact on a particular dispute may sometimes prove decisive. Bushmen of the Kalahari, for example, divide the kill of a hunt according to a highly traditional set of rules, thus avoiding or resolving conflict over who gets the choicest cuts of meat. In modern society, the allocation of scarce goods is more apt to be decided by the forces of supply and demand in competitive economic markets. When such economic forces are working well, housewives in Baltimore are no more apt to feel sharp rivalries with each other at the meat counters of supermarkets than are the Bushmen of Botswana. Sometimes religious oracles or sacred scriptures have been used to provide a framework for avoiding or resolving conflict. Nature also may be viewed as an impersonal third party, in that natural events may heavily influence the resolution of a conflict. For example, we saw in Chapter 13 how an "act of God" (a flood, to be exact) helped decide the county seat dispute in Tom Green County, Texas. More generally, we can see how the resource base may help predetermine the outcome of a conflict—such as in the American Civil War, where the South proved unable to continue after four years of bloody fighting.

Such images of the market, the natural environment, or the special intervention of an Almighty God take us far afield from the mediation or arbitration with which we started this section. The main point to be made is that a more general perspective may enter into conflict resolution in a wide variety of forms. Explicit and direct third party involvements (such as mediation and arbitration) do not exhaust the list of ways that broader considerations may affect the methods used to resolve disputes.

2. General discussions of the countributions of Plato and Aristotle include Barnes and Becker (1938), Ellwood (1938), Chambliss (1954), and Gouldner (1965). The most relevant works for the material of the paragraphs which follow are Plato's *Republic* and Aristotle's *Politics* and *The Nicomachean Ethics*.

3. Rawls (1971).

4. Rawls (1971), p. 60.

5. See, for example, Boudon (1976).

6. See especially Homans (1958) and Homans (1974). The quotation from Aristotle which follows is from *The Nicomachean Ethics*, Book V, Chapter 3, quoted by Homans (1974), p. 249.

7. Adams (1965); Walster et al. (1973, 1978).

8. In many relationships a monetary framework may be applied to assess the value of outcomes. Inputs such as amount of effort, degree of skill, or the value of one's social position are less easy to reduce to a common scale.

A special problem is created when we conceive of the possibility of negative inputs and outcomes. Except for the case of reactions to a harmdoer (including how a harmdoer himself reacts to his exploitation of victims), equity theory has not been systematically applied to negative cases. For the study of social conflict, however, the negative case is especially important to consider. But immediately we have conceptual problems, especially again on the input side. It is easy enough to see how parties to a conflict may give negative outcomes to each other, but what constitutes a negative input? Does a high degree of skill, for example, become a negative input if it is directed to destroying the values of the other party? If so, equity would require that negative inputs be accompanied by negative outcomes—probably by receiving proper punishment from the other party. This pattern may well characterize many cases of social conflict, but do we really wish to describe them as cases of *equity*? It may be poetic justice when two fighters end up with equally bloody noses, or even when the one who starts the brawl ends with a larger injury; but this kind of distributive justice produces a serious strain on our thinking. For one thing, negative inputs are sometimes argued as a basis for *positive* outcomes, as when a nation which succeeds in battle considers it only fair that it reap the victor's rewards. Furthermore, the whole idea of negative justice strains our sense of viewing justice as a positive state. Equity theory makes more natural sense when we limit its application to evaluating relative *gains* (the usual practice of equity theorists) and avoid considering negative inputs or outcomes.

Another key problem for equity theory is that of establishing the basis of comparison for a given actor. Justice in equity theory is ultimately in the eye of the beholder, and as such is evaluated in relationship to whichever other(s) may be in mind. The comparison may be to some person or group not even present in the situation, thereby attaining justice or injustice by purely subjective means. This psychological focus makes it difficult to apply equity theory to more sociological cases, such as for evaluating the claims of justice of structured groups in direct interaction with each other.

9. The threat and security solutions to the bargaining problem come out of formal mathematical theory. They are ways of pointing to rational solutions, given certain assumptions. As such, they (like the theory of John Rawls, but unlike the social psychological equity theorists who follow Homans) fit more into the category of normative theory than of positive theory. They are evaluated as normative theories primarily for their simplicity, comprehensiveness, and logical elegance. On such grounds, most game theorists have come to prefer

Nash's threat solution. However, there has been very little study of how well these logical solutions fit the way persons actually resolve conflicts in the real world. What evidence we have is mixed. For example, Bartos (1974, 1977) found strong evidence in support of the Nash model, but other researchers (such as Heckathorn [1978] or Rapoport and Perner [1974]) report less positive results.

A mathematical game theorist might not worry greatly if his favorite model fails to receive empirical support. He sees the model justified on logical, not empirical, grounds. If people, for instance, fail to apply a threat solution in their bargaining, this may only show that they are not solving their problem in the most rational way.

An empirically based social science, however, cannot deal with this issue so simply. For an empirical scientist, it is important to know what norms people actually use in the process of conflict resolution. Do they in fact follow the Nash model, or is some other model more descriptive? Or, perhaps more to the point, under what kinds of conditions is one model generally descriptive of conflict resolution, and under what conditions is some other model more descriptive? The research evidence is too limited at the present time to do more than point to the central importance of this question.

CHAPTER 15. THE SEARCH FOR PEACE

1. Our discussion in these final four chapters concerning the control and regulation of conflict is admittedly sketchy. For further analysis the reader is referred to such recent works as Wehr (1979) and Himes (1980).

2. Paine (1969), v. 2, p. 242; Condorcet (1955), p. 194.

3. Condorcet (1955), p. 192.

4. Bronowski (1965), p. 46. The quotation which follows is from p. 70.

5. Sherif (1966), p. 89. The quotation in the following paragraph is from p. 173.

6. Our discussion of Quincy Wright's work in Chapter 6 gives only a small start. For an example of more recent work in this area, see Angell (1979).

References

Adams, J. Stacy. "Inequity in Social Exchange," in Leonard Berkowitz (ed.), *Advances in Experimental Social Psychology*, v. 2, pp. 267–299. New York: Academic Press, 1965.

Angell, Robert Cooley. "The Sociology of Human Conflict," in Elton B. McNeil (ed.), *The Nature of Human Conflict*, pp. 91–115. Englewood Cliffs, N.J.: Prentice-Hall, 1965.

———. The Quest for World Order. Ann Arbor: University of Michigan Press, 1979.

Ardrey, Robert. *African Genesis*. New York: Atheneum, 1961.

———. *The Territorial Imperative*. New York: Atheneum, 1966.

Azrin, N. H., D. F. Hake, and R. R. Hutchinson, "Elicitation of Aggression by a Physical Blow," *Journal of the Experimental Analysis of Behavior*, v. 8 (1965), pp. 55–57.

Azrin, N. H., R. R. Hutchinson, and R. D. Sallery. "Pain Aggression Toward Inanimate Objects," *Journal of the Experimental Analysis of Behavior*, v. 7 (1964), pp. 223–227.

Barnes, Harry Elmer. "The Social Philosophy of Ludwig Gumplowicz," in H. E. Barnes (ed.), *An Introduction to the History of Sociology*, pp. 191–206. Chicago: University of Chicago Press, 1948.

Barnes, Harry Elmer, and Howard Becker. *Social Thought from Lore to Science* (2 vols.). Boston: D. C. Heath, 1938.

Bartos, Otomar J. *Process and Outcome of Negotiations*. New York: Columbia University Press, 1974.

———. "Simple Model of Negotiation," *Journal of Conflict Resolution*, v. 21 (1977), pp. 565–579.

Berk, Richard A. "The Emergence of Muted Violence in Crowd Behavior: A Case Study of an Almost Race Riot," in James F. Short, Jr., and Marvin E. Wolfgang (eds.), *Collective Violence*, pp. 309–328. Chicago: Aldine-Atherton, 1972.

———. "A Gaming Approach to Crowd Behavior," *American Sociological Review*, v. 39 (1974), pp. 355–373.

Berkowitz, Leonard. "The Frustration-Aggression Hypothesis Revisited," in L. Berkowitz (ed.), *Roots of Aggression*, pp. 1–28. New York: Atheneum, 1969.

Boudon, Raymond. "Review Essay: *A Theory of Justice*," *Contemporary Sociology*, v. 5 (1976), pp. 102–109.

Boulding, Kenneth E. *Conflict and Defense*. New York: Harper, 1962.

———. *The Economy of Love and Fear*. Belmont, Calif.: Wadsworth, 1973.

———. "Future Directions in Conflict and Peace Studies," *Journal of Conflict Resolution*, V. 22 (1978), 342–354.

Brams, Steven J. *Game Theory and Politics*. New York: Free Press, 1975.

———. "Deception in 2×2 Games," *Journal of Peace Science*, v. 2 (1977), pp. 171–203.

Brams, Steven J., and Donald Wittman. "Nonmyopic Equilibria," paper delivered at the First World Peace Science Congress, Harvard University, June 1980.

Brickman, Philip (ed.). *Social Conflict*. Lexington, Mass.: D. C. Heath, 1974.

Brinton, Crane. *An Anatomy of Revolution* (first published 1938). New York: Prentice-Hall, 1965.

Bronowski, Jacob. *Science and Human Values*, revised edition. New York: Harper, 1965.

Chambliss, Rollin. *Social Thought from Hammurabi to Comte*. New York: Holt, Rinehart & Winston, 1954.

Choucri, Nazli, and Robert C. North. *Nations in Conflict*. San Francisco: W. H. Freeman, 1975.

Clark, Samuel. *Social Origins of the Irish Land War*. Princeton, N.J.: Princeton University Press, 1979.

Condorcet, Antoine-Nicolas de. *Sketch for a Historical Picture of the Progress of the Human Mind* (first published 1795). New York: Noonday Press, 1955.

Coser, Lewis A. *The Functions of Social Conflict*. New York: Free Press, 1956.

———. *Continuities in the Study of Social Conflict*. New York: Free Press, 1967.

Cross, John G. *The Economics of Bargaining*. New York: Basic Books, 1969.

———. "Negotiation as a Learning Process," *Journal of Conflict Resolution*, v. 21 (1977), pp. 581–606.

Croy, Homer. *Corn Country*. New York: Duell, Sloan and Pearce, 1947.

Dahrendorf, Ralf. *Class and Class Conflict in Industrial Society* (first German edition, 1957). Stanford, Calif.: Stanford University Press, 1959.

———. "Toward a Theory of Social Conflict," in Amitai and Eva Etzioni (eds.), *Social Change: Sources, Patterns and Consequences*, pp. 98–111. New York: Basic Books, 1964.

———. *Essays in the Theory of Society*. Stanford, Calif.: Stanford University Press, 1968.

———. *Life Chances.* Chicago: University of Chicago Press, 1979.

Darwin, Charles. *The Descent of Man* (first published 1871). New York: Appleton, 1898.

———. *The Origin of Species* (first published 1859). New York: Macmillan, 1927.

———. *The Autobiography of Charles Darwin* (first published 1876). New York: Harcourt, Brace, 1959.

Davies, James C. "Toward a Theory of Revolution," *American Sociological Review,* v. 6 (1962), pp. 5–19.

——— (ed.). *When Men Revolt—and Why.* New York: Free Press, 1971.

Delgado, Jose M. R. *Physical Control of the Mind.* New York: Harper, 1969.

Deutsch, Morton. *The Resolution of Conflict.* New Haven: Yale University Press, 1973.

Divale, William Tulio, Frosine Chamberis, and Deborah Gangloff. "War, Peace, and Marital Residence in Pre-Industrial Societies," *Journal of Conflict Resolution,* v. 20 (1976), pp. 57–78.

Dollard, John, Leonard W. Doob, Neal Miller, O. Hobart Mowrer, and Robert R. Sears. *Frustration and Aggression.* New Haven: Yale University Press, 1939.

Douglas, Ann. *Industrial Peacemaking.* New York: Columbia University Press, 1962.

Duke, James T. *Conflict and Power in Social Life.* Provo, Utah: Brigham Young University Press, 1976.

Eibl-Eibesfeldt, Irenäus. *Ethology: The Biology of Behavior.* New York: Holt, Rinehart & Winston, 1970.

———. *Love and Hate: The Natural History of Behavior Patterns.* New York: Holt, Rinehart & Winston, 1971.

Ellwood, Charles A. *A History of Social Philosophy.* New York: Prentice-Hall, 1938.

Fanon, Frantz. *The Wretched of the Earth.* New York: Grove Press, 1966.

Feierabend, Ivo K., and Rosalind L. Feierabend. "Aggressive Behaviors within Polities, 1948–1962, a Cross-national Study," *Journal of Conflict Resolution,* v. 10 (1966), pp. 249–271.

Ferris, Wayne H. *The Power Capabilities of Nation-States: International Conflict and War.* Lexington, Mass.: D. C. Heath, 1973.

Fouraker, Lawrence E., and Sidney Siegel. *Bargaining Behavior.* New York: McGraw-Hill, 1963.

Fromm, Erich. *Escape from Freedom.* New York: Rinehart, 1941.

Gamson, William A. *The Strategy of Social Protest.* Homewood, Ill.: Dorsey Press, 1975.

Garnham, David. "Power Parity and Lethal International Violence, 1969–1973, "*Journal of Conflict Resolution,* v. 20 (1976), pp. 379–394.

Gouldner, Alvin W. *Enter Plato.* New York: Basic Books, 1965.

Gumplowicz, Ludwig. *Outlines of Sociology.* New Brunswick, N.J.: Transaction Books, 1980.

Gurr, Ted Robert, "A Comparative Study of Civil Strife," in Hugh D. Graham and Ted Robert Gurr (eds.), *The History of Violence in America,* pp. 572–632. New York: Bantam, 1969.

———. *Why Men Rebel.* Princeton, N.J.: Princeton University Press, 1970.

———. "Sources of Rebellion in Western Societies: Some Quantitative Evidence," in James F. Short, Jr., and Marvin E. Wolfgang (eds.), *Collective Violence,* pp. 132–148. Chicago: Aldine-Atherton, 1972.

Hamermesh, Daniel S. "Who 'Wins' in Wage Bargaining?" *Industrial and Labor Relations Review,* v. 26 (1973), pp. 146–149.

Harris, Marvin. *Cows, Pigs, and Witches: The Riddles of Culture.* New York: Random House, 1974.

Harsanyi, John C. "Games with Incomplete Information Played by 'Bayesian' Players," *Management Science,* v. 14 (1967–68), pp. 159–182, 320–334, and 486–502.

Heckathorn, Douglas. "A Paradigm for Bargaining and a Test of Two Bargaining Models," *Behavioral Science,* v. 23 (1978), pp. 73–85.

Himes, Joseph S. *Conflict and Conflict Management.* Athens: University of Georgia Press, 1980.

Hoffer, Eric. *The True Believer.* New York: Harper, 1951.

Holsti, Ole R. *Crisis Escalation War.* Montreal: McGill-Queen's University Press, 1972.

Homans, George C. "Social Behavior as Exchange," *American Journal of Sociology,* v. 63 (1958), pp. 597–606.

———. *Social Behavior: Its Elementary Forms,* revised edition. New York: Harcourt Brace Jovanovich, 1974.

Howard, Nigel. "Notes on the Harris-Rapoport Controversy," *Psychological Reports,* v. 26 (1970), p. 316.

———. *Paradoxes of Rationality: Theory of Metagames and Political Behavior.* Cambridge, Mass.: M.I.T. Press, 1971.

Isaac, Larry, Elizabeth Mutran, and Sheldon Stryker. "Political Protest Orientations among Black and White Adults," *American Sociological Review,* v. 45 (1980), pp. 191–213.

Janis, Irving L. *Victims of Groupthink.* Boston: Houghton Mifflin, 1972.

Janis, Irving L., and Leon Mann. *Decision Making.* New York: Free Press, 1977.

Kelley, Harold H., and John W. Thibaut. *Interpersonal Relations: A Theory of Interdependence.* New York: Wiley, 1978.

Kennan, George F. *The Cloud of Danger.* Boston: Little, Brown, 1977.

Kissinger, Henry. *Nuclear Weapons and Foreign Policy*. New York: Norton, 1957.

———. *The Necessity for Choice*. New York: Harper, 1961.

———. *White House Years*. Boston: Little, Brown, 1979.

Kriesberg, Louis. *The Sociology of Social Conflicts*. Englewood Cliffs, N.J.: Prentice-Hall, 1973.

LaBarre, Weston. *The Human Animal*. Chicago: University of Chicago Press, 1954.

Levy, Sheldon G. "A 150-year Study of Political Violence in the United States," in Hugh D. Graham and Ted Robert Gurr (eds.), *The History of Violence in America*, pp. 84–100. New York: Bantam, 1969.

Lorenz, Konrad. *On Aggression* (first published 1963). New York: Harcourt, Brace and World, 1966.

Luce, R. Duncan, and Howard Raiffa. *Games and Decisions*. New York: Wiley, 1957.

Machiavelli, Niccolo. *The Prince* (written in 1512). New York: Modern Library, 1950.

Marx, Gary T. "Issueless Riots," *The Annals of the American Academy of Political and Social Science*, v. 391 (1970), pp. 21–33.

McNeil, Elton B. (ed.). *The Nature of Human Conflict*. Englewood Cliffs, N.J.: Prentice-Hall, 1965.

McPhail, Clark "Civil Disorder Participation: A Critical Examination of Recent Research," *American Sociological Review*, v. 36 (1971), pp. 1058–1073.

Milgram, Stanley. *Obedience to Authority*. New York: Harper, 1974.

Miller, Neal. "The Frustration-Aggression Hypothesis," *Psychological Review*, v. 48 (1941), pp. 337–342.

Montagu, M. F. Ashley. *The Nature of Human Aggression*. New York: Oxford University Press, 1976.

Morganthau, Hans J. *In Defense of the National Interest*. New York: Knopf, 1951.

———. *Politics among Nations* (first published 1948). New York: Knopf, 1973.

Morris, Desmond. *The Naked Ape*. New York: McGraw-Hill, 1967.

Moyer, Kenneth E. *The Physiology of Hostility*. Chicago: Markham, 1971.

Nash, J. F. "The Bargaining Problem," *Econometrica*, v. 18 (1950), pp. 155–162.

———. "Two-person Cooperative Games," *Econometrica*, v. 21 (1953), pp. 128–140.

Nisbett, Richard E., and Lee Ross. *Human Inference: Strategies and Shortcomings of Social Judgment*. Englewood Cliffs, N.J.: Prentice-Hall, 1980.

Oberschall, Anthony. *Social Conflict and Social Movements.* Englewood Cliffs, N.J.: Prentice-Hall, 1973.

Oskamp, Stuart. "Effects of Programmed Strategies on Cooperation in the Prisoner's Dilemma and Other Mixed-Motive Games," *Journal of Conflict Resolution,* v. 15 (1971), pp. 225–259.

Paine, Thomas. *The Complete Writings of Thomas Paine* (edited by Philip S. Foner). New York: Citadel Press, 1969.

Payne, Pierre Stephen Robert. *Marx.* New York: Simon & Schuster, 1968.

Portes, Alejandro. "Political Primitivism, Differential Socialization, and Lower-class Leftist Radicalism," *American Sociological Review,* v. 36 (1971a), pp. 820–835.

———. "On the Logic of Post-factum Explanations: The Hypothesis of Lower-class Frustration as the Cause of Leftist Radicalism," *Social Forces,* v. 50 (1971b), pp. 26–44.

Pruitt, Dean G., and Melvin J. Kimmel. "Twenty Years of Experimental Gaming: Critique, Synthesis, and Suggestions for the Future," in Mark R. Rosenzweig and Lyman R. Porter (eds.), *Annual Review of Psychology,* v. 28, pp. 363–392. Palo Alto, Calif.: Annual Reviews, 1977.

Rapoport, Anatol. *Fights, Games, and Debates.* Ann Arbor: University of Michigan Press, 1960.

———. *Two-person Game Theory: The Essential Ideas.* Ann Arbor: University of Michigan Press, 1966.

———. *N-person Game Theory: Concepts and Applications.* Ann Arbor: University of Michigan Press, 1970.

———. *Conflict in Man-made Environment.* Harmondsworth, England: Penguin Books, 1974.

Rapoport, Anatol, and Albert M. Chammah. *Prisoner's Dilemma.* Ann Arbor: University of Michigan Press, 1965.

Rapoport, Anatol, Melvin J. Guyer, and David G. Gordon. *The 2 ×2 Game.* Ann Arbor: University of Michigan Press, 1976.

Rapoport, Anatol, and J. Perner. "Testing Nash's Solution of the Cooperative Game," in Anatol Rapoport (ed.), *Game Theory as a Theory of Conflict Resolution,* pp. 103–115. Dordrecht, Holland: D. Reidel, 1974.

Rawls, John. *A Theory of Justice.* Cambridge, Mass.: Harvard University Press, 1971.

Richardson, Lewis F. "Variation of the Frequency of Fatal Quarrels with Magnitude," *Journal of the American Statistical Association,* v. 43 (1948), pp. 523–546.

———. *Arms and Insecurity.* Pittsburgh: Boxwood Press, 1960a.

———. *Statistics of Deadly Quarrels.* Chicago: Quadrangle Books, 1960b.

Rubin, Jeffrey Z., and Bert R. Brown. *The Social Psychology of Bargaining and Negotiation.* New York: Academic Press, 1975.

Sahlins, Marshall. *The Use and Abuse of Biology.* Ann Arbor: University of Michigan Press, 1976.

Schellenberg, James A. "County Seat Wars: A Preliminary Analysis," *Journal of Conflict Resolution,* v. 14 (1970), pp. 345–352.

———. "Courthouse Coups d'Etat: County Seat Wars in the Old West," *The American West,* v. 10 (1973), pp. 33–37, 62–63.

———. "Conflict Resolution in County Seat Wars," *Journal of the West,* v. 13 (1974), pp. 69–78.

———. "2 × 2 Primitive Games," *Psychological Reports,* v. 47 (1980), pp. 301–302.

Schelling, Thomas C. *The Strategy of Conflict.* New York: Oxford University Press, 1963.

———. *Arms and Influence.* New Haven: Yale University Press, 1966.

Schwartz, Lola Romanucci. "Conflict without Violence and Violence without Conflict in a Mexican Mestizo Village," in James F. Short, Jr., and Marvin E. Wolfgang (eds.), *Collective Violence,* pp. 149–158. Chicago: Aldine-Atherton, 1972.

Scott, John Paul. *Aggression,* second edition. Chicago: University of Chicago Press, 1975.

Sherif, Muzafer. *In Common Predicament.* Boston: Houghton Mifflin, 1966.

Siegel, Sidney, and Lawrence E. Fouraker. *Bargaining and Group Decision Making: Experiments in Bilateral Monopoly.* New York: McGraw-Hill, 1960.

Simmel, Georg. *Conflict* and *The Web of Group Affiliations.* New York: Free Press, 1955.

Simon, Herbert A. *Models of Man.* New York: Wiley, 1957.

Singer, J. David. "The 'Correlates of War' Project: Interim Report and Rationale," *World Politics,* v. 24 (1972), pp. 243–270.

——— (ed.). *Explaining War.* Beverly Hills, Calif.: Sage Publications, 1979a.

———. *The Correlates of War: I.* New York: Free Press, 1979b.

———. *The Correlates of War: II.* New York: Free Press, 1980.

Singer, J. David, Stuart Bremer, and John Stuckey. "Capability Distribution, Uncertainty, and Major Power War, 1820–1965," in Bruce M. Russett (ed.), *Peace, War, and Numbers,* pp. 19–48. Beverly Hills, Calif.: Sage Publications, 1972.

Singer J. David, and Melvin Small. *The Wages of War 1816–1965: A Statistical Handbook.* New York: Wiley, 1972.

Smelser, Neil J. *Theory of Collective Behavior.* New York: Free Press, 1963.

Smith, Adam. *An Inquiry into the Nature and Causes of the Wealth of Nations* (first published 1776). New York: E. P. Dutton (2 vols.), 1910.

———. *Adam Smith's Moral and Political Philosophy* (edited by Herbert W. Schneider). New York: Harper, 1970.

———. *The Theory of Moral Sentiments* (first published 1759). London: Oxford University Press, 1976.

Smith, Clagett G. (ed.). *Conflict Resolution: Contributions of the Behavioral Sciences.* Notre Dame, Ind.: University of Notre Dame Press, 1971.

Smith, J. Maynard, and G. R. Price. "The Logic of Animal Conflict," *Nature,* v. 246 (1973), pp. 15–18.

Snyder, David, and Charles Tilly. "Hardship and Collective Violence in France, 1830–1960," *American Sociological Review,* v. 37 (1972), pp. 520–532.

Snyder, Glen H., and Paul Diesing. *Conflict among Nations.* Princeton, N.J.: Princeton University Press, 1977.

Spilerman, Seymour. "The Causes of Racial Disturbances: A Comparison of Alternative Explanations," *American Sociological Review,* v. 35 (1970), pp. 627–649.

————. "The Causes of Racial Disturbances: Tests of an Explanation," *American Sociological Review,* v. 36 (1971), pp. 427–441.

Stoll, Richard J., and Michael Champion. "Predicting the Escalation of Serious Disputes to International War: Some Preliminary Findings," paper read at the North American Peace Science Conference, Philadelphia, November 1977.

Strauss, Anselm. *Negotiations.* San Francisco: Jossey-Bass, 1978.

Tilly, Charles. *From Mobilization to Revolution.* Reading, Mass.: Addison-Wesley, 1978.

Tilly, Charles, Louise Tilly, and Richard Tilly. *The Rebellious Century: 1830–1930.* Cambridge, Mass.: Harvard University Press, 1975.

Tocqueville, Alexis de. *The Old Regime and the French Revolution* (first published 1856). Garden City, N.Y.: Doubleday, 1955.

Tucker, Robert C. (ed.). *The Marx-Engels Reader,* second edition. New York: Norton, 1978.

Tversky, Amos, and Daniel Kahneman, "Judgment under Uncertainty: Heuristics and Biases," *Science,* v. 185 (1974), pp. 1124–1131.

Ulrich, Roger E., and Nathan H. Azrin. "Reflexive Fighting in Response to Aversive Stimulation," *Journal of the Experimental Analysis of Behavior,* v. 5 (1962), pp. 511–520.

Vernon, Walter, and Roger Ulrich, "Classical Conditioning of Pain-elicited Aggression," *Science,* v. 152 (1966), pp. 668–669.

von Neumann, John, and Oskar Morgenstern. *Theory of Games and Economic Behavior.* Princeton, N.J.: Princeton University Press, 1944.

Walster, Elaine, Ellen Berscheid, and G. William Walster. "New Directions in Equity Research," *Journal of Personality and Social Psychology,* v. 25 (1973), pp. 151–176.

Walster, Elaine, G. William Walster, and Ellen Berscheid. *Equity: Theory and Research.* Boston: Allyn and Bacon, 1978.

Walton, Richard E., and Robert B. McKersie. *A Behavioral Theory of Labor Negotiations.* New York: McGraw-Hill, 1965.

Weber, Max. *The Theory of Social and Economic Organization* (edited by Talcott Parsons). Glencoe, Ill.: Free Press, 1947.

――――. *Economy and Society* (edited by Guenther Roth and Claus Wittich), 3 vols. New York: Bedminster Press, 1968.

Wehr, Paul, *Conflict Regulation.* Boulder, Colo.: Westview Press, 1979.

Wilson, Edward O. *Sociobiology: The New Synthesis.* Cambridge, Mass.: Harvard University Press, 1975.

――――. *On Human Nature.* Cambridge, Mass.: Harvard University Press, 1978.

Wright, Quincy. *A Study of War* (first published 1942). Chicago: University of Chicago Press, 1965.

Zartman, I. William. "Negotiation as a Joint Decision-making Process," *Journal of Conflict Resolution,* v. 21 (1977), pp. 619–638.

Index